CODE GAMERS DEVELOPMENT 2-IN-1 VALUE BUNDLE

CODE GAMERS DEVELOPMENT: ESSENTIALS + CODE GAMERS DEVELOPMENT: LUA ESSENTIALS

YOUR #1 BOOK SET TO JUMP START YOUR VIDEO GAME PROGRAMMING CAREER

A.E. COLONNA

CONTENTS

CODE GAMERS DEVELOPMENT: ESSENTIALS
A 9-Week Beginner's Guide to Start Your Game-Development Career
A.E. Colonna

CODE GAMERS DEVELOPMENT: LUA ESSENTIALS
A step-by-step beginners guide to start developing games with Lua
A.E. Colonna

CODE GAMERS
DEVELOPMENT: ESSENTIALS

A 9-WEEK BEGINNER'S GUIDE TO START
YOUR GAME-DEVELOPMENT CAREER

A.E. COLONNA

INTRODUCTION

Video games are an inherent feature of modern society. According to WePC.com, the gaming industry is worth a shocking $178 billion in 2021 and is estimated to grow to more than $260 billion by 2026 (Padilla, 2018). With more than 3 billion gamers across the globe, it is no surprise that game development is a flourishing career. In recent years, the gaming industry has expanded to include various platforms, including console, PC, and mobile gaming. The gaming industry is not limited to gamers and game developers either. Video games have become popular as a form of visual entertainment, with gamers sharing their experiences through streaming platforms and Let's Plays. People who are not interested in playing video games for themselves can now enjoy them through other people, opening the market to a whole new demographic. It is no small wonder that game developers have more opportunities and enjoy exposure beyond the traditional expectations.

Many game developers start as gamers or game enthusiasts. They might wonder how a game works or how their favorite game was developed. They might even wonder if they can make a game for others to enjoy. Many things could encourage someone to try their hand at being a game developer. They might recognize it as the opportunity it is. With the rapid growth of the gaming industry, there is an ever-growing demand for developers.

There are, however, just as many things that might discourage someone from pursuing a career as a game developer. Many people believe that game development is only for those who know what they are doing. They might think there is no hope of becoming a developer if they have not had formal education or years of experience in programming. They might find themselves wondering if they are smart enough, if they are qualified, or if they have what it takes.

This book will show you that anyone can become a game developer. You do not need a fancy education or the best computer on the market. You definitely do not need years of experience. The only things you need are passion and a willingness to learn.

Being self-taught is not a handicap in programming or game development. Some might even argue that it is an asset. Anyone can be taught how to code or how to build games. The best programmers and developers are the ones who are willing to explore and learn on their own. True skill comes with wanting to understand what you are doing.

Game development is a diverse and dynamic field. We are nowhere near the limits of technology or computer science. Every day, new advancements are made. With every new development, comes a shift in programming culture. With every shift in programming culture, comes new avenues of game development. Technology develops rapidly and constantly. Game engines get better with every new generation of games. It is only natural then that developers have to evolve with them. This is where being self-taught is an asset. Good developers need to be able to grow and adapt. Being capable of teaching yourself is a skill that will help you in your career.

That might seem intimidating. Rest assured; you won't be going at it alone. As a self-taught game developer, I am fully aware of how difficult getting started can be. There are many programming languages and game engines available to any potential developer. You are immediately assaulted with new information, and it can be overwhelming. This book will help guide you along your journey to becoming a game developer and get you started building your very first game. In this book, we will explore some programming basics, introduce you to programming languages, and give you the skills you will need for your new career. We will explore game engines and their function in game development. Once you are more comfortable with the basics, we will take you through building your first game step-by-step.

A big part of game development and programming, in general, is problem-solving. You will see that we place a lot of focus on problem-solving in this book. You might feel inclined to gloss over those parts. Like many others, you might feel it is an unnecessary part of the process you can avoid by simply not making mistakes. After all, who needs problem-solving if there are not any problems to solve?

We are taught that mistakes are bad and should be avoided. Errors feel like mistakes, but they are not. Errors are not glaring mistakes we must avoid at all costs or even something to fix as soon as they pop up. Errors are an inescapable part of any programming process. They are unavoidable. Not even the most experienced developers and programmers code without errors. It is important to learn to work with them instead of working against them. One of the first and most essential skills of programming is knowing that errors are not something to be scared of. Errors are a valuable tool in making your game run as smoothly as possible.

At the end of this book, you will find a Glossary. All the relevant terms will be explained in detail as we go through the material. If you ever feel lost or uncertain, refer to the Glossary and refresh your knowledge. If you are ever unsure, go back through previous chapters. Programming is about building on fundamentals and applying technical knowledge to create something worthwhile. This book is here for you to use as a reference guide.

There are few things as rewarding as the completion of your first successful project. It is made all the sweeter for having reached that point by yourself; no one understands that better than someone who's been where you are. From one self-taught student to another, it is not impossible to learn. The best learners are the ones willing to figure it out for themselves.

With that said, let's begin.

1

WELCOME TO CODE GAMERS

WHAT IS PROGRAMMING?

The Collins Dictionary defines programming as "the act or process of writing a program so that data may be processed by a computer." (Collins Dictionary, n.d.). However, there's more to programming than the idea of merely creating a program. Modern programming is a complex series of actions aimed at the creation of a system. It encompasses a wide variety of different activities. Coding is one of those activities. So are direct manipulation and hardware management.

Blackwell considers the key to defining programming to lie with the person that does the programming and not in the actions performed (Blackwell, 2002). In his view, programming is determined by who performs the actions associated with programming and in what context they perform them. For example, anyone can code. Anyone with the right knowledge can put code into a system and get a result. That doesn't make them a programmer. Similarly, a professional programmer can input code into a spreadsheet without it being considered programming. The key lies in recognizing that programming actions need to be performed in a programming context by someone with programming intent. Only then should it be considered programming.

Programming cannot be defined simply through its tasks, who performs them, or what they encompass. There are no strict confines to what does and does not qualify as programming. Programming is whatever it needs to be to create a program. Therefore, there is no limit to who can be a programmer.

In short, programming is the application of programming techniques to create a computer program. Similarly, game programming is simply the process of using programming techniques to construct a system that will later become a game.

PROGRAMMING LANGUAGES

Programming languages are used by developers to convey instructions to a computer or system. It is what developers use to define the elements that make up a video game. It is how developers define settings, determine mechanics, and handle events. Basically, it is the language a developer uses to communicate with computers and systems. They allow us to construct the code that makes up the backbone of games and programs.

There are many different programming languages to choose from. Each one has a unique set of rules and uses. Each language has its own pros and cons. Some languages are better suited for game development than others.

That being said, programming logic is fairly universal. The logic you apply in constructing code is separate from the language you convey it with. That logic can be applied to any of the various languages. It is simply a matter of learning the rules and syntax for any language and then applying that logic to it.

Which language you choose will largely depend on the nature of the project you are working on. The things we need to construct a game are somewhat different from what we will need to build a website or to develop music software, for example.

Here are some of the more popular languages used in game development:

C++

C++ is one of the most popular programming languages for game development and is used by many AAA game companies and developers. It is most commonly used in developing game engines and larger, more complex video games. It is also the language of choice for modifying existing game engines.

C++ offers great control over hardware and system assets. This makes it the language of choice for high-function and high-spec games. It was designed to optimize computer functionality. It features fast game execution and results in less delay during gameplay.

C++ is an Object-Oriented Programming (OOP) language. That means that code using C++ is structured in a particular way. In OOP languages, code is organized using objects or classes rather than functions. At its most basic, OOP is a method of structuring code in a manner that prioritizes reusability and efficiency.

Most importantly, C++ is compatible with most game engines. Since it is such a popular language for game development, users have access to a lot of tools, including open-source libraries. To top it all off, it is compatible with most other programming languages.

The only problem with C++ is that it is tough to learn and is not a particularly beginner-friendly language. At the same time, its steep learning curve makes it a rewarding language to master.

Some famous games you might recognize that were built with C++ are *Counter-Strike*, *Maple Story*, and *World of Warcraft*.

In short, C++ is the language you choose when you want to build a game from scratch or when you want a great degree of freedom in asset management. It is also the language you use when you want to build a game engine or modify an existing game engine.

C#

C# (pronounced C Sharp) is an OOP language and was released in 2002. Some might refer to it as a simpler, lighter-weight alternative to C++. C# was developed to take all the good things of other programming languages and improve them. It was designed to be simple and flexible.

C# is very popular in game development. Unlike C++, it is easy to learn and beginner friendly. It is popular among Indie game developers and smaller development companies.

C# employs an assortment of data structures and uncomplicated syntax to encourage code reutilization. Additionally, you will encounter a broader scope of errors using C#. This, simultaneously reduces run-time issues and allows the developer to have greater insight into their code. Most importantly, C# can be used on all platforms and is compatible with a variety of other languages and game engines.

Famous games you might recognize that use C# include *Temple Run* and *Pokemon Go*.

In short, C# is the language you use when you want to use existing structures and game engines. It is easier to learn, and a developer can expect to get working more quickly using C#.

JavaScript

JavaScript is perhaps the most popular language for web development. In game development, it is mostly used to ensure interactivity with web elements. Outside the game development sphere, JavaScript is often used hand-in-hand with HTML and CSS to create functioning web pages.

JavaScript is behind most browser games and the majority of interactive elements found on web pages. If you have ever used a search bar or refreshed a page, odds are it was powered by JavaScript. That's not to say JavaScript is limited to browsers, however.

It is an easy language to learn and is often cited as something every developer should be acquainted with. Since it is so popular with users, there are tons of resources for anyone wanting to learn JavaScript. You can use JavaScript to develop mobile games and apps.

Famous games made with JavaScript are *Angry Birds*, *CrossCode*, and *Little Alchemy*.

Java

Java is best known for its almost universal compatibility. It will run on anything from washing machines to mobile phones and everything in between. As such, it is highly versatile and dynamic.

Of all the programming languages, Java has perhaps the widest scope of application. You would think that a language like that would be complex and hard to learn but it is not. In fact, it is considered one of the easiest languages to learn.

Its ease of use and versatility has made it one of the most popular programming languages. It is closely related in style to C++.

Some notable features of Java are multithreading and socket programming. Multithreading refers to when a system is capable of processing separate sets of instructions simultaneously. Game developers often prefer to separate tasks into multiple different threads, and Java is capable of processing more than one of them at a time. Socket programming is a feature that allows for two-way communication with servers, something that is helpful when creating multiplayer games.

Java allows for the game to be hosted on a virtual system, separate from the host computer. This not only guarantees better general performance but also ensures better and simpler growth of the system in the future.

Famous games that were built using Java include *Minecraft* and *RuneScape*.

In short, Java is the language you choose when you want versatility and compatibility.

Python

Python is different from the other languages on this list, for the simple reason that it is not commonly used in game development. However, Python is perhaps the easiest language to learn if you are new to programming and is often used as a teaching tool for software development.

Python is another OOP language. It boasts uncomplicated syntax and easy execution. It is touted to be the closest to actual English, which makes it simple to read and learn.

While it is not the go-to language for game developers, it is still capable of producing games. It has an open game library called PyGame that shares game-development tools for Python. Python is not a preferred game development language because it is much slower than languages like C++ or Java.

Despite that, however, many developers will utilize Python to build prototypes. While the compiling and execution might be slower, coding in Python tends to be quicker and thus optimal for creating models and testing ideas.

In short, Python is not your typical game-development programming language. It is perfect for learning to code and for developing game ideas.

Lua

Lua is a less popular programming language but is worth mentioning nonetheless.

Like Java, Lua can run on a virtual machine, making it memory-friendly. It is lightweight and easy to use.

Lua's main draw is being highly embeddable. Developers will often use multiple languages to get exactly what they want in their game. Lua is easy to integrate into other applications.

Lua is also used in several game engines, making it a viable language for any game developer.

GAME ENGINES

What Is a Game Engine?

A game engine is a structured environment within which a game developer can build a game. They provide developers with the technological tools they need to create well-rounded games. They function as a single gathering place for all essential game elements. Most game engines make provision for graphics, physics, sound, and player event management. Game engines are built with the intent to simplify and optimize what could otherwise be a complicated process.

Why are Game Engines Important?

Game engines play an essential role in making game development more accessible as a career. Without game engines, the process of video game development can be time-consuming and costly. Without their support, a developer would have to dedicate time and focus to the development of every possible element of that game. You would have to make provision for all the little details involved in physics management, graphics rendering, movement of game objects, etc. Game engines cut out a lot of that work.

Game engines allow developers more freedom in where they focus their attention. They are also a means of opportunity for small development teams and solo developers. Independent developers will always be at a disadvantage when compared to large companies. A handful of people or one person cannot compete with a well-developed team backed by funding and company support. Game engines can take some of that load and even the playing field a little. Even more important, game engines make it easier for nonprofessionals to get a start as game developers by providing beginners with resources and learning opportunities.

That being said, game engines are optional. You do not have to use them. Many developers do not. However, they are a great asset to beginners and professionals alike.

Popular Game Engines

There are quite a few game engines available for use. While some of them are more suited to specific types of games, there are several that can be used to develop just about any game imaginable. Here are some of the most popular ones available today.

Unity

Unity is by far the most popular game engine on the market. More than 60% of developers claim to prefer Unity over other game engines (MOOC Blog Team, 2021). According to Unity, 71% of all mobile games were developed using their engine (Kean, 2022). This is quite an accomplishment when you consider just how many engines there are to choose from.

The main language used on Unity is C#, but it also allows for a few other languages.

Unity is easy to download and offers a host of learning opportunities through affiliated tutorials and courses. It proffers a free subscription, and anyone with that subscription has full access to their asset store. It is compatible with most gaming platforms and can develop 2D and 3D games.

Unity can be used to develop more than just games. It can be used to create any software that requires some aspect of visual simulation, ranging from business software to training simulators.

Unreal Engine

Unreal prides itself on being one of the best tools on the market for advanced visual development. The application of Unreal extends beyond game development. It can also be used to develop software for architectural and automotive visualization and even films.

Multiple subscriptions are available to users in the form of licenses, and most of them are free. Each subscription gives its user access to all of Unreal's features. It even gives them access to its source code for further customization.

It is the engine of choice for high-level developers and even commercial companies. Unreal is the go-to engine for anyone who wants to develop large-scale, high-spec games.

GoDot

GoDot offers an easier learning curve and a wider range of compatible languages than most other engines. It makes use of common tools, something that makes it ideal for beginners. It is entirely free to use.

GoDot has a large community of developers which results in the constant development of the engine itself. Users can find a lot of support from this community and could find plenty of help in the form of learning aids.

All in all, GoDot is one of the best options for absolute beginners.

GameMaker

GameMaker is somewhat unique in that it uses a point-and-click system to enable its users to avoid coding altogether. Developers with no interest in coding are still able to make their own games using this engine. It allows for rapid game development of 2D games and is the ideal choice for someone who wants to get a game up and running quickly.

Naturally, that means it has some limitations in its application. While you can make fairly complex games with GameMaker, coding allows for a wider range of options and freedom that you won't find with this engine. Additionally, while it offers free subscriptions, you would need a paid subscription to really make use of all its features.

WHAT WE WILL BE USING AND WHY

For the purposes of this book, we will be using Unity and C# to build your first game.

Unity is one of the best options for beginner game developers. It is aimed at providing developers of all levels of experience with as many tools as possible. Furthermore, its compatibility with C# and other simpler languages makes it ideal for coding beginners. That doesn't mean Unity is only useful to beginners, however. Unity is suitable for novices and experts alike. It is an engine you can use to learn and keep using well into your career. After all, it is the engine of choice for more than half the developers out there.

Unity provides simplicity and versatility in its interface and development options. It supports a wide variety of audio and visual formats, making asset importation easier. It offers the best blend of options and interactions.

Most importantly, Unity offers access to what is considered to be the best collection of assets for our use—for free. Unity's free subscription provides an opportunity to learn and experiment at no cost and it does so without limiting your options.

To top it all off, there's tons of support for Unity users, from both Unity and the immense community of developers who use it.

C# is the most commonly used language in Unity. It is a simple language that's fast to learn and easy to use, making it perfect for our use for this project.

2

UNITY IS LIFE

INSTALLING UNITY

Before we can do any work, you need to install the correct software. While Unity will likely run on most computers, it is always a good idea to check that you meet Unity's hardware prerequisites.

Step 1: Go to unity.com and click on the "Get Started" button in the upper right-hand corner. You will be redirected to their store where you will see "Plans and Pricing."

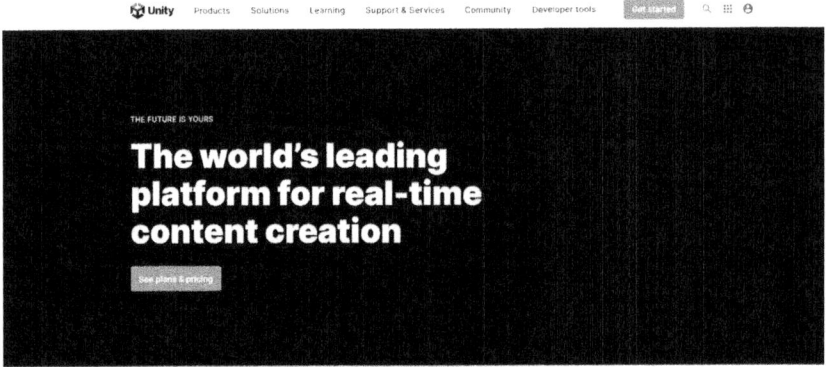

Unity for all industries

Step 2: Go to the Individual tab and select one of the accounts. The Personal Plan is the one best suited for our purpose. Once you decide on an account, click "Get started."

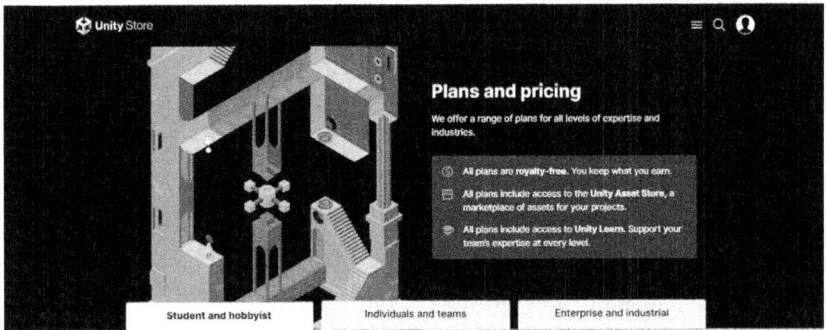

Step 3: Download Unity Hub for your Operating System (OS), and run the application file once the download is complete. Follow the installer prompts. When the installation has finished, you can open Unity Hub.

Step 4: Unity Hub will prompt you to sign in before letting you go further. If you do not already have a Unity account, create one. After confirming your email address, you can sign in.

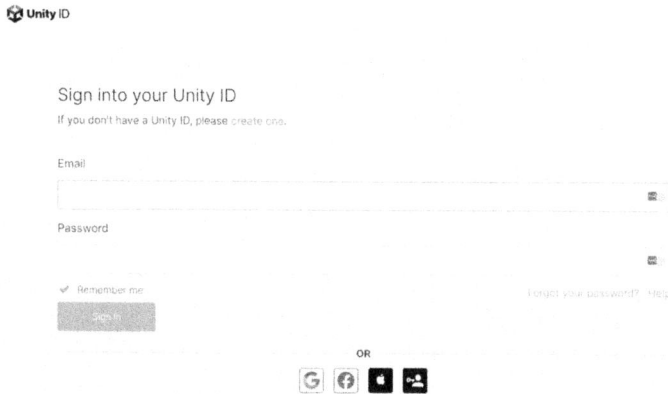

Step 5: After successfully signing in, install the Unity Editor. Ensure that you get a version with Long-Term Support (LTS).

Congratulations! You now have Unity installed.

CREATING A NEW PROJECT

Upon opening the Unity Hub, you will see multiple tabs. In the Projects tab, you will be able to see and create projects. Simply click the "New project" button.

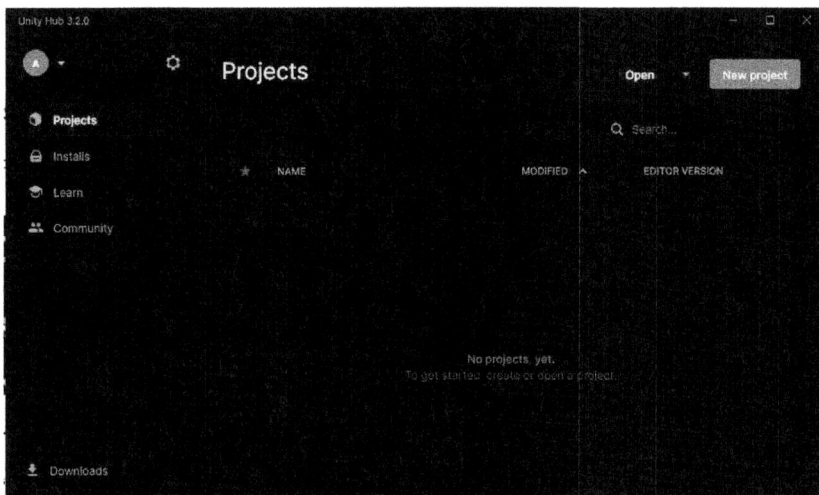

You will be met with options about the project you want to create. Choose an appropriate name for your project. It is important to get into the habit of naming your projects appropriately. Choose project names that will let you recognize them at first glance. This is vital to maintaining good organization and will help you when you start accumulating multiple project files.

Next, set the project location. Choose where the file will be saved. Again, it is good to get used to proper storage management early. Do not just dump your files at random wherever you find space. Project files accumulate quickly, and you want to be able to navigate your files with ease.

Finally, select either 2D or 3D. Click "Create Project" and wait for Unity to configure your project files. Once the files are ready, Unity Editor will be launched, and you can get started.

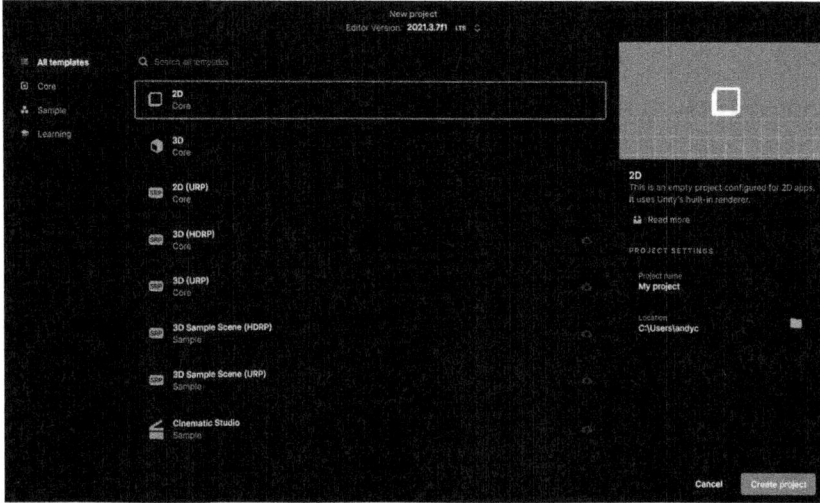

THE UNITY INTERFACE

Once your new project has opened, you will see the Unity Editor interface.

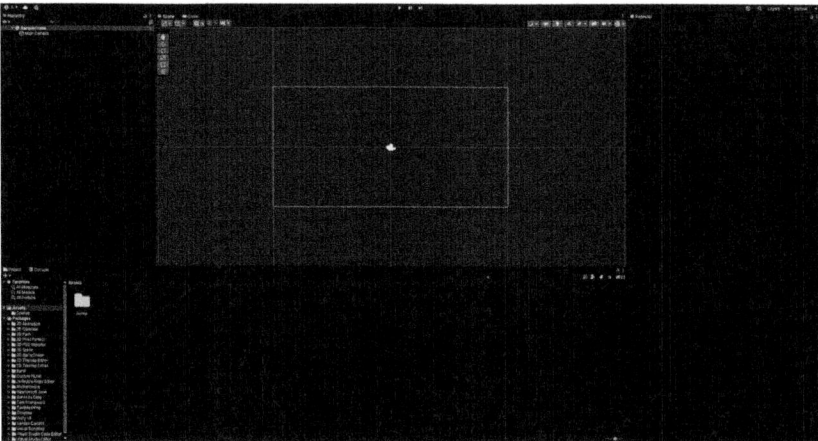

Scene View

The scene view is where you construct the scene in which the game takes place. Think of this as your game's set. This is where you can add and change GameObjects and move through your terrain. The scene is where you control what happens in your game. You can manipulate objects like cameras, landscapes, characters, and lights in the scene.

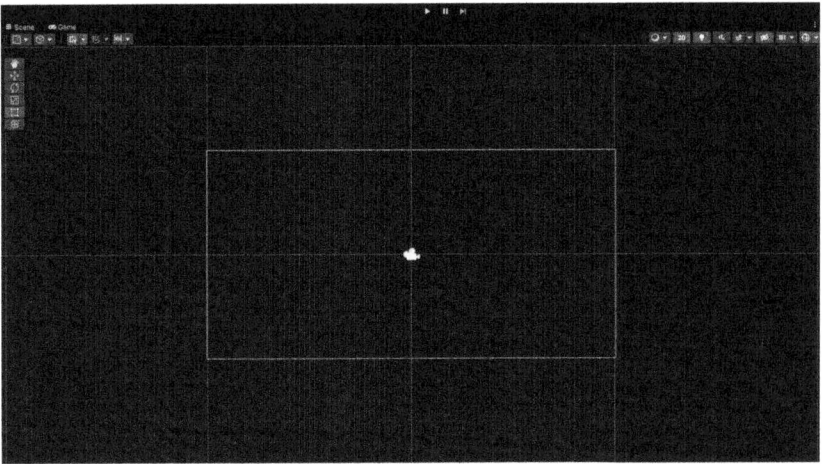

Game View

Here, you can preview what a player will see when they play the game. Think of this as your end product. In the Game View, you can experience the game mechanics as though you were a player. You can adjust the aspect ratio and resolution to ensure your game looks good.

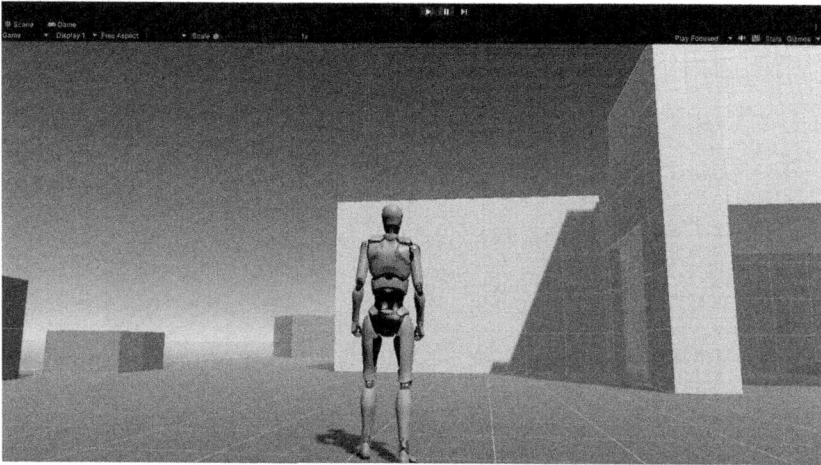

Hierarchy Window

The Hierarchy is where you can see a list of all the GameObjects you have added to the game. This window will help you keep track of all the objects in your scene. Even the most rudimentary game can amass all sorts of objects. Instead of combing through the scene when looking for a specific element, you can use the Hierarchy and its search function.

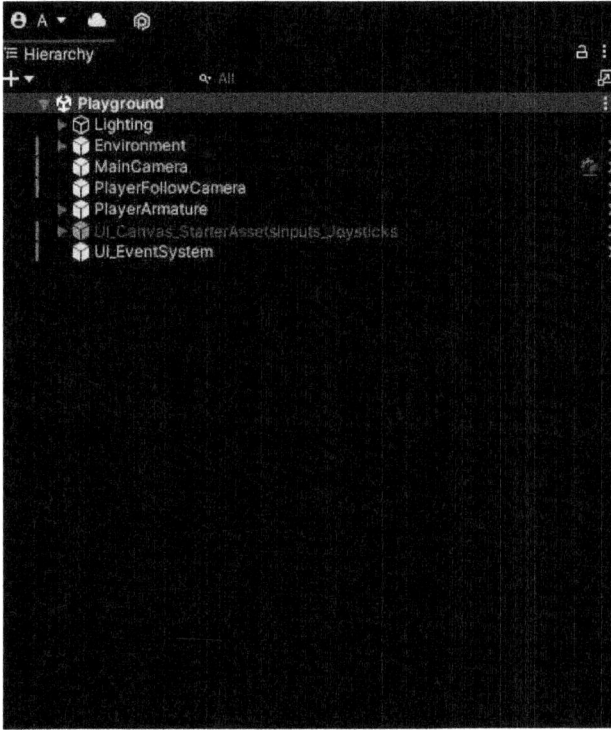

Project Window

Where the Hierarchy lists the objects in your scene, the Project Window lets you see your available assets. To add an asset to your game, locate it in the Project Window and drag it to the scene. If you want to import a file from your computer, you can drag it into the Project Window and Unity will automatically add it as an asset.

Bear in mind that Unity organizes the Project Window to mimic the files on your computer. Moving asset files via your OS file manager will mess with Unity's system and break the asset metadata. Try not to fiddle with your files to avoid this. If you need to move asset files, do so through the project window.

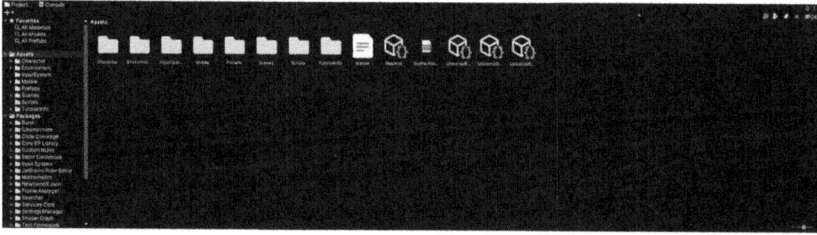

Inspector Window

Each GameObject has its own set of properties and components. You can manipulate them through the inspector Window. If you want to change an object's colors, textures, or other properties, you do so through the Inspector.

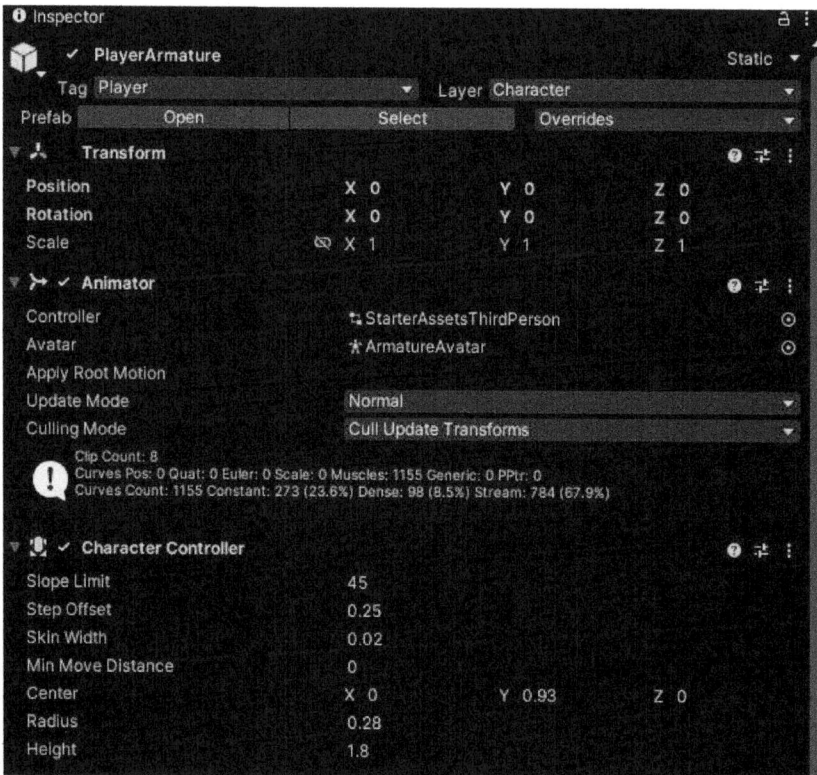

The Play Buttons

By now, you have probably noticed the tempting play, pause, and step buttons.

As you might expect, the play button lets you run the game, and the pause button pauses the gameplay. The step button is a handy feature to let you move through the game step-by-step. It allows you to observe the game frame-by-frame and see precisely what is happening to objects.

These three buttons allow you to run the game and experience what it does from a player's perspective. You can make changes to the game as it is running. However, these changes will disappear as soon as you stop the game. This feature allows you to experiment with changes you are unsure of without permanently affecting the project file. Basically, this lets you play around with ideas without affecting the work you have already done. If you change something and want to keep it, make a note of it and go change it permanently once the game has stopped.

Miscellaneous Buttons

These are extra elements you can add to the project. These features let you customize and enrich your experience as a whole. You can add additional services, change game settings, and even invite others to work on your project with you.

The Layers drop-down lets you add layers to your scene. This can be useful if you want different environments, want specific objects not to interact with others, or general organization.

The Layout drop-down lets you customize how your interface is spread out. Here, you can change the order of the windows, change which windows are on screen, and resize the windows. You can even save custom layouts to make it easier to switch between different aspects of the development process.

GAME OBJECTS AND COMPONENTS

Simply put, GameObjects are the objects you have added to the game. A GameObject is a defined space within which you set and manipulate components. In other words, a GameObject is a container within which components are kept. Components are the properties and values we assign to objects. Everything in your game is a GameObject. Cameras, lights, trees, characters, and collectibles are all GameObjects. Without the components assigned to them, GameObjects have no function or value. Different combinations of components can create different objects.

If you find these concepts hard to understand, consider them through an example. Imagine you want to eat some food. The dishware you use is your GameObject. The ingredients that make up the food are the components. If you use a different combination of ingredients, you will get a different meal.

To create a new empty GameObject, click the GameObject tab on your menu bar. From the drop-down menu, select "Create Empty."

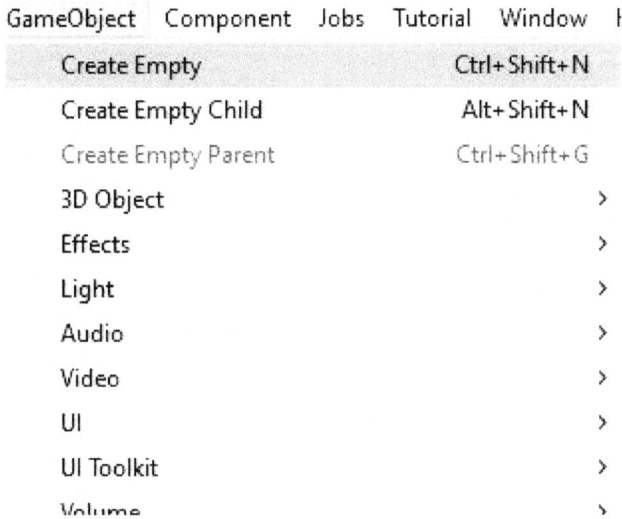

GameObject	Component	Jobs	Tutorial	Window	
Create Empty			Ctrl+Shift+N		
Create Empty Child			Alt+Shift+N		
Create Empty Parent			Ctrl+Shift+G		
3D Object				>	
Effects				>	
Light				>	
Audio				>	
Video				>	
UI				>	
UI Toolkit				>	
Volume				>	

To add components to the empty object, select that object in the Hierarchy and open the Components tab on your menu bar. You will notice a variety of component categories. For this example, you can select any combination of options. If you choose Physics and Rigidbody, a Rigidbody component will appear in the Inspector window. Alternatively, you can add a component through the Inspector by clicking "Add Component" and searching for the correct option.

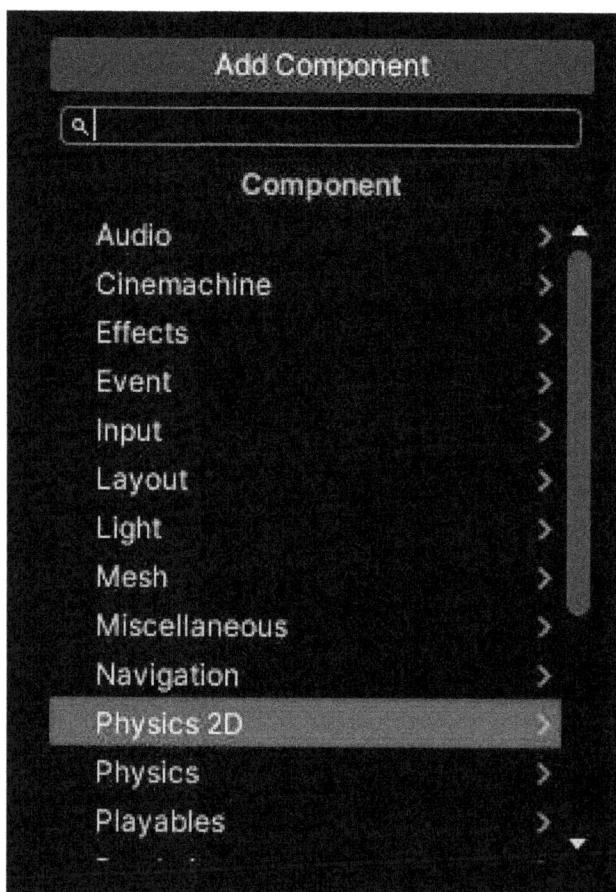

We can control GameObjects and components using direct manipulation or scripts/code.

TRANSFORMING TOOLS

Transform is a vital component of all objects. All objects have a transform component by default. Without the transform component, an object cannot be moved or scaled. Transform can be manipulated through either code or by using the Transform Tools.

There are six transform tools. We will discuss them all briefly. However, the best way to learn is by doing. In your test project, add an object and play around with it. The object will provide a visual representation of what each tool does.

First, **the Hand tool** lets you manipulate your field of view. To pan around the scene, select the Hand tool, hold the left mouse button and drag the cursor around the screen. Hold the right mouse button and drag the cursor to change your perspective and get a look at things from another perspective.

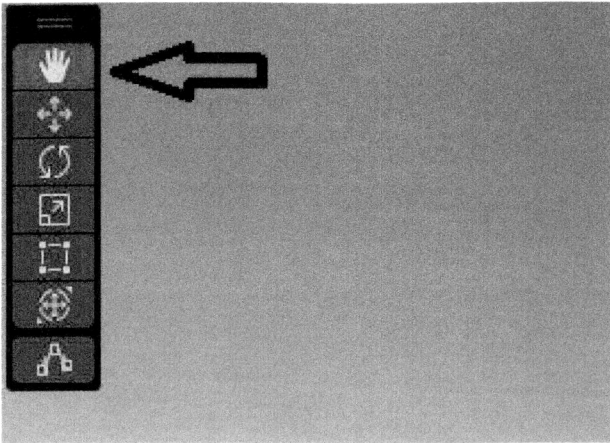

To traverse the scene, hold the right mouse button and move with WASD. This will let you move through the scene as though you were a character in it. Similarly, holding the right mouse button and using the Q and E keys will let you move up and down.

Next, **the Move/Translate tool** lets you move objects. When you select an object, you will notice three colored arrows that meet in the middle. This is called a Gizmo. The Gizmo is a visual representation of the object's geometry. Each arrow represents a directional axis. They can offer you a lot of information. To move an object using the Move tool, click one of the arrows and drag the object in the indicated direction.

If you look closely, you will also notice three colored squares at the center of the Gizmo. Where the arrows allow movement along a single axis, the squares let you move along planes. When using the squares, you will get a more dynamic translation since it is moving along two axes instead of just one.

Thirdly, the function of **the Rotate tool** is fairly self-explanatory. It lets you rotate objects. When you select an object with the Rotate tool, you will notice several colored circles around the object. The circles represent the axes of rotation, and you can rotate the object however you want with them.

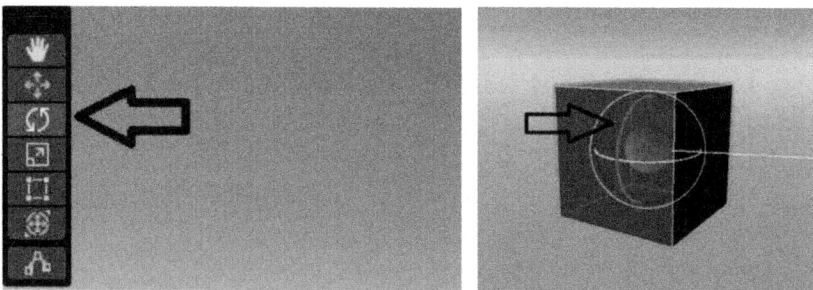

Fourth, **the Scale tool** lets you adjust the size and scale of an object. Using this tool, you will be met with another Gizmo. You can scale an object along any of the axes. Select the shape at the center of the Gizmo and drag your mouse forward or backward to scale the object as a whole.

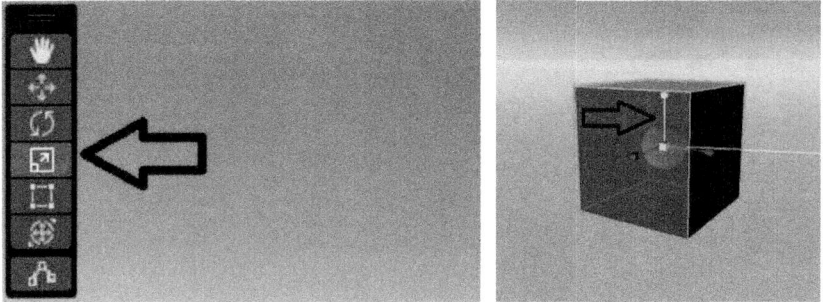

Fifth, **the Rect Transform tool** is used to scale, rotate, and resize 2D objects. We use this tool largely in 2D development or for User Interface (UI) elements.

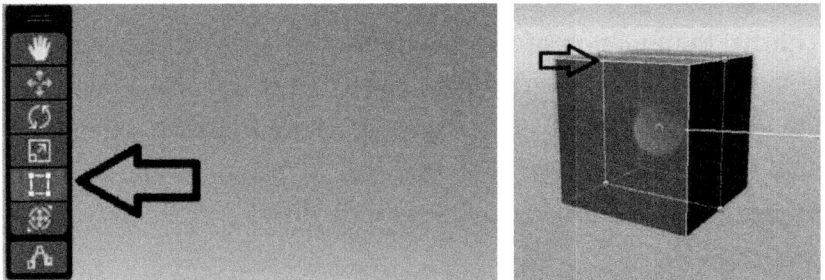

Last but certainly not least, is **the Transform tool**. This tool combines moving, scaling, and rotation into one mechanism.

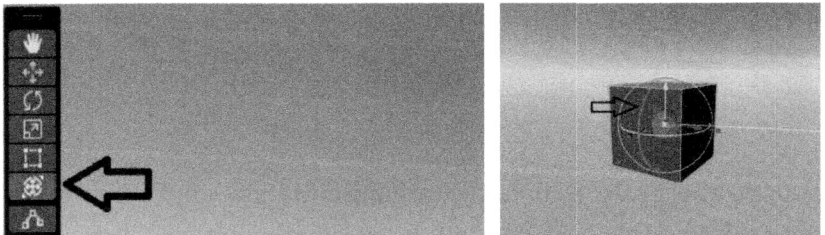

Also on the toolbar are some Gizmo control options. The first lets you toggle the Gizmo's positioning. When set to Center, the Gizmo is placed in the middle of selected GameObjects. When set to Pivot, the Gizmo is placed in the object's pivot point.

The second lets you toggle the Gizmo orientation. On Local, the Gizmo is oriented in relevance to the GameObject. When set to Global, the Gizmo is aligned to the scene's orientation. This might seem like a superficial distinction, but objects move during gameplay. The Gizmo's orientation determines the direction of movement, rotation, and scaling. For example, if a character is upside down and jumps, does it jump toward the floor or the sky? The Gizmo's orientation will determine that.

CREATING 2D AND 3D OBJECTS

Unity has a few primitive 2D and 3D objects available for users without them having to import assets. These are simple, geometric shapes. To add a 2D or 3D object to your project, go to the GameObjects tab on the menu bar. From there, select either "Create 2D object" or "Create 3D object." Click on whichever one you want and choose a shape from the available list.

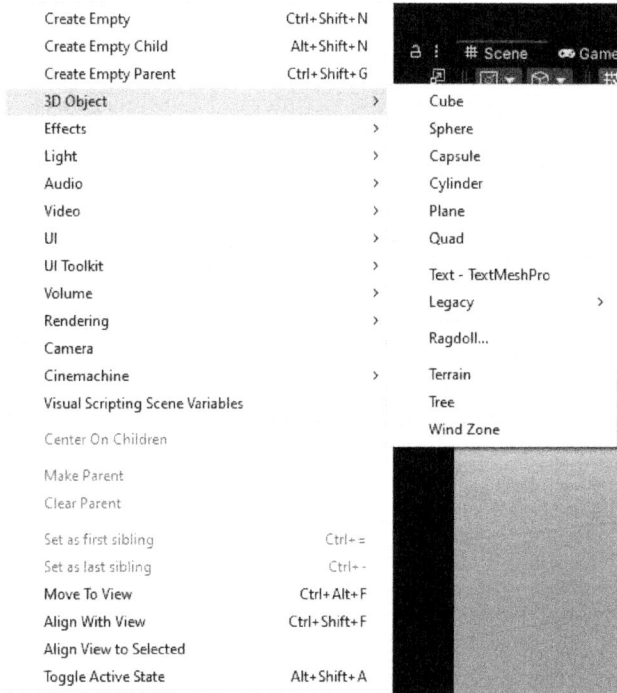

The object you have chosen will appear in your scene. You will also be able to see the shape listed in your Hierarchy. By selecting the object, you can change its properties and components.

PREFABS

Prefabs act as templates for configured GameObjects. They let you save an object's child objects, values, and component configuration to your assets. That way, you can easily add duplicates or replace accidentally lost objects. You can also create a duplicate object to experiment on if you want to try out some changes but do not want to permanently change the original object.

To make a Prefab, simply select the desired object in the Hierarchy and drag it to the Project window. Simple as that. This saves the object configuration as a Prefab, and you can now add a new object to the scene directly from the Project window.

Using Prefabs, you can create Prefab Instances and Prefab Variants. Instances are carbon copies of the original Prefab. If you want to create a crowd of people by duplicating one model, those duplicates will be Instances. Variants are objects created from the Prefab and adjusted. An example of a Variant would be a door made from a Prefab with textures added to make it appear older.

If you want to edit an existing Prefab, there are two ways of going about it. Firstly, you can edit a Prefab in Prefab mode. You can enter Prefab mode by double-clicking the Prefab file in the Project window or clicking the arrow next to the Prefab object in the Hierarchy. To exit Prefab mode, you can simply click the back arrow at the top of the screen.

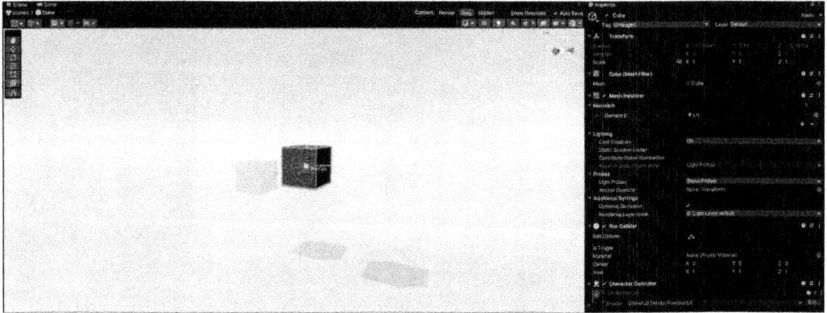

Alternatively, you can select the Prefab object, change its components and then click apply in the Inspector. Bear in mind that doing this will not only edit the Prefab file but will also apply that change to all Instances. Clicking Apply sets the Prefab file configuration to reflect that of the object you have selected.

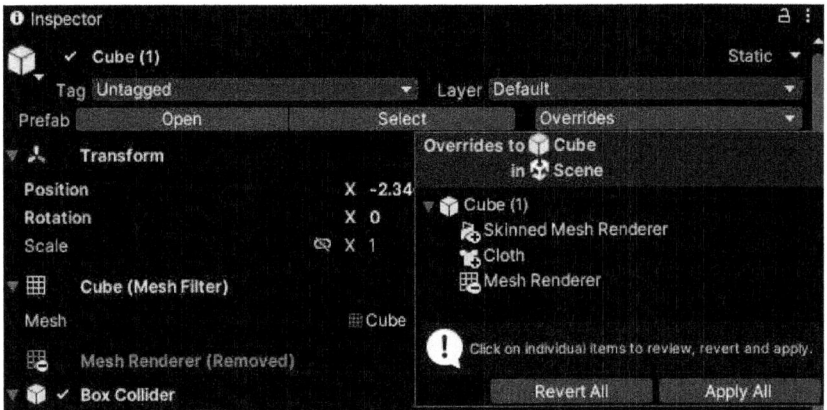

Next to the Apply button in the Inspector, you will also find the Select and Revert buttons. Select lets you locate the file in the Project window. Revert lets you revert the selected object to the Prefab configuration. Revert can be extremely useful if you are experimenting with changes and do not like what you have done.

Prefabs have a lot more uses than you might originally think. Aside from the obvious duplication benefits, Prefabs can help you preserve the integrity of your single-use objects. If you are juggling multiple objects, it can be easy to delete one by accident and not notice until it is too late to undo the mistake. By regularly updating your Prefabs you can add the lost object back to the game instead of rebuilding it from scratch.

For Prefabs to be effective, you need to update them. It is a good idea to create Prefabs for all your custom objects. It is surprisingly easy to lose track of things, and it is always better to have a failsafe.

3

INTRODUCING C#

W e took a brief look at what C# is and why we will use it. It is the main language used with Unity and also one of the most-popular programming languages in general. It was released in 2002 by Microsoft and was built on the .Net Framework. Since then, C# has grown as a language, with newer versions changing the way we use C#. The most recent version of C# (C# 10) cuts down on the amount of code we need to initialize a project. Older versions of C# required several lines of code to provide the necessary structure for a C# project to run. Most of that has now been integrated into the framework to provide a smoother experience for software development.

There are multiple motivators to learning C#. Its popularity among Unity developers makes it a favorable language for game development. It is also a common language for web development and Windows-based software. With it being so popular, there's a vast community of C# programmers willing to help each other. There are plenty of online tools for learning and support beyond the official tools offered by Microsoft.

C# is best learned and used through an Integrated Development Environment (IDE). IDEs provide all the necessary tools for creating a functional program, including a compiler and a debugger. There are multiple options to choose from when picking an IDE. The most-commonly recommended one is Visual Studio since it is free and can compile most programming languages.

Do not be disheartened if you begin to feel overwhelmed at any point during this chapter. Programming is best learned through doing. You will find that most concepts are hard to understand until you have tried to apply them. Keep at it, and things will click into place eventually.

HELLOWORLD AND C# TEMPLATE STRUCTURE

It is something of a programming tradition to introduce new programmers to coding with a HelloWorld program. Go ahead and copy the following code:

```
using System;

namespace HelloGamers
//NameSpace declaration
{
    class Gamers
    //Class Declaration
    {
        static void Main ()
        //Main method declaration
        {
            Console.WriteLine ("Hello Gamers!");
            //Executable code
            //Most Functional code is placed into main

        }
    }
}
```

This shows the basic template for a C# console app and illustrates the structure of C# programs. You will notice a few things when looking at the above example.

Firstly, the using statements are used to link a project to pre-existing namespaces and public libraries. This lets your program access the integrated features of the .Net Framework.

Next, there is a namespace declaration. Namespaces are containers for classes. They serve to enclose specific objects into a contained space where they can interact with each other. Namespaces allow us to create interactivity between classes in a project without having it affect other projects or other namespaces in the same project.

Within a namespace, we have a class. Classes are containers of members and structures around which our code functions.

Finally, we have a method called Main. Most functional code for basic programs is placed in Main. Main is a method that is executed when the program starts up. Everything in the Main method is executed at that time. Inside Main, we have our display statement. In this example, the message "Hello Gamers!" is printed onto the console.

With .Net 6 and C# 10, the basic template is no longer necessary for basic programs that have only one class. The namespace declaration has been integrated into the framework, and with it, the other declarations fall away. If you do not specify differently, anything you code is placed into Main. However, most learning resources still include the template since older versions of C# still require the inclusion of this structure.

STATEMENTS AND COMMENTS

Statements, Blocks, and Expressions

Code is made up of multiple statements. Statements are lines of text that include executable instructions. Each statement is ended with a semicolon, much like English sentences are ended with punctuation. A single statement can span multiple lines on the screen, so it is necessary to have an indication of where one statement ends and another begins. The semicolon is that indicator.

We can group statements together using curly brackets {}. Statements encased in curly brackets form a block. This is usually to indicate object grouping, such as for classes. The curly brackets indicate where an object's block begins and ends. The curly brackets also allow us to nest objects within each other.

Statements consist of expressions. An expression is any combination of an operator and an operand that can result in a value. An operator is a symbol with an attributed meaning relating to an operation. For example, + is an operator. An operand is the subject of an operation undertaken by an operator. For example, in 3+4, the numbers are operands.

To that effect, there are two main kinds of statements: declaration statements and expression statements. Declaration statements are used to declare something and expression statements are used to express values.

Comments

For the most part, if any text is added to code, the computer will try to execute it. We do not always want all text to be executable, however. That's where we use comments. Comments are text added to code that does not form part of the functional code but serves as notes to other programmers. They are predominantly used to explain complex bits of code. You will see comments used this way frequently in this book. They can also be used as a means of experimentation. They let you remove specific statements from play without needing to delete them. This is a great help if you are trying something new or trying to find which statement, in particular, is causing problems in execution.

There are two ways to make comments:

- Single line comments follow after //
- Comments spanning multiple lines are enclosed between /* and */

```
//This is a comment

/* This is also
a comment */
```

It is recommended to not overuse comments. Comments are there to make your code more intelligible. You do not want the majority of your code to consist of comments. The best comments are short and to the point. As a rule of thumb, do not explain "how" in your comments. Rather use them to explain "why" a statement is there.

VARIABLES

Variables are containers for data. They act as placeholders for information in your program. Programming variables are similar to mathematical variables in that they represent the information you do not have. They also represent information that is not constant. We cannot always account for all the potential data our programs could manage, so we use placeholders instead of defined data. Think of variables as an empty box you can keep something in. Even while empty, the box retains its shape and acts as a place where you can store something.

Variables consist of two parts: a name and a value. A variable name is a unique identifier by which we can call a variable. A value is what we assign that variable to contain.

Variable names must always be unique. Note also that names are case-sensitive. The names "myname" and "MyName" are different identifiers and cannot be used interchangeably. It is good practice to use Camel case when assigning names. Camel case is when the first letter of each word in a compound word is capitalized, for instance, FirstName or PhoneNumber. Alternatively, you can keep the first word lowercase and then capitalize the first letter of the second word, for example, firstName or phoneNumber. Either way, keep a consistent style to the way you assign names. That way, you won't have to go double-check as often.

Data Types

C# is considered to be a strongly typed language. C# code relies heavily on distinct data types. This regulates what kind of data can be stored in variables and also how we use that data. Data types are not unique to C#. Most programming languages differentiate data in some kind of way, and some data types are universal.

There are many different kinds of variables, but the ones you will likely use the most are:

- **int:** Integers are used to store whole numbers between -2,147,483,648 and 2,147,483,647.
- **short:** Short integers ranging from -32768 to 32767 are stored in short variables.

- **long:** Long integers store whole numbers of a more extensive range than integers. Long can store integers of up to 19-digits long.
- **byte:** Bytes are essentially much shorter integers. They store whole numbers between the values 0–255. As you can see, only positive values can be assigned to a byte.
- **sbyte:** Similar to bytes, sbytes have a much smaller range. They can store whole numbers between -128 and 127. Unlike bytes, they can store negative numbers.
- **char:** Character types are different from the above variables in that they store single letters rather than numbers. Where an integer type would be 12 or 26, a character type would be a or f. Take note that char variables are initialized with single quotation marks.
- **bool:** Booleans are unique. The only values a boolean can hold are true or false.
- **float:** Float variables can store fractional values up to the 7th decimal. When initialized, float values are followed by the suffix f or F. When the suffix is excluded, the value will default to double.
- **double:** Double variables can store fractional values up to the 14th or 15th decimal point. Unlike floats, doubles require no suffix.
- **string:** String variables contain sequences of Unicode characters. In other words, strings store words and sentences. They can also include numbers and symbols but not in a way that can be used for calculations.

There are other types of variables aside from the ones mentioned. Unless you are absolutely sure what value your variables will be using, it is best to provide for all possible eventualities. At the same time, each variable is assigned a certain amount of memory space. While that space is negligible, it is good practice not to assign the max range variables since they occupy a larger space in memory.

Declaring Variables

To use variables, we need to declare them. This can be done anywhere within a class structure. Variables can also be initialized when they are declared. For clarity, declaring a variable means creating one and determining what DataType it has. Initializing means assigning a value to a variable. Variables do not have to be initialized at the time of declaration. If no value is assigned to them, variables receive a default value of zero (0) or null.

When declaring and initializing a variable, you can use this formula: DataType [name] = [value].

```
//How to declare variables

int EgNum1 = 41;
short EgNum2 = 23;
long EgNum3 = 89462;
char Char = 'e';
bool EgBoolean = true;
float EgNum4 = 3.984f;
double Egnum 5 = 2.4237561;
string EgString = "Hello Developers";
```

ARRAYS

Arrays are structures that can contain multiple variables of the same data type. They act as a database of sorts for related variables. Each entry into an array is called an element and is identified by an index number. Array elements must be of the same data type. You cannot, for example, store integers and strings in the same array.

Arrays are useful when your program needs to be able to store and process multiple instances of similar data. For example, if your program needs to collect and manage a variety of phone numbers, an array can store and index each individual number while keeping it in the same structure. Arrays let us use multiple variable values without needing to create and assign separate variables. As per the above example, you can store each individual phone number in the array instead of having to provide a variable for every one of them.

Array elements are characterized and identified by an index number. They are called individually by the array's name and the index number. Index numbers start from zero (0) with the first element. For example, an array of the months in a year would look like this: months[0] = "January", months[1] = "February", months[2] = "March", months[3] = "April", and so forth. If you wanted to recall February, you would use months[1].

Just like any other variable, arrays need to be declared before values can be assigned to them. We can declare arrays according to this formula: DataType [] ArrayName.

The number of elements in an array is referred to as its length. The length is either set by the programmer or automatically defaulted to the number of elements added to it. New elements are created using this formula: ArrayName = new DataType[length]. If you want ten elements, you put 10 between the square brackets. If you do not want to assign a particular length, leave the brackets empty, and the length will default.

```
string [] DaysoftheWeek = new String [7]

{"Mon", "Tues", "Wed", "Thur", "Fri", "Sat", "Sun"};
//Above array has a determined length of 7

int [] RandomNum = {4, 58, 9, 27, 6};
//Above array's length is determined by the number of elements added – 5
```

Arrays can be initialized in the same statements as they are declared, or they can be initialized separately.

```
int [] Numbers; //here an array is declared by not initialized

//We can initialize separately
Numbers = new int [5] {1, 2, 3, 4, 5};
```

Alternatively, array elements could be initialized individually. Note, however, that this method requires you to write a statement for each element.

```
string [] Days = new String [7]
//Array is declared and 7 elements are created but no initialized

Days[0] = "Mon";
Days[1] = "Tue";
Days[2] = "Wed";
Days[3] = "Thur";
Days[4] = "Fri";
Days[5] = "Sat";
Days[6] = "Sun";

//Each element has been individually assigned a value
```

OPERATORS

As previously mentioned, operators are symbols that are associated with the execution of certain functions. These operations are executed on operands, the subjects of operations. Consider 2 + 3. In this example, the numbers are operands, and the + is an operator.

Operators have assigned functions and usually serve that function exclusively. Symbols reserved for operations cannot be used for anything else but that function. Here are some of the most common operators:

- To assign values we use =
- **Arithmetic operators:** These are operators we use when we want to execute equations

○ + is used for addition. This operator is somewhat unique. It is used in mathematical addition and to construct code. We can use + to add expressions to a statement or when building strings

○ – is used for subtraction

○ * is used for multiplication

○ / is used for division

- **Relational or Comparative operators:** These operators compare two values and return a true or false value

○ == means equal to

○ > means greater than

○ < means less than

○ >= means greater than equal to

○ <= less than equal to

○ != not equal to

- **Boolean Logical operators:** These operators return a true or false value regarding the

○ && (and) is used when two conditions are evaluated, and both conditions must be true. For example, x && y is only true when both x and y are true

○ || (or) is used when either of two conditions must be true. For example, x || y is true when either x or y is true

- ++ indicates that a value should be increased by one
- –– indicates that a value should be decreased by one

CONDITIONAL AND SWITCH STATEMENTS

Conditional statements allow us to branch our code to provide for possible eventualities. Some programs need the capacity for decision-making and consequential execution. There are two main conditional statements: if statements and switch statements.

If Statements

If statements are fairly straightforward. They provide instructions for if a condition is true. If statements are built on boolean results. If a condition returns a result of true, the code block is executed. If the condition results in false, an alternative instruction can be executed, or the program will move on to the next statement.

We write If statements with this formula:

```
if (condition)
{ /*Statements to be executed*/ }
```

Anything contained within the curly brackets is considered part of the code block for the If statement. It can be a single statement or multiple statements.

Using an If-Else statement, you would be able to make provision for both a true and false result. An If-Else statement looks like this:

if (condition)

```
{ /*Statements to be executed*/ }
else {executable code};
```

For example, if your program needs to separate adults from minors, it would need to weigh their age. An If statement would let you test the presented age against the age of adulthood–18. That scenario would look like this:

```
class Program
{
    static void Main ()
    {
        int age = 25;
        // We create a variable to record a person's age

        if (age >= 18)
        //This condition tests if the age is greater than or equal to 18.
        {
            Console.WriteLine ("You are an adult!");
            //This condition is met and the program does something
        }

        else
            Console.WriteLine ("You are not
            an adult!");
    }
}
```

More intricate If statements would provide for more eventualities. An Else-If statement would let us offer another condition for consideration if the initial condition returned false. In this way, programs can make more complicated decisions.

```
static void Main ()
{
    int number = 4;
    //Variable is declared and initialized

    if (number < 0) //Tests if the number is negative and returns a false value
    {
        Console.WriteLine ("This number is negative");
    }
    else if (number == 0) //Tests if the number is zero and returns a false value
    {
        Console.WriteLine ("This number is zero");
    {
    else if (number > 0)//Tests if the number is positive and returns a false value
    {
        Console.WriteLine ("This number is positive");
    {

    /* Example sourced from https://www.softwaretestinghelp.com/c-sharp/csharp-
    conditional-and-decision-statements/ *Retrieved in Aug 2022*/
```

Making provision for every possible outcome like this could end up in complex and overly long code. There is another way to offer the ability to choose between multiple options; the Switch statement.

Switch Statements

Switch statements are similar to If statements. The main difference is that If statements deal with true/false decisions while Switch statements make provision for multiple options. We use Switch statements when there are more than two potential branches from a condition. Where If statements are the programming equivalent of "chicken or beef?" Switch statements are the menus of the programming world.

Using a Switch statement, we can match the value of specific data to available possibilities. Each possibility is given its own set of executable instructions. The following example shows how a Switch statement might look.

```
string color = "red";
// a variable is declared and initialized

switch (color)
    /* we compare the value of the variable to the values below if a matching value is found,
    the relevant block is executed*/
{
    case "blue":
        Console.WriteLine ("You have choosen blue!");
        break;
        /* It's mandatory to have 'break;' after each case in a switch statement
        Its shows where that block ends instead of having to add { } around each block */

    case "orange":
        Console.WriteLine ("You have choosen orange!");
        break;

    case "yellow":
        Console.WriteLine ("You have choosen yellow!");
        break;

    case "green":
        Console.WriteLine ("You have choosen green!");
        break;

    case "red":
        Console.WriteLine ("You have choosen red!");
        break;
}
```

LOOPS

We use loops when certain pieces of code need to be executed multiple times. Instead of copying and pasting the same code as many times as it needs to run, we use a loop. This lets us keep our code shorter and easier to read. Loops are useful when code needs to be executed multiple times, but the exact number of repeats is unknown.

Loops function by using conditions. As long as the loop condition is false, the code will keep repeating. Loop conditions work much the same as conditional statements. The condition produces a true or false result, and we use that result to initiate the instructions within the loop. If the condition returns a true value, the code within the block is executed, and the loop starts again. The condition is tested again and again until it eventually returns false. Once the condition returns a false value, the loop is exited, and the program moves on to the next statement.

There are two different types of loops depending on the placement of the condition. In the first type, the condition is placed before the code. This means that the condition is tested before the code is executed. We call these **Entry Controlled Loops**. There are two entry-controlled loops:

- For loop
- While loop

The condition can also be placed after the loop statements. This would mean that the code is executed once before the statement is ever tested. If the condition is met, the code is executed a second time. If it is not met, the loop ends. This is called an **Exit Controlled Loop,** and we only have one of those:

- Do-while loop

Loops are an integral part of managing arrays. Without them, we would have to write code for each element. We can use loops with arrays by using a variable to represent the index value. With each iteration, the index variable will be increased, and the block will be applied to the next element in the array.

For Loop

We use this loop for as long as the condition returns true. For loops utilize a local counter variable that is increased with each iteration. The counter is declared within the loop parameters. That counter has only one purpose: to act as a progress tracker for how many times the loop repeats.

For loops are extremely useful when you know exactly how many times a loop should repeat or if you can determine how many repeats there will be. For loops are often used alongside arrays since we can easily determine exactly how many elements are in an array using the .length property.

For loops can be constructed with this formula:

```
for (initializer; condition; iterator)
{ /*statements to be executed*/ }
```

You will notice three values in the brackets following the word for. These are the loop's parameters. The initializer is the variable we will be using to run the loop. It is declared and initialized here and will only be available to the loop. The counter is only initialized once at the beginning of the loop. For example, int i = 0.

The condition is the part of the loop that tests the value of our variable to get the true/false result. For example, i < 10. If i starts at zero, the loop will keep repeating until that value becomes 10. For this to work, the counter needs to be increased with every iteration.

The iterator is where we change the counter value. This is the first of the executable instructions that will be executed if the condition returns true. For example, i++. This is what differentiates the For loop from the others. Its counter creates an environment where we are in control of how many times it executes. The counter can only increase until the condition is met and no further. Similarly, the loop won't stop repeating until the counter has increased the determined number of times. If we provide x number of iterations, the loop will execute x amount of times, no more and no less.

```
for (int i = 0; i < 10; i++)
    //We declare i and assign the value 0
    //The condition tests if i has a value less than 10 and returns true      //The iterator then increased i
to 1
{
    Console.WriteLine ("i = " + i);
}

/* Code adapted from https://www.tutorialsteacher.com/csharp/csharp-for-loop Retrieved Aug 2022 */
```

While Loop

While loops function very similarly to For loops. While the condition remains true, the While loop will keep repeating. Once the condition returns a false result, the loop ends, and the program moves on. The main difference between For and While loops is that the For loop creates a local variable for its condition. The While loop, on the other hand, uses a separate variable to test a condition. That doesn't mean we cannot use a counter in a While loop, however. That counter will just have to be declared and initialized somewhere outside the loop.

The While loop is good for when we cannot determine precisely how many times a loop will repeat. All we need for a While loop is a condition.

Unlike For loops, While loops provide for the eventuality of being unable to determine the exact number of iterations. Since any counter variable would be an external one, it can be affected by other parts of the code.

While loops can be constructed using this formula:

```
while (condition)
{ /*Statements to be executed*/ }
```

As you can see, it has one sole parameter. If you want to use a counter within a While loop condition, it is prudent to note that you would need to increase it within the loop's block of code. Otherwise, the same value will be tested over and over again. This loop will keep on running until the condition becomes false.

```
int i = 0;
// i is declared and initialized

while (i < 10)
    // The condition tests whether the value of i is less than 10 and returns true
{
    Console.WriteLine ("The value of i is: " + i);
    i++; // the value of i is increased by 1
}

/* Code sourced from https://www.knowledgehut.com/csharp/csharp-loops
Retrieved Aug 2022*/
```

Do... While Loop

This loop operates on the same logic as the While loop. However, the Do-While loop places the condition after the block. This means that the condition is tested for the first time only after the code has been executed once. With the For and While loops, code could only be run if the condition returned true. In the Do-While loop, the code is executed before the condition is even tested. That means that the code will be executed even if the condition returns false on the first iteration.

This loop is used when you want the code block to be executed at least once, no matter what. The other two loops will only execute code if the condition is met. The code provided in those loops can possibly execute zero times. With a Do-While loop, the code will be executed even if only once.

Do-While loops can be constructed using this formula:

```
do
{ /*Statements to be executed*/ } while
(condition);
```

```
int i = 15; //Variable declared and initialized for loop

do
/* An example of a do-while that will return true and execute a few times until the condition returns false */
{

    Console.WriteLine ("The value of i is: " +i);   i++;

} while (i < 20);

int k = 23; //variable declared and initialized for loop

do //an example of a do-while that will return false at the first test {

    Console.WriteLine ("The value of k is: " + k);
    k++;
    //These statements will execute even though the condition will be false

} while (k < 20);

/*Code adapted from https://www.geekforgeeks.org/loops-in-c-sharp/ Retrieved Aug 2022*/
```

CLASSES AND FIELDS

In programming, classes are used to structure code around objects. They can act as containers for data and methods. We can use classes to store blueprints for the objects we want to create. Consider it through the following example: A car consists of a collection of traits. If you think about it, there are many elements that work together to make a particular car distinct. The majority of those elements are also traits you will see in other cars. Think of features like color, the number of doors, max speed, and the car brand. These are all properties with a specific value we can utilize to make a blueprint of cars as objects.

A class can be used as a collection of the traits that make up an object. In that class, we can create variables to act as placeholders for the properties. We call these variables fields. Fields differ from traditional variables in that a single variable can hold one value. Fields represent that value for distinct objects. Using the above example, we can create multiple cars. Each of those cars would have a color field with a corresponding value. If the color field was to be a traditional variable, its value would change with each object, and the previous value would be lost.

Every element you add to a class is considered a member of that class.

Objects

The process of creating an object from a class blueprint is called instantiating. Instantiating an object involves calling the originating class, allocating an object name, and assigning unique values to the fields. Each object consists of three elements:

- Identity: An object's identity is the name you assign it when it is instantiated.
- States/Attributes: These are traits that all objects of this class have in common. These traits reflect the properties of the object. Attributes are represented by the values of each field.
- Behaviors: Behavior is represented by the methods associated with the object.

Suppose a dog is an object. Dogs each have a name that can be used to identify them and by which to call them. Dogs have attributes like fur color, age, and breed. Dogs are also associated with behaviors like barking, sleeping, or eating.

Static Classes and Fields

Classes and objects generally make use of instance values. This just means that each object of a class has its own copy of that value. Fields are instance values. Each object has a different value for any given field. Sometimes, however, values need to be the same across the board. That's where static comes in.

Static is a keyword we can use to modify programming structures. The word static indicates that there should be only one copy of the element in question. What this means is that its value remains unchanged by accessing members.

Classes can be static as well. Static classes are different from non-static classes in that they cannot be used to instantiate objects. They function as a collection point for related methods and members. All members of a static class must be static themselves. While you can create static members in non-static classes, you cannot have non-static members in a static class.

Static class members can still be accessed outside the class. One could say that static members are the property of their classes. To access a static member, you must call the class it resides in first. You do so like this: ClassName.MemberName.

Non-static classes can contain static fields. However, a static field will give instantiated objects the same value. Something like a color field would never be static.

DECLARING AND DEFINING CLASSES

Let's take a look at how to declare a class. Like every other structure in programming, classes need a unique name by which they can be referenced. When working in Unity, classes are automatically created when you open a new script. The class name in that case would be the same as the name of the file. If you change one, you will have to change the other to match.

For our example, let's say we make a game that features multiple different characters. Each character has its own set of stats and abilities. We can use a class to create a template from which to make objects for each character. Now, consider what stats a basic playable character would have: HP, defense, attack power, and type. We would need a field to represent each of these stats. Following that, we can instantiate objects for each character.

```
public class Character // class contains the variable to determine new character properties {

    public string name;
    public string type;
    public int hp;
    public int def;
    public int atk;

}

public class Play
{
    private Characters knight;
    // A new character knight is created

    void Build ()
    {
        knight = new Characters ();
        knight.name = "Sir Lance";
        knight.type = "Tank";
        knight.hp = 4000;
        knight.def = 2000;
        knight.atk = 600;
        //Our knight is assigned values as per the properties set out in the characters class
    }
}
```

We now have an object to represent one of our game characters. This object can be used and manipulated in our code. As you can imagine, if we had to create every object of the Character class in this way, our code would become tediously long. We can use constructors instead.

CONSTRUCTORS

Constructors are simple methods that can be called to instantiate objects. They take the same name as the class they are instantiating. If we have a class called Characters, the constructor will also be called Characters.

When a constructor is defined, parameters are assigned as per the fields of the class. Each parameter will be linked to one of the fields. If a class has x amount of fields, the constructor will have x amount of parameters. When calling the constructor to instantiate an object, we put the values we want to assign to fields as parameters.

For this purpose, we create local variables to act as placeholders and store the values. We cannot create variables of the exact same name as the fields, but it is convenient to allocate matching names. Slight variations in capitalization would be enough to distinguish them. For example, if we have a field called FirstName, we can create a corresponding variable called firstName. Similarly, if a field is called LastName, we can name the affiliated variable last-Name. It is a good idea to use the same capitalization convention for all fields and a different one for all corresponding variables to avoid confusion later.

Use this formula when defining a constructor:

```
public ConstructorName (DataType field1,
DataType field2)
{
Field1 = field1;
Field2 = field2;
}
```

The parameter variables are equated to the fields in the block. This is what instructs the constructor on what to do with the values given to it.

Using the above example, here's how the creation of a Character object would look using a constructor:

```
public class Character // class contains the variable to determine new character properties
{
    public string name;
    public string type;
    public int hp;
    public int def;
    public int atk;

    public Characters (string Name, string Type, int Hp, int Def, int Atk)
    // a constructor is created with field equivalent variables as parameters
    {
        name = Name;
        type = Type;
        hp = Hp;
        def = Def;
        atk = Atk;
        // The fields are assigned the values of the equivalent variables
    }
}

public class Play
{
    Characters knight = new Characters ("Sir Lance", "Tank", 4000, 2000, 600);
    // a new character object knight is instantiated with the fields values as parameters
}
```

DESTRUCTORS

As you might expect, destructors are used to destroy objects once they are no longer needed. Destructors are an implicit part of the .Net Framework and work as garbage collectors. They are called when the program closes and destroys the objects from the machine's memory. Destructors can only be used in the class they are defined in and cannot destroy objects instantiated from another class.

Destructors have no parameters and take the name of the class they are in. To distinguish them from constructors of the same class, their names are preceded by a tilde (~). You can construct them like this:

```
~ClassName ( )
{ /*executable code*/}
```

INHERITANCE

Inheritance is one of the main features of OOP and one of the reasons it is preferred over other paradigms. Inheritance occurs when one class has access to another class's members. This is inherent in ensuring code reusability.

There are two sides to an inheritance relationship:

- Base/Parent Class: The class from which the data and methods are inherited.
- Derived/Child Class: The class that inherits the data or methods.

The inheritance relationship is indicated in code by the use of a colon (:). The colon is an operator that signifies that the class on the left is to inherit from the class on the right. Inheritance is indicated when the derived class is declared. It looks like this:

```
class DerivedClass : BaseClass
```

There are multiple types of inheritance relationships. The first is **Single Inheritance**. This is when a single derived class inherits from a single base class.

Multilevel Inheritance is where a derived class inherits from a base class and then acts as the base class for a third class. What's interesting about this type of inheritance is that all the classes in this relationship are linked. You can have a chain of five classes and the last one would still have access to the first one, even though they are not in a direct inheritance relationship.

Hierarchical Inheritance is where one base class can act as the parent class to multiple derived classes.

Lastly, **Multiple Inheritance** is when one derived class inherits from multiple base classes.

METHODS

Methods are blocks of code aimed at completing a specific task grouped under one identifier. That task only gets completed once the method is called. As such, methods act as tools for keeping our code organized and making code reusable. Using methods, you can define the method and its block somewhere else and call it when needed. This is incredibly useful if your program needs to execute the same task multiple times.

Whenever a method is called, the program jumps to where it was created and executes the code it finds there. When it is done with the method block, the program will go back to where it left off and continue onwards.

Whenever you start a new program from a template, you will find a static method called Main. That method forms part of the C# structure and is executed when the program starts running. When making basic programs, most of your code will be used here. C# has many built-in methods. For example, sqrt is a method used to determine the square root of a number.

Methods can serve many purposes. Some of them are just collections of task-related statements, while others process data. Some of them even return values. The type of method will determine what it can do.

Types of Methods

There are a lot of different methods. We will take a quick look at the ones relevant to us and see what they can do and, most importantly, what we can use them for.

The first we will look at is **Parameterless Methods**. These methods serve to group statements aimed at fulfilling a function. They have no parameters and receive no data when called. For example, a method SayHi is called to display a hello message.

```
static void Main () //Main method called at the activation of the program {

    SayHi(); //Our custom method SayHi is called and executed
}

static void SayHi() //Custom method is declared {

    //You can put as many statement here as is needed to achieve the method's goal
    Console.WriteLine ("Hello Gamer");
}

/* Code adapted from https://www.mikedane.com/programming
languages/csharp/methods Retrieved Aug 2022*/
```

Next is the **Parameterized Method**. These methods can receive data to process or use through parameters when called. These methods utilize the data received as parameters in the execution of their block. For example, when using the SayHi method, we can provide a particular value to be included in the hello. We can input any name or value, and the display would change accordingly.

```
static void Main () //Main method called at the activation of the program {

    SayHi ("Gamer");
    //Our custom method SayHi is called and executed
    //In this example, the method is given the parameter "Gamer" to display
}

static void SayHi( string name)
//Custom method is declared and a parameter variable created to store the data it receives {

    Console.WriteLine ("Hello " + name);
}

/* Code adapted from https://www.mikedane.com/programming languages/
csharp/methods Retrieved Aug 2022*/
```

Parameter and Return Methods. Up to now, we've been using a lot of void methods. The keyword void indicates that the thing it refers to, holds no returnable value. Non-void methods can return a value when they are called. We mostly use these methods when they contain logic that needs to be applied to data. The following example shows a method where a number is taken to the method, displayed, and returned as is. Note, however, that we can do all sorts of things with that number. We could increase it and return the value of 16, or decrease it and return the value of 14.

```
static void Main () //Main method called at the activation of the program {


    ReturnValue(15);
    //Our Custom method ReturnValue is called and executed
}

static int ReturnValue (int num)
 //Custom method is declared and a parameter variable created to store the data it receives {

    Console.WriteLine ("This is the value " + num);
return num;
}

/* Code adapted from https://tutorialslink.com/articles/different-types-of-method-in-c/1164
Retrieved Aug 2022*/
```

The word "return" indicates the value that should be returned to where the method was called. In this way, we can use methods to do calculations and assign their value to a variable like this: int result = Calculate(5). The Calculate method would take the value it was given, run it through the calculations and return the answer to the variable result.

Lastly, **Virtual Methods.** These are methods that can be defined in a base class and overridden in a derived class. They allow us to adapt default methods to suit a particular class's needs. We will discuss virtual methods more when discussing polymorphism.

ACCESS MODIFIERS

Modifiers are keywords we use to describe the state of members. Access modifiers are specifically aimed at describing the accessibility of members. They specify who can have access to the member they define. A particular method might need to be available to all other classes in that project, or it might need to remain completely inaccessible to anything outside the class it is in.

The most common access modifiers are:

- **Public**: A public object can be accessed by anyone within that project. Basically, public objects are accessible to the entire program. This is the most accessible type of object.
- **Private**: A private object can be accessed only by other members of the class it was created in. Only other members of that class can use it. This is the least accessible type of object.
- **Protected**: These objects can be accessed by other members from the same class or from classes derived from it. Protected members are like private members that can be inherited.

There are, of course, other access modifiers available, but these are sufficient for our purpose.

Why use access modifiers? If all structures in a program are public, data could get out of hand quickly. Some DataTypes and methods ought to remain inaccessible to maintain data integrity and functionality. Having some structures remain private means they won't interfere in the functioning of other areas while ensuring their usefulness to the class they exist in.

SCOPE OF VARIABLES

The accessibility of variables is determined by their scope. This correlates to where variables can be used and who can access them. The scope of a variable is dependent on where it is declared. There are three categories of scope for variables:

- Class Level Scope: Class level variables are declared in a class outside any method or block. These variables can be used anywhere in the class. These types of variables make up fields and act as members of that class.
- Method Level Scope: These variables are declared in a method. They are available for use anywhere within that method but not outside of it. They are created when the method is called and ceases to exist afterward. They are considered local variables to that method and everything in it.
- Block Level Scope: block level variables are declared within a block and can only be used inside that block. The best example of a block variable is the counter variable we use in For loops. They are most prominently used in For and While loops and, as a result, are often called loop variables.

```
class Method
{
    //Here is where class level scope starts. Variable created here are class level variables   int
ClassVariable = 1;

    static void Main ()
    {
        //Here is where the method level scope starts. Variables created here are method level variables  int
        MethodVariable = 2;

        for (int i = 0; i < 10; i++)
        {
            //Here is where block level scope starts. Variables here are block
variables      // In this case, i is a block variable
        }
    }
}
```

EVENTS

Whenever something that requires attention happens in a program, an event is raised. Events can be induced by various things, including user interaction, program notifications, or machine interruptions. Events are used to enable classes to communicate with each other. It also allows for easier expansion of the program.

Most programs, and games especially, need to be upgraded or patched at some point. Even something as simple as adding a method to notify the user of something could result in multiple errors. Whenever the code is changed, the relevant classes need to be recompiled. If that change affects other classes, it could result in all sorts of problems you might not have provided for. An easy way to bypass this risk is to use events.

Events allow one class to call on other classes when something happens that requires a follow-up action. The class in which the event takes place and where the event is raised is called the publisher. The classes that react are called subscribers. Subscribers are classes that have been registered to handle the event. They contain the statements that would respond to the event.

This is better understood with an example. Our example program is used to run a food-ordering service. A customer would input their order, and the program would create an object representing the order in the system. The order would be sent to a class that handles food preparation. Once the food has been prepared, the system would be informed that the order is complete, and the user would be notified in turn. Different notifications are managed by separate classes. To get those classes to alert the user, the food preparation class would have to communicate with those classes, creating a specific relationship. This could cause problems if we later want to change the notification process.

Instead of creating a relationship between those classes, we can use an event instead. Instead of the preparation class communicating directly with the notification classes, the preparation class could raise an event, and the notification classes can respond. This would be equivalent to a chef ringing a bell and a waiter responding instead of the chef needing to talk to the waiter personally.

In this scenario, the preparation class is the publisher, and the notification classes are subscribers. With no direct relationship between a publisher and subscribers, we can change the subscribers as much as we want without affecting the publisher at all. If we need to change the notification system in the future, we would simply change who responds to the event.

Setting Up The Publisher

In order to set up an event for a publisher to raise, we need to:

- define a delegate
- define an event based on that delegate
- provide for the publication of that event

We define a delegate to take care of the event handling. Delegates are a type of reference variable in C# used to call methods by their signatures. They allow us to call methods as parameters to other methods and offer event handling.

Delegates are defined by using the delegate keyword to indicate their type. They are usually public void and are given a unique name. Delegates are conventionally given a descriptive name followed by "EventHandler," e.g. FoodPreparedEventHandler. Event delegates take two parameters. The first is generally "object source" to indicate the publisher when called. The second is a variable of type EventArgs that contains event information. If there is no event information specified, its value is EventArgs.Empty or null. The delegate can be defined outside any class or inside the publisher class.

Secondly, an event is declared related to the delegate. The event is of the type of the delegate and contains the delegate's name in its declaration. It is conventionally given a matching name, e.g., FoodPrepared.

Lastly, we make provision for the event in the publisher class. This means creating a protected virtual void method related to the event. It is usually named "On" followed by the name of the event, e.g. OnFoodPrepared. The event is called in that method.

```
public class FoodOrderingService {

    public delegate void FoodPreparedEventHandler (object source, EventArgs e);

//A delegate is defined
    public event FoodPreparedEventHandler FoodPrepared;
    //the consequent event is created

    public void prepareOrder ()
    //Method to notify that the order is being made
/*if this were an actual program, this would be where the program starts the food preparation
process */
{
    Console.WriteLine ("Your order is being prepared..." );
    OnFoodprepared(); //We call the method that would raise the event

}

    protected virtual void OnFoodPrepared ()
       //This is the handler method where the event will be raised once the order has been prepared
       {
       if (FoodPrepared != null)
           FoodPrepared (this, null);
    //The null is the above statements is only because we don't have event info
       }
}

/* Code sources and adapted from https://code-maze.com/csharp-events/ retrieved Aug 2022 */
```

Next, we need to register subscriber classes to deal with the event.

Setting Up Subscribers

Subscribers deal with the event. When an event is triggered, the program needs to respond. In a game-development context, events would be triggered by user interaction like pressing the spacebar to make a character jump. In response, the program would need to make the character jump. The code to respond to an event is contained in the subscriber classes. As such, we need them to subscribe to the event.

Firstly, if the responding code hasn't already been created, we need to provide the code that will be executed in the response. A method is defined that the delegate can call in response to the event. You will notice in the following example that it has the same name as the method in which the event was raised. The response method has the same parameters as the delegate, and that links them. When the event is raised, the delegate will automatically call the method that matches its signature, i.e., the method with the same parameters. The name of the method doesn't matter.

```
public class NotifyService
//This is a class we want to register as subscriber to the event
{
    public void OnFoodPrepared (object source, EventArgs e)
    //We create a method with the same parameters as the delegate
    {
        Console.WriteLine ("Your food is ready!");
    }

/* Code sourced and adapted from https://code-maze.com/csharp-event/ Retrieved
Aug 2022*/
```

When the method is set up, we equate the event to the handling method. To do this, we use the += operator. Linking the event and the handling method automatically links the class in which that method is declared, thus subscribing the class to the event. This takes place where your core processing happens. This is often in the Main method and doesn't have to be in either the publisher or subscriber.

In the following example, the publisher and subscriber classes are instantiated to create variables to represent the classes in the Main method. The event defined in the publisher is equated to the corresponding method in the subscriber. Thereafter, the method responsible for creating the order is called. When the order has been completed, the event will be called and handled.

```
static void Main ()
{
    //We create variables to instantiate the publisher and subscriber classes
    var orderService = new FoodOrderingService ();
    var notifyService = new NotifyService ();

    orderService.FoodPrepared += notifyService.OnFoodPrepared;
    /* Here is where the event is subscribed to += is an operator used to point
    the event to the method it is handled in */
}

/* Code soureced and adapted from https://code-maze/csharp-events/ Retrieved Aug
2022 */
```

EventHandler<TEventArgs>

The illustrations above are not how we usually handle events in functional programs, but it serves to demonstrate how the process works. C# has a built-in delegate called EventHandler that manages events for us. This means that we do not have to define a custom delegate for every event we create. If we are not creating custom delegates, we also are not creating events of their type. Instead, our events are defined to be of the type EventHandler<TEventArgs>. The event declaration from the above example would look like this: public event EventHandler<TEventArgs> FoodPrepared.

TEventArgs is a parameter holding the event information to pass event data to the EventHandler. We can create custom event data by creating a class that inherits from the built-in EventArgs. This class is conventionally named something descriptive followed by "EventArgs," e.g., FoodPreparedEventArgs. We can now change event handling methods to use this class as a parameter by replacing EventArgs with FoodPreparedEventArgs.

Additionally, using the built-in EventHandler, we can use Event?.Invoke ( ) in the method where the event is raised instead of the more complex if statement. This solution is more secure and less intricate.

POLYMORPHISM

Polymorphism is one of the main features of OOP and comes hand-in-hand with inheritance. When one class inherits from another, they have access to their members. Polymorphism takes this a step further in allowing those members to be used in ways that go beyond inheritance. Having more than one use for a singular object is the basis of polymorphism.

Polymorphism allows us to create more than one use for the methods and objects in our programs. It also allows our objects to take on multiple forms. Functional programs need to be capable of some degree of decision-making. We see this in conditional statements. A program needs to do different things based on what its users do. This might involve being able to adapt a method to a slightly different context. Polymorphism enables us to create a base class containing a basic method that derived classes can adapt to fulfill their own purpose.

For example, a program that calculates the area of a shape based on a user's input would need to be capable of calculating the area of various shapes. The area of a triangle is calculated differently than the area of a square is calculated. Of course, you could create separate methods to calculate each shape and use conditional statements to determine which one should be used. However, with polymorphism, there's another option. We could create a base class that would contain the standard method Area. This method would do the work of gathering the input data and processing it. Now we can create derived classes for each shape that would inherit Area and its variables. Each class would be able to adapt the Area method for its shape by overriding it.

As you can imagine, polymorphism comes with its own set of potential issues. If one object has multiple forms, how does the program know which of them to use? This will depend on the type of polymorphism at play. Polymorphism creates the potential for an object to have multiple forms. This doesn't mean that polymorphic objects have more than one form at all times. Methods, for example, only take on another form when they are called in the right context, and that other form doesn't exist anywhere else. At the same time, not all objects are automatically polymorphic. Only the objects you create more than one form of will be polymorphic.

Static Polymorphism

Static polymorphism is also known as early binding or Compile Time Polymorphism. It is resolved when the program is compiled. This kind of polymorphism occurs when multiple methods are given the same name but assigned different parameters. We call this overloading. Despite having the same name, these methods are intended to complete separate tasks. At the time of compiling, the compiler can decide which method is referred to when the shared name is called by considering their signatures and the context. By the time the program is run, the decision has already been made. This is a faster manner of resolution since the decision of which method is being called is made early on and not in the moment.

Dynamic Polymorphism

Dynamic polymorphism is also known as late binding or Run Time Polymorphism. This refers to polymorphism that's resolved when the program is run. This is referred to as overriding. This occurs when methods of the same name and signature exist in separate contexts. These methods usually have the same purpose but different execution. The above example of calculating the area of shapes is an example of overriding.

This type of polymorphism cannot be resolved at the time of compiling since all forms of the polymorphic method need to be available and functional. Where static polymorphism involves multiple options for one execution, dynamic polymorphism involves one option being adjusted to fit numerous functions. As such, the resolution occurs when the method is called to change.

This is also where virtual methods fit in. Virtual methods serve the purpose of being overridden. In order to maintain code integrity, we cannot just allow all methods to be overridden. Some methods need to remain as they are. Of course, we can set these methods to private so derived classes won't be able to access them. That doesn't, however, protect methods that need to be accessible for the functionality of the program. Thus, virtual methods. Having a distinct type of method that can be overridden provides security for methods that need to be accessible but not changeable. Only virtual methods can be overridden.

4

CODE GAMERS BEST PRACTICES

Now that we've had some time to get familiar with C#, it is time to apply that knowledge to the Unity context. Coding in Unity is done through scripts. While we use C# in Unity, we do not necessarily use it in the same way as we would with general programming.

WORKING WITH SCRIPTS IN UNITY

If you will remember, GameObjects are containers for components. Components are adjusted in the Inspector or through the application of scripts. Scripts in Unity are another component we can attach to any given GameObject.

In general programming, classes are often in the same file. In Unity, a new class is assigned to each new script, and you will have a separate script for each class. In this way, classes are linked to specific GameObjects. That doesn't mean you cannot have multiple classes per file, but it is not recommended.

Creating a New Script

If a GameObject needs to be manipulated through code, it requires a linked script. Creating a new script is fairly easy, and there are multiple ways to do it. The first way is to select the object you want to attach a script to and select Add Component from the Inspector. You will find an option for a new script when you search for any component. The script is automatically attached to the object and will appear in your Assets folder.

Another way of creating a new script is to add one through the Project window. Go to the folder you want the script saved in and right-click in the folder space. Select Create and choose C# Script. Now you can drag the file from the Project window to the object you want to attach it to. Alternatively, go to the Assets tab on the menu bar and hit Create and then C# Script. This will create a file in your project folder that can be dragged onto an object.

Once attached, the script will execute when you run your project.

Unity automatically adds a template to the file and creates a class of the same name as the file. If the names do not match, you won't be able to attach the script to an object. Assign the correct name from the start so you can avoid the hassle of changing it later. Be sure to give your file a suitable name.

Working in Scripts

You will need an external code editor or IDE to edit a script. Unity uses Visual Studio by default, but you can change that under Preferences. From the menu bar, select Edit > Preferences, and then open External Tools. You will be able to set which external editor you want to use. If you do not already have a preferred code editor or IDE, Visual Studio comes highly recommended. You can download the Visual Studio Installer from Microsoft's website. The community version of Visual Studio is free. When installing any IDE, confirm that it supports the .Net Framework and C#. If you are using Visual Studio, make sure you have the .Net Framework workspace added as well as the Unity workspace.

When you open the script for the first time, you will see the Unity template. It looks like this:

```
using System.Collections;
using System.Collections.Generic;
using UnityEngine;

public class TestingScripts: MonoBehavior
{
    //Start is called before the first frame update
    void Start ()
    {

    }

//Update is called once per frame
    void Update ()
    {

    }
}
```

All scripts in Unity inherit from the built-in class MonoBehaviour. Note that it uses the British spelling for the word behavior. MonoBehaviour is a library that contains most, if not all, of the basic properties you will need for scripting in Unity. It provides the framework for manipulating components and for attaching scripts to objects.

You will notice two methods that appear in all Unity scripts. These are the Start and Update methods. Start is called automatically when the object the script is attached to becomes active. It is akin to the Main method in traditional programming. This method is commonly used to initialize variables and other members. This method runs only once.

Update is used to manage the object's frame updates. Depending on the game's build, the game will be updated once per frame. For a 60-fps game, the game will update 60 times per second. The code is scanned once per frame for code that has become relevant since the previous scan. That code is then applied. It is an automatic process and thus extremely useful for functional code.

COMPILING SCRIPTS

Since you will have separate files for each class, you will have several files scattered across multiple folders. These all need to be compiled into one functional program.

Assemblies

Unity automatically sorts through all project folders and compiles files into an assembly. An assembly is essentially a library of successfully compiled scripts. You can either stick with the default assembly or create unique assembly definitions. The downside to using the default assembly is that every time you edit a file, the entire library will need to recompile. The compile time increases with each individual script.

Instead, you can set up custom assemblies. One project can have multiple assemblies. By defining them yourself, you have more control over the time it takes to compile your project. Grouping scripts into smaller libraries will result in not needing to recompile the entire project if one of the files is changed. Only the assembly containing the edited file will need to recompile.

Another benefit of defining custom assemblies is that it will provide more security as regards object accessibility. The access modifier "public" gives access to all classes in an assembly. If all your files are in the same assembly, all classes would have access to public variables. Custom assemblies maximize interactivity without overexposing data.

To define a new assembly, create an assembly definition file from the Project window. Sort the scripts you want to group together into a separate folder under Assets, and add an Assembly Definition file to that folder. The scripts contained in this folder will compile into the defined assembly.

You can change the assembly name in the Inspector of the assembly definition. The name of the definition file and the folder it is hosted in has no effect on the assembly's name. You can also set Preferences and other properties in the Inspector.

Conditional Compilation

Unity utilizes directives to provide an opportunity for the compiler to elect whether or not code should be compiled. This decision is based on a condition, much like in conditional statements. Conditional statements let a program decide whether or not to execute code at run-time. Directives let the compiler decide whether or not parts of the code should be compiled at all.

If we want to create cross-platform games, we will have to make allowance for each of those systems. There are disparities between the different platforms, and we must adjust our games accordingly. At the same time, we cannot simply make a copy for each available platform and make the relevant adjustments. That would involve duplication. Instead, we can utilize directives to instruct the compiler to compile specified code only under specific circumstances.

For example, using #if UNITY_STANDALONE_WIN {/*code*/} #endif, would let the compiler test if the program is for a Windows stand-alone. If it is, the compiler can compile the code. If it is not, the code is ignored.

Directives are indicated using a hash (#). There are numerous conditions that can be used in this way.

Special Files and Compilation Order

Unity reserves several file and folder names for their use. Folders like Assets and Plugins serve a specific function in the project and indicate the purpose of their files. You can store your files inside these directories, but you cannot and should not create folders with the same names. Suffice it to say these folders have been reserved for a reason.

Unity compiles in four separate stages. Where in the timeline a script is compiled depends on its location in the Project directory. The stages work as follows:

- First, **Assembly-CSharp-firstpass:** The first files to be compiled are the run-time files found in the Standard Assets, Pro Standard Assets, and Plugins folders.
- Secondly, **Assembly-CSharp-Editor-firstpass:** Next, Unity will compile scripts in all folders named Editor located in the top-level directories of the Standard Assets, Pro Standard Assets, and Plugins folders.
- Thirdly, **Assembly-CSharp:** all remaining scripts outside Editor folders will be compiled.
- Lastly, **Assembly-CSharp-Editor:** All scripts that have not been compiled by this point will now be compiled.

CODING CONVENTIONS

We briefly discussed naming conventions in Chapter 3, but there's more to coding conventions than how we name our objects. There are also conventional guides for how to structure code, how to use space to our advantage, and how to use comments.

Coding conventions are not mandatory. No one is going to force you to apply them. However, there is a reason why programming has adopted certain conventions. Conventions are supported and upheld because they make things easier for everyone.

Very few projects are built in isolation. It might just be you and your computer for now, but you will eventually find yourself in a community looking for help or offering advice. You might even end up working in teams to complete larger-scale projects. At some point in your career, you will start making contributions to online libraries or working in someone else's code. When that happens, you need to be capable of producing readable and comprehensible code. It would mean coding in a conventional style or even adopting another style entirely.

The key to coding well is consistency. When coding in a particular style, it is important to apply that style throughout the entire project. This applies to both working alone and working in a group. If you name objects in a specific way, name all your objects the same way. Consistency leads to quicker and more accurate coding. The more settled you are in a style, the less you have to actively think about it. This also improves team relations. When there's a consistent style, there's less time spent on trying to figure out what other members were doing and less time spent butting heads. Consistency makes code readable and easier to understand.

There are numerous Microsoft publications on C# conventions, but they won't all apply to Unity conventions. General C# conventions were not developed with Unity's structure in mind, and as such, we need to adjust them.

Naming Conventions

Naming conventions offer guidelines for how we assign names for our code objects and how we name files. Part of naming conventions is capitalization styles.

There are two main case styles in programming, Camel case, and Pascal case. Both refer to the capitalization of each word in a compound name. However, with Camel case, you can elect to keep the first word lowercase. In Pascal case, the first word is always capitalized. From here on, whenever we refer to Camel case, it will mean keeping the first word lowercase, e.g., firstName. When mentioning Pascal case, we refer to the first word being capitalized, e.g., FirstName. For the sake of clarity, we will use camelCase and PascalCase.

C# general conventions forbear the use of hyphens (-) and underscores (_) in object names. Of course, you can still use them, but it is convention not to. The convention carries over to Unity scripts. In particular, it is recommended to avoid hyphens and underscores when working in Mono libraries.

Use PascalCase when assigning names to classes and methods and camelCase when assigning names to variables and fields. This is a great way to imply the functionality of members with similar names. All names in code are case-sensitive. That means that FirstName, firstName, and firstname are distinct names and can be used in the same code. This distinction of case styles means you can use similar names for objects that exist in a relationship.

Always use descriptive names where possible. Choosing generic names could confuse both you and anyone reading your code. Assign names that imply the object's purpose and functionality. Some variables inherently take generic names because of their function. For example, counters in For loops will almost always be

i. That being said, you do not want to find yourself combing through your code trying to find what the purpose of this or that object was. Avoid generic names like string1 or MethodA.

It is useful to include function-related suffixes to objects that serve a specific purpose. Delegates, for example, usually take the suffix EventHandler or CallBack depending on their intended purpose. This serves to create a distinction between delegates that handle events and delegates that are assigned to methods. This also applies to other members.

When saving your files, pick a case convention to use on all your files. Give your files appropriate and descriptive names. Unity scripts especially, need to be named carefully. The name given to the file is the name that will be assigned to the class. You will have multiple script files and as such, need to name them in a way that indicates their purpose.

Style Conventions

Style conventions relate to how screen space is utilized and how code is displayed. It also relates to how code is structured within that space. Blocks can become convoluted and are easier to make sense of when structured appropriately. You will notice this in the code examples.

We can break code down into a hierarchy of sorts. Everything on the same level is displayed on the same vertical line. Whenever a new block opens within another block, it is indented to form a new level in the hierarchy. This way, you can easily tell what level something is on by where it sits on the screen.

A good rule of thumb is to use blank space for clarity. Computers and compilers automatically ignore the blank spaces between lines and instead rely on syntax to determine the beginning and end of blocks and statements. Add blank lines on either side of a method. You can group block members by function and use a blank line to distinguish them from other statements. For example, group all variable declarations together at the top of a block and add a line to separate them from the rest of the block. This makes it easier to keep track of all the variables in one block.

Keep curly brackets on their own lines, especially the closing brackets. Some IDEs automatically place brackets in new lines when you open them and hit enter in between. The brackets are usually in line with the declaring statement of the block and everything inside them is indented. The opening brackets can be on a separate line or in line with the block declaration for the sake of maintaining vertical space. Having each bracket on its own line makes it easy to keep track of them and see if brackets are closed properly.

For example, they can be displayed like this:

```
static void Main ( )
{
//code
}
Or like this:
static void Main ( ) {
//code
}
```

On the topic of brackets, it is preferable to use brackets even when you do not technically need to. If a method only has one statement, you do not technically need brackets. However, it is recommended to use brackets anyway. This makes it easier to add to the method later and keeps things neat.

If you are ever in a situation where one line becomes too long, you can wrap the text to begin on a new line. In that scenario, indent the code to show that it is a continuation and not a new statement. C# allocates 180 spaces per line, but it is good to have your code fit the screen. Make it so that you do not have to use the horizontal scroll bar to read your lines. In the case of parameters crossing multiple lines, indent them to start in line with the brackets.

To illustrate, it is easier to read this:

```
namespace Program
{
  public class Hello Gamers

  static int ReturnAdd (int num1, int num2)
  {
    return num1 + num2;
  }

  static void main ()
  {
    Random rnd = new Random();
    int firstNum = rnd.Next(0,10);
    int secondNum = rnd.Next(0,10);

    Console.WriteLine(ReturnAdd(firstNum, secondNum));

  }
  }
}
```

Then it is to read this:

```
namespace Program
{public class Hello Gamers
static int ReturnAdd (int num1, int num2
{ return num1 + num2;}
  static void main ()
  { Random rnd = new Random();
int firstNum = rnd.Next(0,10);
int secondNum = rnd.Next(0,10);
Console.WriteLine(ReturnAdd(firstNum, secondNum)); } } }
```

Note that it is actually quite difficult to have bad structure. You'd have to go out of your way to circumvent most IDEs' automatic structuring of code.

Another aspect of style conventions is how you utilize comments. Each programmer uses comments differently. In this book, comments are used to illustrate the code examples. Comments are not usually used to this degree in practice. How you use them in your own code is up to you. Comments do not need to be grammatically correct and contain full sentences. It is up to you to decide if you want to use consecutive lines of //comments or always use /*comments*/. Regardless of how you use them, use them.

GENERAL BEST PRACTICES

Avoid using string variables for anything other than display values. We rarely refer to objects by their file names using a variable, and as such, string variables are not used much in Unity code. If you must use strings, use them as constant variables so their values won't be changeable.

Do not use arrays for objects in Unity scripts. In general programming, arrays can be linked to simulate databases. You can link arrays so that Name[3], PhoneNumber[3], and Age[3] all refer to the same person. That doesn't work as effortlessly with Unity. Instead of using linked arrays, use object instances with field properties. Arrays are difficult to set up in the Inspector, and as such, it is better to avoid them. Of course, there are exceptions to this rule.

Having multiple files with their own unique class has certain drawbacks. For one, you won't have everything in one document; instead, information would be contained in multiple separate files. To make it easier to find specific information, add a descriptive header to your scripts. In this header, give a brief overview of what's contained in the class and to what the class relates. The header consists of a few lines of code at the top of the file above the using statements or just below them.

If you are making significant contributions to public files or making your code available online, add your details to the header so others can give you due credit. Do not publicize personal information like home addresses for safety reasons. If you use someone else's work in your code, cite them. Plagiarism in programming is complex since there are only so many ways in which one can code, and duplication is unavoidable. If you didn't personally come up with code, cite it. It doesn't matter too much if you are just coding as a personal project. However, if you are planning on publishing or selling your code, cite sources. Most programmers share their code freely, but be respectful.

Lastly, when instantiating a new object, use the DataType var if the class name is included on the right side of =. When instantiating a class object, we first need to create a new object of that class. To do so, we define an object name and equate it to a new ClassName. If you are only creating the variable do: ClassName ObjectName; and if you are initializing it do: var ObjectName = new ClassName;

GENERAL TROUBLESHOOTING

Problem-solving is inherent to programming. Code seldom runs perfectly on the first try. If your code is not executing the way it should, here are some general troubleshooting tips:

- Scan your code for highlights. Most IDEs or code editors will highlight or underline errors and possible flaws. If your code is not working right, scan through it to see if there are highlights.
- Check spelling and name consistency. It is incredibly easy to make typos and not notice them. This counts for both names and commands. These will most likely pop up as highlights, but it doesn't hurt to double-check.

- Make sure that every opening bracket has a corresponding closing bracket. You can also check that statements are enclosed in the right set of brackets. If a method is not returning the value it should, it could be that one of its statements is outside the method block. To this end, it is better to type the brackets before building the statements.
- Lastly, make sure that each statement ends in a semi-colon. Compilers are not foolproof.

When all else fails, try again. Programming can be complex, and there's often more than one way to approach a solution. If your code doesn't work no matter what you do, try approaching the problem from a different angle.

THINGS TO REMEMBER WHEN SCRIPTING

Use descriptive names where you can, and include headers in your scripts to provide an overview of what each file contains.

Keep your scripts modular. While it is possible to have more than one class per script, it is not recommended. Each script will be attached to a GameObject so stick to code that's relevant to the object a script will be attached to. Organize your scripts into related assemblies to reduce compile time.

Most IDEs have an autocomplete function. You do not have to type out each word letter-by-letter. Keep an eye on the screen, and make use of the pop-up suggestions. On a similar note, if you need to look at your hands while typing, make sure to look at your code every once in a while. It is easier to fix typos as they happen than it is to try to find mistakes later. Most IDEs check syntax, but they do not always pick up spelling mistakes or general typos.

Create a separate folder on your desktop where you can stash useful code snippets as you come across them. Having a personal library full of useful code can save a lot of time and effort. Keep this folder separate from your project files. This collection doesn't need to be code files. It can be as simple as an indexed Word document or text file. Make sure to keep the folder organized.

Use empty GameObjects to organize your Hierarchy and scene. This is useful for managing big groups of objects in a script. If you have a crowd of spawned enemies and want to disable them, it is easier to disable a parent object than it is to individually disable each spawn. In this way, you can use empty parent objects like folders in a directory. This will help you maintain order in your Hierarchy. Do not just leave all objects as single entries in your Hierarchy. The less scrolling you have to do to navigate it, the better.

Remember to save unique object configurations as Prefabs. Simultaneously, remember to update your Prefabs regularly. There are few things as disheartening as losing a masterpiece and then having to build it again from scratch.

Most importantly, maintain workspace organization. Just because everything you work with is contained to a computer does not mean it won't get chaotic. Maintain directory structures. Do not let it get out of hand by thinking "it's fine, I'll just tidy up later." Here are some tips for maintaining an organized workspace:

- Do not store files in the root directories, especially not in the Assets folder. The location of your files will affect the order of compilation. The compiler shifts through the root directories first. Having all your files in there will slow down the process.

- Do not dump your files in the first available space. Take the extra time to find/create an appropriate place to store each file. The order of compilation is dependent on proper folder hierarchy.
- Make sure to save files at regular intervals to avoid losing progress.

Lastly, something interesting to think about. When playing a game, you are bound to certain rules and limitations. As a developer, you do not have to be bound to the same limitations when testing your game. Game cheats and editor cheats can help you test a game in ways it wouldn't otherwise be tested. For example, if you are building a combat game that involves a lot of character respawn, there's no reason to limit the number of lives you have available.

5

SCRIPTING TIME

UNITY REFRESHER

L et's take another quick look at the Unity Editor interface. If you need a more in-depth refresher, head back to Chapter 2. Remember, you can change the layout of the Editor to fit your preferences.

The important windows are:

- The Scene View where you build your game scenes
- The Game View where you can see what a player will see
- The Project window where you access your project files
- The Hierarchy window where the objects added to your game are listed
- The Inspector window where you can set and manipulate object components
- The Transforming tools toolbar where you can access the transforming tools

To create new projects or open existing projects, open the Unity Hub. In the projects tab, you will find your existing projects and the option for creating a new project.

CREATING YOUR FIRST CLASSES

As a reminder, classes in Unity each have their own file. Remember that class names must be the same as the script file names. Classes can be used to create a blueprint for objects, and objects can be created from them through instantiation.

Follow along and build your first class using Unity. We will create a class called Database that will act as a collection point for all your game items. Items will be instantiated from separate blueprint classes called Weapons and Armor.

In a new project, create an empty GameObject called Database. This object will serve to contain our Database class and attach it to the game. In the Project window, create a suitable folder under Assets in which to save your scripts. In that folder, create a new script and name it Database. If you cannot remember how to create a script, turn back to the section on creating scripts in Chapter 4. Once the script has been created, drag it onto the object in the Hierarchy.

In the same folder, create two new scripts called Weapons and Armor respectively. Do not attach these to the object. These classes will contain our object blueprints and do not form part of the game functionality. We will only use them to instantiate item objects.

Your Editor will look something like this:

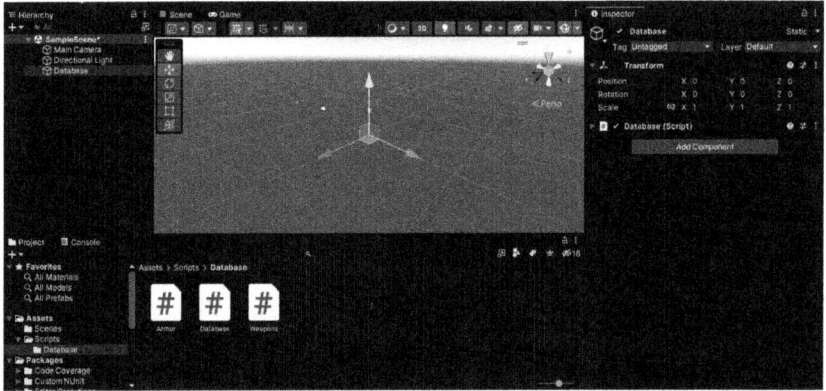

Notice the GameObject in the Hierarchy and the script component in its Inspector.

Go ahead and open the scripts. For now, leave the Database script as it is. Let's start in Armor. Firstly, since the Armor class is not needed for game functionality and won't be attached to a GameObject, remove the inheritance from MonoBehaviour. Above the class declaration, add [System.Serializable]. This will allow us to assign values to the objects from the Inspector.

```
using System.Collections;
using System.Collections.Generic;
using UnityEngine;

[System.Serializable]
public class Armor
{
    //Start is called before the first frame update
    void Start ()
    {

    }

    //Update us called once per frame
    void Update ()
    {

    }
}
```

Go ahead and repeat these steps in the Weapons class.

```
using System.Collections;
using System.Collections.Generic;
using UnityEngine;

[System.Serializable]
public class Weapons
{
    //Start is called before the first frame update
    void Start ()
    {

    }

    //Update us called once per frame
    void Update ()
    {

    }
}
```

Next, we can create fields inside these classes to create stats for our items. We will only create a few fields to illustrate how this works. You can create as many fields as needed to reflect the properties of the objects you want to create. In Armor, declare public integer fields for defense, resistance, and dodge attributes.

```
using System.Collections;
using System.Collections.Generic;
using UnityEngine;

[System.Serializable]
public class Armor
{
    public int defense;
    public int resistance;
    public int dodge;

    //Start is called before the first frame update
    void Start ()
    {

    }

    //Update us called once per frame
    void Update ()
    {

    }
}
/* Code sources from https://medium.com/nerd-for-tech/what-are-classes-in-unity-
620e467fd4f Retrieved Aug 2022*/
```

Similarly, in Weapons, declare public integer fields for damage, attack speed, and range properties. These fields are all declared integers because their values will be whole numbers. These fields could be of any DataType to suit the values they represent.

```
using System.Collections;
using System.Collections.Generic;
using UnityEngine;

[System.Serializable]
public class Weapons
{
    public int damage;
    public int attackSpeed;
    public int range;

    //Start is called before the first frame update
    void Start ()
    {

    }

    //Update us called once per frame
    void Update ()
    {

    }
}
/* Code sources from https://medium.com/nerd-for-tech/what-are-classes-in-unity-
620e467fd4f Retrieved Aug 2022*/
```

Make sure to save script files whenever you make changes to them. The changes will only reflect in Unity once the files have been saved.

Now that our blueprints are ready, it is time to create objects to represent some game items. For this example, let's create two Armor items (helmet and chestplate) and three Weapons items (sword, knife, and axe). In the Database class, define three new objects using the following formula: public Class ObjectName. Ensure that the Database still inherits from MonoBehaviour. Your script will look like this:

```
using System.Collections;
using System.Collections.Generic;
using UnityEngine;

public class Database : MonoBehaviour
{
    public Armor helmet;
    public Armor chestplate;
    public Weapons sword;
    public Weapons knife;
    public Weapons axe;

    //Start is called before the first frame update
    void Start ()
    {

    }

    //Update us called once per frame
    void Update ()
    {

    }
}
/* Code sources from https://medium.com/nerd-for-tech/what-are-classes-in-unity-
620e467fd4f Retrieved Aug 2022*/
```

It is not necessary to assign values to these objects in the scripts. Using the System.Serializable command in the blueprint classes allows us to assign values to fields directly from the Inspector. Once all your files are saved, you will be able to see the items in the Database script component. You can add values from here.

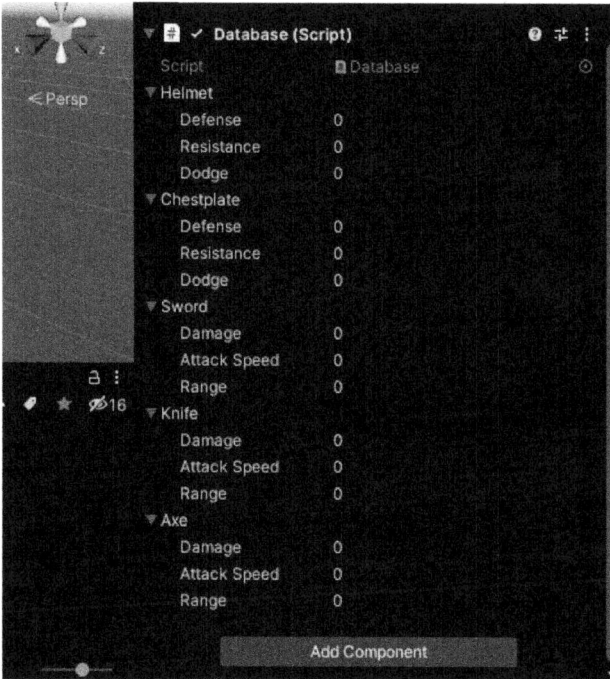

Static Classes in Unity

In Unity, static classes are often used to control workflow. Static classes must contain static members and cannot be used to instantiate objects. Since only one version of the information in a static class can exist, they are useful for keeping track of progress data and other important game information. Other classes would still have access to the information and methods contained in a static class but will not be able to unilaterally change the values of its members.

If your game is dependent on player progress to unlock features, your game would need to track that progress. Other classes would need to have access to progress information without changing it. Using a static value would be the most secure way of achieving this.

Static classes are created in the same way as other classes in Unity. Create a new script and open it. You will see a regular Unity public class template. Add the keyword static to the class declaration after the word public so that it reads: public static class. Remember that all members created in this class must also be static. Simply add the keyword static to all member declarations. Instead of a public int variable, we would have a public static int variable.

To access static members from another class, call the class before calling the member. For example, if we have a static method called Load in a static class called Progress, we would call Load using Progress.Load.

CREATING YOUR FIRST METHODS

In the last chapter, we took a brief look at the two methods added to Unity classes. Start is a method that's called when the object the script is attached to first becomes active. Update is called once per frame and ensures that the game remains current. These two methods cover the majority of the game's functionality, but we are not limited to them. Just like in general programming, we can create custom methods.

In the same project as before, create another empty GameObject and name it MethodTest. This object will contain a script that will illustrate how methods are created and used. Create and attach a script component and name it Methods. Open it. In this script, we will create two methods and use them in the Start method to display a message.

Until now, we've been using the command Console.WriteLn to present output. Unity can display messages in a similar manner. Instead of displaying to a console app, we can print messages to the Debug Console. Messages can be shown in the Debug Log without appearing in the game, and as such, can be used to test values and methods. Instead of Console.WriteLn ( ), use Debug.Log ( ).

HelloWorld in Unity

Normally, we wouldn't create a method for a single display statement. The statement can be used in Start on its own to achieve the same result. For the sake of illustrating methods, however, we will create a separate method and call it in Start instead.

In the Methods script, define a method called Hello and write the statement to display a message. Thereafter, call the method in Start.

```
public class Methods : MonoBehaviour
{
    void Hello ()
    {
        Debug.Log ("Hello Gamers!");
    }

    //Start is called before the first frame update
    void Start ()
    {
        Hello ();

    }

    //Update us called once per frame
    void Update ()
    {

    }
}
```

When you run the project in Unity, the message will appear on the console like this:

ApplyDamage

The second method we will make is called ApplyDamage. This method will receive the amount of damage taken and subtract it from the player's health.

In the same script, create a return method and define variables to represent the damage and health values. The method will return the value of the player's current health. Now the method is ready to be called. In Start, define a variable that will call the method and store its result using the following statement: int x = ApplyDamage (5, 100). Next, display the calculated value with a suitable message.

```
public class Methods : MonoBehaviour {

    void Hello ()
    {
        Debug.Log ("Hello Gamers!");
    }

    int ApplyDamage (int damageTaken, int health)
    //Method that receives total health and damage taken as parameters to calculate player health

    {
        return health – damageTaken;
    }

        //Start is called before the first frame update
()
    void Start    {
        Hello ();

        int x = ApplyDamage (5,100);
        Debug.Log ("Player health is: " + x);
    //Variable x is declared and initialized to contain value returned from ApplyDamage method

    }

    //Update us called once per frame
void Update ()
    {

    }
}

/* ApplyDamage sourced from https://www.c-sharpcorner.com/blogs/creating-and-calling-methods-in-unity
Retrieved Aug 2022 */
```

When you run the game in Unity, your console should look like this:

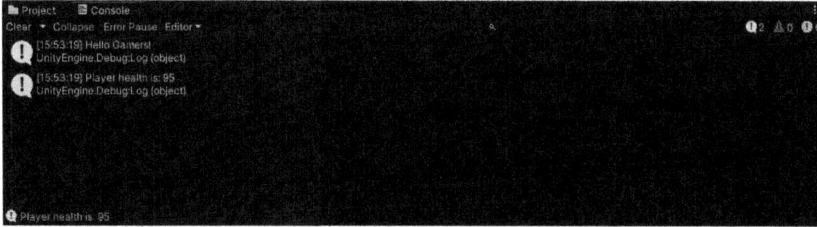

COMMON MISTAKES WHEN CODING IN UNITY

The game development process is complex. Mistakes are inevitable, more so when coupled with inexperience. Here are a few things that other developers have learned through experience:

- Do not underestimate the amount of planning that's needed. It is crucial to have a plan before starting a new project. Games are intricate. There are lots of elements that require attention, and it is easy for some to slip through the cracks; especially when you are working without a plan. Take some time to map out the details of your game.
- Keep device performance in mind during development. Modern devices are capable of a lot, but that doesn't mean your game should not be optimized for the best performance possible. Do not wait until the last stage to consider performance concerns either. Optimize your processes from the start so you won't have to compromise on work you have already done for the sake of performance.
- When working on something that's affected by physics, consider the effect of the world as a whole.

- Do not try to manually test every single feature of your game. It is a lot of fun to play a game you have created, but the gratification wears out quickly when you are testing every minute detail manually. Unity has automated testing tools you can use. Focus on testing features that require manual testing, and let Unity deal with the rest.
- If your game is not working the way you want it to, do not give up. No one's projects work perfectly from the outset. Pay attention to the error messages you get, and try to resolve them. Double-check the details, and make sure everything is where it should be.
- If all else fails, remember that you have the whole internet at your disposal. Google the things you are struggling with. There are countless online communities where programmers and developers can share what they are stuck on. If you cannot find a solution through research, try posting in one of the many programming forums. There is always someone willing to offer some advice.

Common Code Errors

Errors are unavoidable. Instead of trying to avoid errors, learn how to use them to your advantage. The first step to resolving an error is to read the error message. It will tell you what the error is and where it occurred.

Here are some of the most common errors and how to resolve them:

- "Unknown identifier" means that the object referenced cannot be identified. This can be anything from a typo to an accessibility issue. Check that the referred object's name is spelled correctly and that the object is accessible to the class in which it was referenced.

- "; expected" is perhaps the most common code error. It means that there is a semicolon missing from the referenced statement.
- Any variation of "expecting... found..." refers to missing syntax. Simply go to the referenced line and replace the missing syntax.
- "Overload for method _ is not compatible" refers to the wrong DataType being passed as a method parameter. If a method is expecting an integer and you give it a string, you will get a compatibility error.

These are only a few of the errors you might encounter. If you cannot make sense of the error you are seeing, copy that error and look it up.

6

LET'S BUILD A GAME

I n the next few chapters, we will be going through the steps of building a simple 2D tap game. The game will feature mouse-click interaction, a collision system, rigidbodies, a User Interface (UI), and a scoring system. The objective of the game will be to click on a spawned character to kill it.

You will be shown an example, but you are not obligated to follow it exactly. Choose your own character, background, and elements. You will need:

- One background image
- One character sprite
- UI elements
- Sound effects

You do not need to have all the assets gathered before we start, but it is always good to have them prepared. Below are some recommendations for where you can find assets. Take some time to browse through the available selections.

- For a background image and character sprite image, go to spriters-resource.com or opengameart.org. The art found on the above websites is free to use. If you use art from somewhere else, ensure that it is available for use without copyright infringement.
- For UI assets, visit Unity's asset store or the above-mentioned websites. You can do this through any browser. In the Asset Store, browse Unity's collection of UI Elements. Once you have found a package you like, select Add to My Assets and download the package. Next, import the package to your project.
- Sound clips can be sourced from freesound.org, opengameart.org, and sounds-resource.org.

Gather all your assets in a folder from where you can import them as needed later.

Create a new 2D project and follow along.

ADDING A SPRITE

A sprite is a 2D object we can use as a game character. Sprites are images overlaid on objects to offer the appearance of a character. For this book, the word sprite is used to reference the game character.

To create a sprite, we need an image. Import the image you want to use for your character. In the Project window, create a folder named Sprites or Images in the Assets directory. Right-click inside that folder and scroll down to Import New Asset. You can now choose the image from your computer.

Once the image has been imported, you can create a sprite for your game. Drag the image from the Project window and drop it into the Hierarchy. Rename the sprite to something appropriate in the Inspector.

Next, take a look at the sprite through the GameView. Make sure it looks good from the player's perspective after each change.

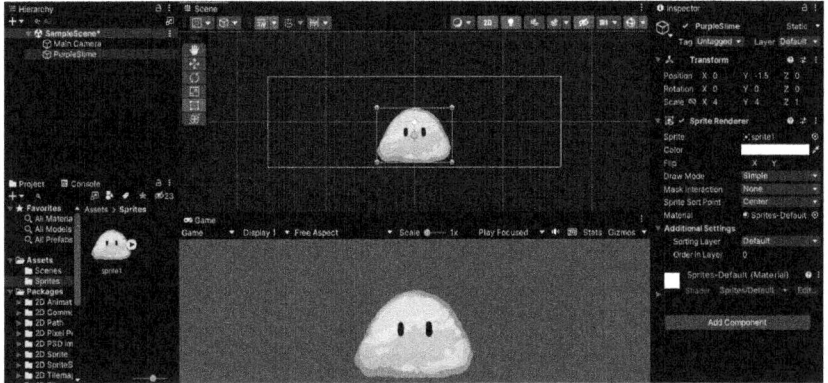

In the above example, a slime sprite was added to the game and named PurpleSlime.

Sprites automatically have two components. The first is the Transform component that all objects have. The second is the Sprite Renderer.

Transform

The Transform component shows three properties: position, rotation, and scale.

Position refers to the object's positioning in relation to the scene. Its values depend on where it is anchored. The anchor point holds the value (0,0). The X value is the object's horizontal position in reference to zero (0), and the Y value references its vertical position. To move the sprite left or down, enter a negative value. To move it right or up, enter a positive value. For example, you will notice that the slime has a position Y value of -1.5 while anchored in the center. This moves the slime downwards from the middle and places it closer to the bottom of the Game View.

Rotation determines an object's orientation. We won't work with these values much for now, so play around with them and see how they affect your sprite.

Scale relates to the object's size. Scale can be adjusted on three axes. Since this is a 2D game and object, we will only work with the first two values. X refers to its width and Y to its height. The slime was resized to X = 4 and Y = 4. Play around with your sprite's scale. Try adjusting it to the correct size manually and see what the values are in the component. There are no correct values. Do what looks right on your screen.

Sprite Renderer

The Sprite Renderer component contains the following properties:

- Sprite: This property refers to the asset used to create the object. If you want to change the sprite's image, change this property by selecting another image. This is the source for the object.
- Color: Here, you can add a color overlay to the image. It doesn't recolor the image but instead adds a tint to it. Try changing the color to black and see what happens. To return the sprite to its original color, set the Color property to white.
- Flip: This is where you can mirror your sprite. X flips the image horizontally, and Y flips it vertically.
- Additional Settings let you determine on what layer the object will sit if you add multiple layers to a scene.

CANVAS

The canvas is an object in the Hierarchy that contains all objects related to the UI like backgrounds, buttons, and text. To add a canvas object, right-click in the Hierarchy and select UI. A menu will appear that contains all the UI-related objects.

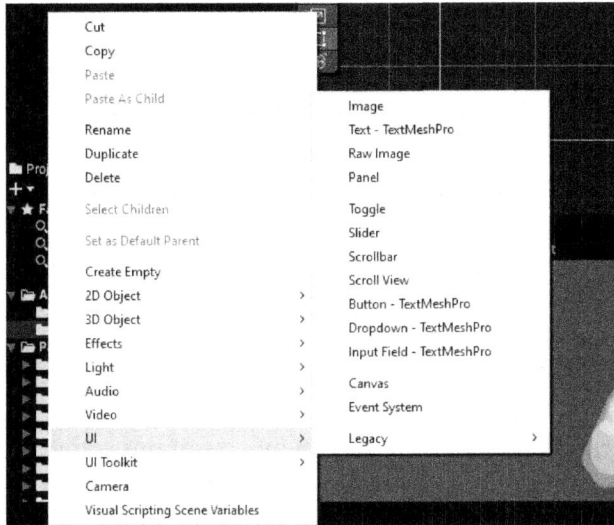

Among them, you will find the canvas. If you create any of the other objects without a canvas, Unity will automatically create a canvas. Unity also automatically adds an Event System whenever a canvas is created. Go ahead and create a canvas.

The canvas has four components: Rect Transform, Canvas, Canvas Scaler, and Graphics Raycaster.

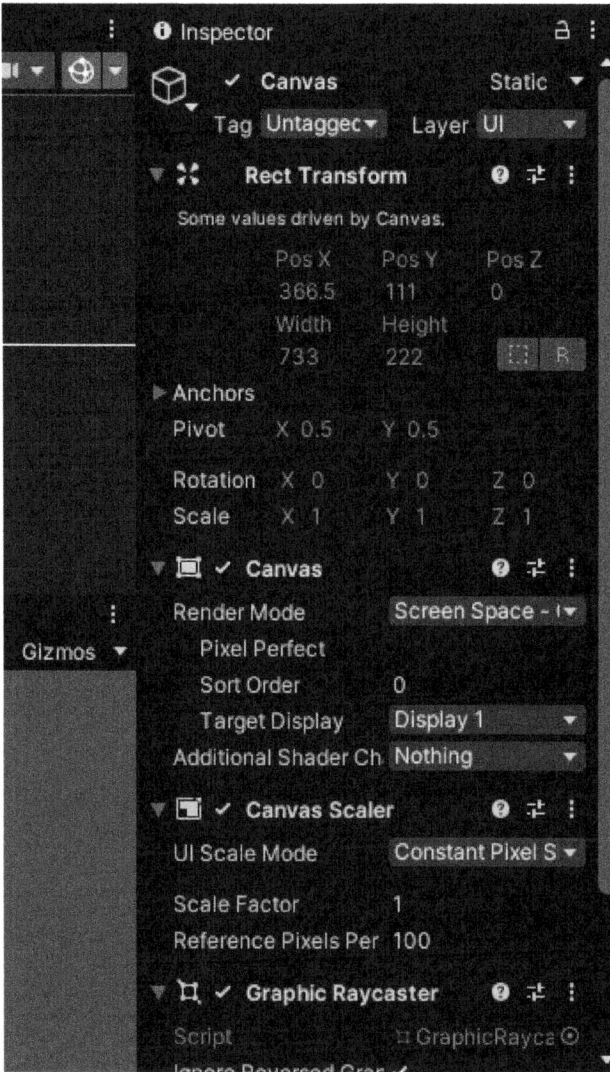

Rect Transform

Rect Transform is the 2D equivalent of the Transform component and is mostly used for UI elements. It will be grayed out as it is positioned by the scene itself.

Canvas

Canvas elements are controlled and contained via this component. All UI objects are canvas child objects and are collected at this point.

When it is first created, the canvas doesn't appear in the Game View the way it does in the Scene View. For the time being, it is nothing more than a possibility, but if you add a Text object to the canvas, you will notice that it shows up differently. To overlay the canvas properly, change the Render Mode property to Screen Space - Camera. Now drag the main camera from the Hierarchy to the Render Camera property. The canvas will now be overlaid properly.

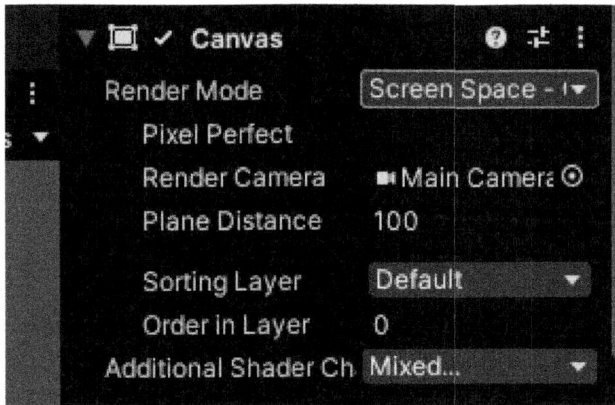

Canvas Scaler

Canvas Scaler lets you adjust the way the UI is scaled when changing the aspect ratio to fit different devices. Change the UI Scale Mode property to Scale with Screen.

Reference Resolution lets us assign a resolution value for the canvas to reference when changing scale.

Graphic Raycaster

This component deals with how the game detects graphics. It basically scans the game for graphics and catalogs what it finds.

ADDING UI ELEMENTS

Background Image

Import the background image from your computer using the same steps as for the sprite asset. Create a UI object image by right-clicking in the Hierarchy, selecting UI, and then Image. Drag it into the canvas. Select the image and change its name to backgroundImage in the Inspector. Find the image component for that object. Once you have it, drag the imported image to the Source Image property to set it as your background. If the size is off, scroll down the same component until you find a button that says Set Native Size. As its label implies, this will reset your image to its native size.

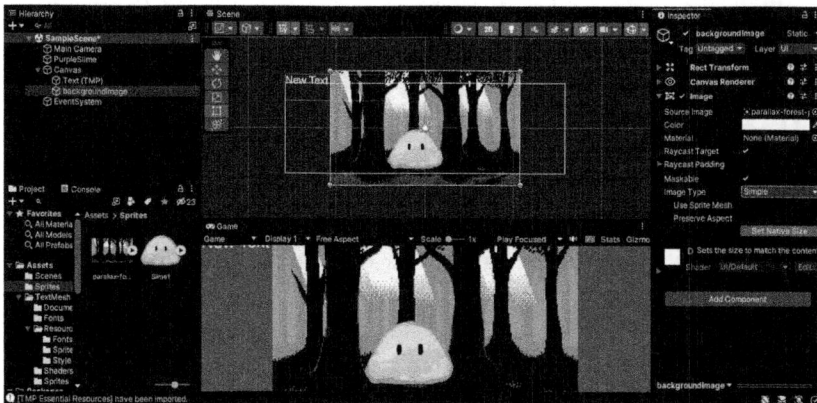

From here, go back to the Canvas component of the canvas object, and set the Reference Resolution to the image's original size. If you

are unsure what the image's size was, go to the folder you saved it in through your computer's file manager. Right-click the image, select Properties, and then Details. There, you will be able to see the original dimensions of the image. Copy those values into the Reference Resolution property. If this throws off your image, simply go back and hit Set Native again.

Next, adjust the background's anchor points. By default, the image is anchored at its center. To change this, go to the image object's Rect Transform component and click on the square next to the values. You will be given options for what your anchor should be. Select what works best for your image. In the example, the anchor point was set to bottom center. To also apply the new anchor, hold the alt key when selecting the option you want.

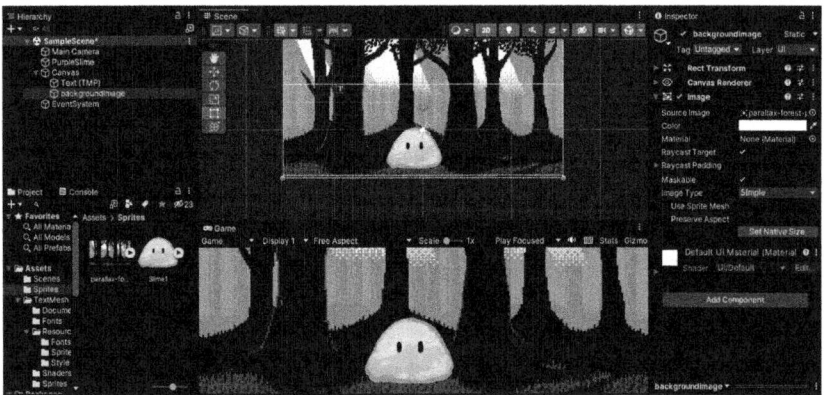

Remember to keep an eye on your Game View to judge what adjustments need to be made. If the image still looks wrong, manually adjust it until it looks good.

Text

Add a text object to the canvas by right-clicking in the Hierarchy and going to UI and then Text. The Text object will have its own components where you can change its appearance. You can change the font size, color, and style. Take a moment to play around with it.

Drag the object into the top center of your game. Adjust the text to display a message. We will be adding a button to resize the character next, so adjust the text to reflect that.

Button

Buttons can be used to add functionality to the game. To add one, right-click in the Hierarchy, select UI, and then Button. Drag the button into the canvas object.

Every button is automatically created with a text object to act as its label. If you want to change what text is displayed on the button, you will have to change it in the text's components.

If you look in the button's Inspector, you will see a Button and Image component. The Image component relates to the button's appearance in the game. You can change the button's color to suit your sprite and background.

The Button component relates to its functionality. Here, you will see an event called OnClick. This will control what happens when the button is clicked. As is, the button is just another graphic in the game. If you run the game and click it, nothing will happen. To make a button functional, we will need to add a script.

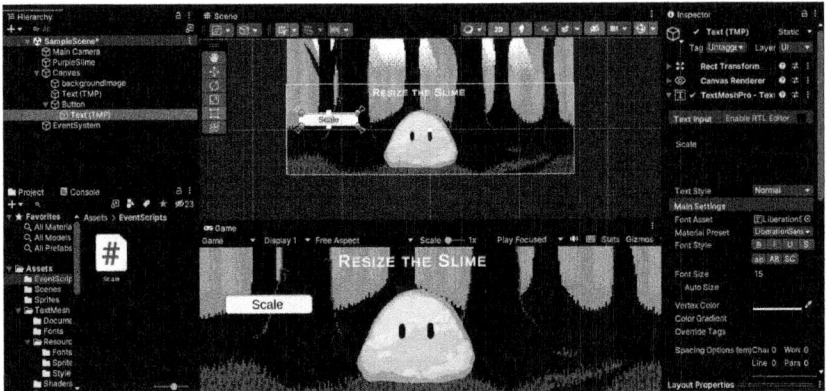

EVENT SYSTEM

The Event System lets us manage events triggered by user interactions. To make a game respond to clicks and keypresses, we rely on the Event System. Without the Event System object, our game wouldn't be able to process user input or trigger a reaction.

In this example, the event would occur when the Scale button is clicked. To affect this, we need to create a script that would provide the necessary code. Create a new folder in Assets called Scripts. Next, create a new script called Scale, and attach it to the button in the Hierarchy. Once ready, open it.

EVENT SCRIPT

In the Scale script, define a variable of the GameObject type by using the following statement: GameObject name. Assign whatever name is suitable for your object.

Next, in the Start method, use the GameObject.Find command to link the sprite to the variable. Find lets us call an object by its name. In parameters, use the name assigned to your sprite by copying it from the Inspector and pasting it into the brackets. Use

126 | A.E. COLONNA

double quotation marks as it is a string value. The system will take that name, compare it to the objects in the scene, and find the one with a matching name. For example, the slime is called PurpleSlime, and the code can assign it to a slime variable through the "PurpleSlime" parameter.

Create a public void method called ScaleDown. In this method, we will provide a statement that will change the object's scale values. For example, PurpleSlime was set to X=4 and Y=4. The code will change it to X=2 and Y=2. Whatever your sprite's values are, reduce that number to use in the method statement.

```
public class Scale : MonoBehaviour {

    GameObject slime;
    //We create a GameObject reference for our slime

    void Start ()
    {
        slime = GameObject.Find("PurpleSlime");
    //We assigned the game slime to our code object slime by finding the name of the game object   }

    public void ScaleDown ()
    //This is the method we'll call when the button is clicked to scale the slime
    {

        slime.gameObject.transform.localScale = new Vector3 (2, 2, 0.0f);
        //This statement calls the transform component and reassigns the value of its scale property
        //Vector3 calls the third set of Transform values i.e. the scale values
    }

    //Update is called once per frame
    void Update ()
    {

    }
}

/* Code adapted from https://blog.sentry.io/2022/03/21/unity-tutorial-what-you-need-to-know-
before-developing-your-first-unity-game#introduction-to-the-unity-editor-interface  Retrieved Aug
2022*/
```

Save the script and return to Unity. Open the button's Button component and find the OnClick event. Click on the +. You will see items under OnClick now.

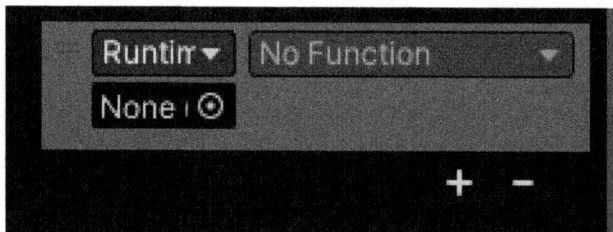

The box on the second row is the source. Since the script has been attached to the button, drag the button from the Hierarchy into that source.

The next step is to select which of the methods this event will be using. From the function drop-down, select Scale, and find ScaleDown from the list that pops up. Finally, make sure that the first drop-down is set to include runtime.

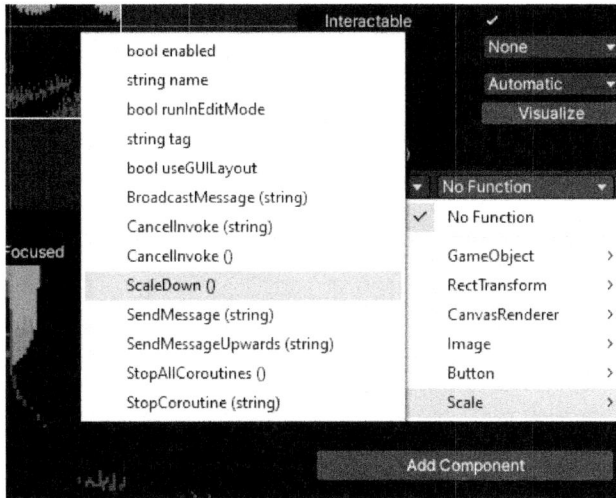

Save everything one last time and hit the play button. Here's the slime before clicking the button:

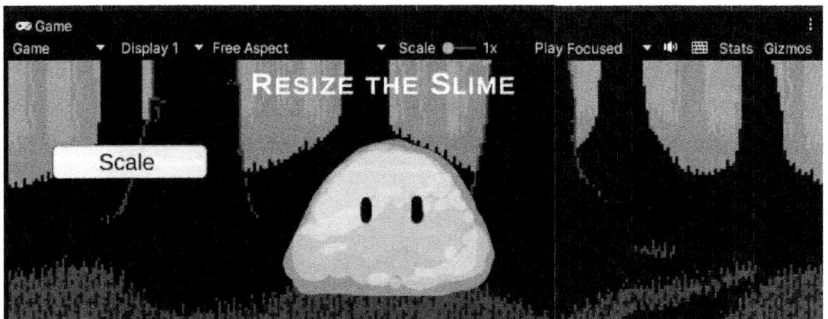

And here's the slime after clicking it:

7

YOUR GAME PART 1—SETTING THE SCENE

Now that you have the necessary foundations, it is time to buckle down and build a functional game. To recap, the game we will be building will include a UI with a menu, game mechanics, sounds, and a scoring system. The objective of this game will be to tap/click on the characters as they spawn in order to kill them.

To do this, we need to set up a character that can be destroyed and that will repeatedly respawn. We will need to keep track of the number of kills. For the UI, we need to create a separate menu screen and play and pause buttons that will respond to user interaction.

You will be building this game in the same project file as the previous chapter's scale scene. You can use the same sprite and background or completely different ones, it is up to you. The examples will be using the same slime as Chapter 6 but on a different background. It is also recommended to browse for play and pause button assets as well as a panel image.

If you are using different assets, make sure they are all imported to the project. Without further ado, let's jump into it.

CREATE A NEW SCENE

First, we need to create a new scene to host the game-play elements for the game. In the Scenes folder under Assets, right-click and select Create > Scene. Name it TapGame.

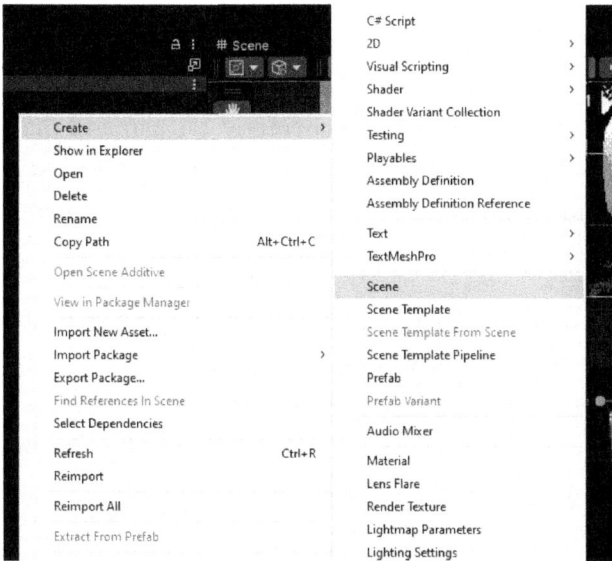

Next, create a canvas for the UI elements of this scene. You will need to set it up again. Set the Render Mode to Screen Space - Camera and drag the camera into the source. Set the UI Scale property to Scale with Screen. If you cannot remember how to do this, turn back to Chapter 6, where the steps were outlined in more detail.

Create a UI Image object, and drag it onto the canvas in the Hierarchy. This scene will contain another canvas child image so rename this object to something appropriate like

BackgroundImage. Drag the image you want to use as a background into the Image Source property. Go through the steps to set the image up. Set its size to native and anchor it as needed. Go back to the canvas and set its Reference Resolution to the size of the image. Again, the steps are described in more detail in Chapter 6. Go back to them if needed.

Remember to take a look at the Game View to verify how the game appears from the player's perspective.

ADDING THE SPRITE

Once the background is set up correctly, we can add the sprite for our game character. Drag the image you want to use from the Project window into the Hierarchy and name it accordingly. Like last time, the example sprite is named PurpleSlime.

There's no need to move the sprite, but you can relocate it to the top of the screen if you want to. It needs to be much smaller than in the last scene, so scale it down. We will later have a bunch of them on the screen, so the sprite cannot be too big. In the example below, the sprite is still a bit too big and will later be scaled down to X = 1 and Y = 1.

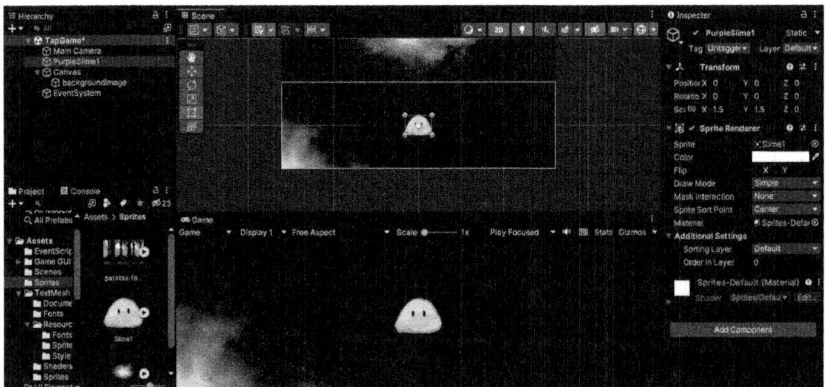

Two essential components are needed to make the sprite subject to physics: Collider and Rigidbody.

Collider 2D

A Collider will determine the susceptible shape of the sprite. It determines, in essence, the area of effect of the sprite. There are different options available depending on the general shape of your sprite. The slime is somewhat rectangular, so the Box Collider is added to the example.

Select the sprite, and click Add Component in the Inspector. Search Collider 2D, and choose from the available shapes. It is important to use a Collider 2D since Collider is used for 3D objects.

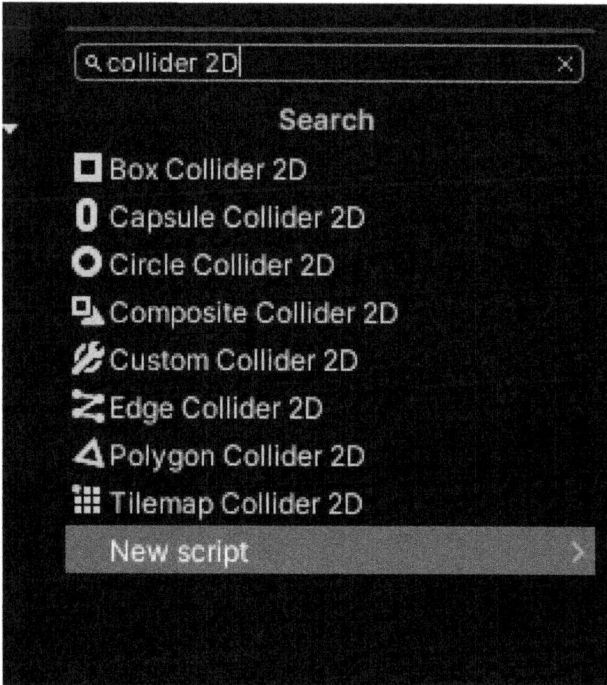

Pick whichever best fits your sprite. Choose Circle Collider for round shapes, Polygon for complex shapes, or Box for square/rectangular shapes. Edge colliders are for when you are using flat surfaces. Once you have picked one, it will look like this in the Inspector:

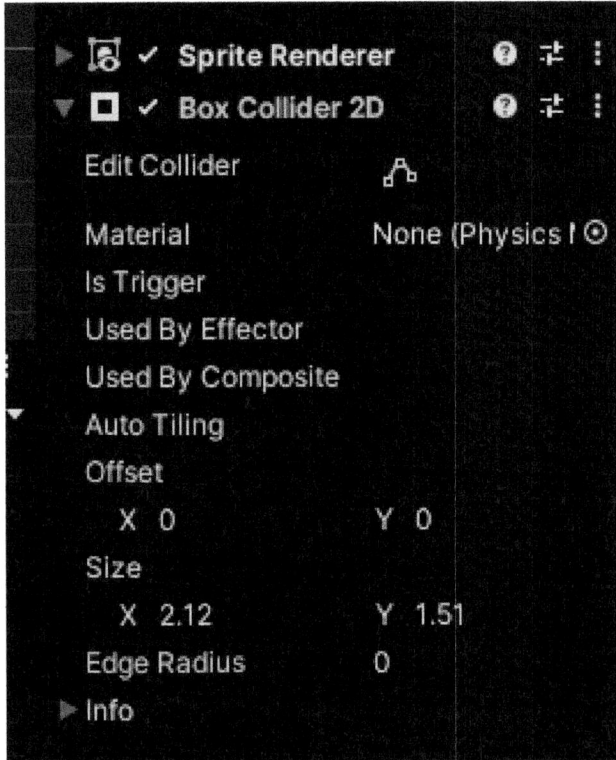

When the component is selected, a green outline will appear around the sprite in the Scene View. This is the collider's edges and determines the area of effect. You can manually adjust the collider to fit your sprite better by using Edit Collider. However, if you change it, you will likely notice the Offset values change. When the edges touch the sprite, those values will be zero.

Material is somewhat self-explanatory. It refers to the material used by the collider and affects what can happen to the sprite. For example, different materials bounce differently.

IsTrigger determines whether or not the object is considered a trigger as it relates to other objects. This affects methods concerning collisions, such as OnTriggerEnter and OnTriggerExit. Leave it unchecked.

Rigidbody 2D

This is the component that will subject your sprite to Unity's physics engine. Hit Add Component, and search for Rigidbody 2D. Once it is added, click play before changing anything else to see what happens. Your sprite will start falling from its position and disappear from the game. This is because the sprite is now influenced by gravity.

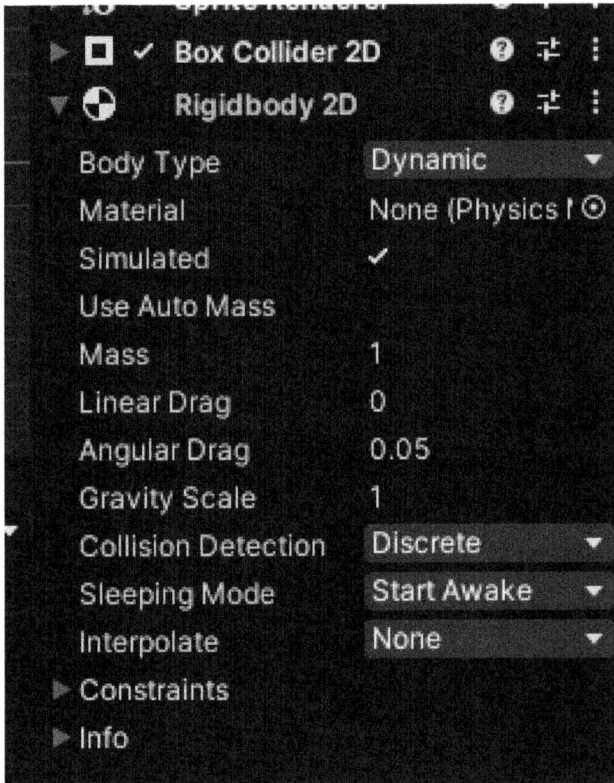

The Body Type property will determine how the object is affected by physics. There are three different Body Types.

The first, **Dynamic Body Type**, is the most interactive of them. This type will apply physics force to your sprite.

The Simulated property is what determines whether or not your sprite is affected by forces like gravity. If unchecked, the sprite won't be subject to physics. It is checked by default.

Auto Mass sets the sprite's mass to what the Collider determines it to be. Mass, on the other hand, lets you specify a specific mass.

Linear and Angular Drag determine the position and rotational coefficients for the sprite respectively.

The Gravity Scale property references the degree to which gravity affects the object in question. A value of one means the object is affected by gravity normally. If you want an object to fall slower, set the value to less than one. Similarly, if you want the object to fall faster, set the value to higher than one.

Collision Detection determines what will happen when two objects collide. Discrete lets objects pass through each other after collisions and Continuous means they won't.

The **Kinetic Body Type** is a body type that won't be affected by the forces of physics or other objects. A Kinetic object will likely move faster than a Dynamic type because it is not affected by things like resistance. Full Kinematic lets it interact with other objects. In that scenario, the Kinematic will be an immovable object since it cannot be affected by any forces exerted by other objects.

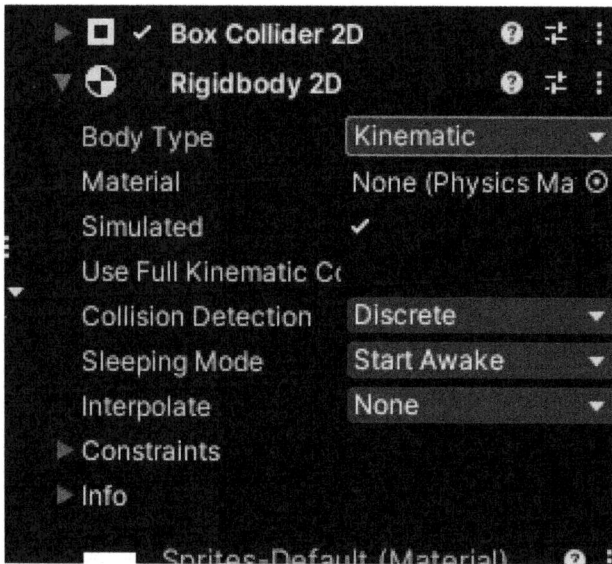

Lastly, the **Static Body Type** is a body that won't move at all. It can interact with Dynamic types, but won't move.

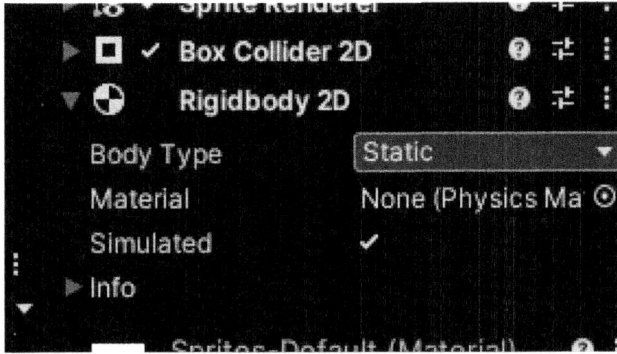

For our game, select the Body Type Dynamic and set the Gravity Scale to 0.3. The sprite needs to be able to fall at a slower than normal rate.

DESTROYING A GAMEOBJECT

For this game to work, the sprite needs to be destroyable. In the Scripts folder, create a new script and name it appropriately, e.g., KillSlime. Attach it to the sprite by dragging it into the sprite's Inspector or onto the sprite in the Hierarchy.

In the script, create a new public void method called OnMouseDown. Type the statement Destroy(gameObject) inside the method. This will destroy the object to which the script is attached.

```
void OnMouseDown ()
//This method will determine what happens to the sprite once its clicked in-game
    {
        Destroy (gameObject);
        //This will destroy the gameObject this script is attached to
    }
}
/* Code sourced from https://blog.sentry.io/2022/04/01/unity-tutorial-developing-
your-first-unity-game-part-1  Retrieved Aug 2022 */
```

Save the script and return to Unity. Keep your IDE open since we will be going back and forth a lot. In Unity, make sure the script is attached to the sprite. Run the game and click on the sprite to see it disappear.

Next, we can add an animation effect for when the sprite is destroyed.

ADDING A DESTROY EFFECT

Open the Unity Asset Store, and browse for an effect from one of their packages. The example uses the Cartoon FX Free package (Moreno, 2019) as it offers a variety of different effects. You will need two separate effects, one for the sprite being destroyed and another for later when we add a different destruction function.

Cartoon FX Free
Jean Moreno
★★★★★ (351) ♥ 4326)
FREE
1199 views in the past week

Add to My Assets

License agreement	Standard Unity Asset Store EULA
License type	Extension Asset
File size	2.6 MB
Latest version	1.03
Latest release date	Mar 20, 2019
Supported Unity versions	5.6.7 or higher
Support	Visit site

Once you have found a package you like, add it to your assets, and return to Unity. From the Window tab in the menu bar, open the Package Manager.

bject   Component   Jobs   Window   Help

Panels	>	
Next Window	Ctrl+Tab	
Previous Window	Ctrl+Shift+Tab	
Layouts	>	
Search	>	
JMO Assets	>	
Collaborate		
Plastic SCM		
Cartoon FX Easy Editor		
Asset Store		
Package Manager		
Asset Management	>	

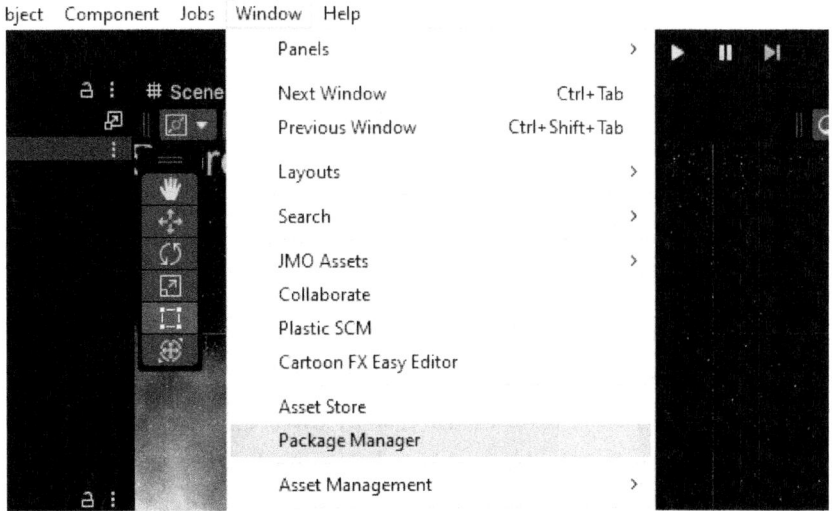

You will see all the packages added to your assets from the Unity Store. Download the one you want, and import it to your project. You will now have a JMO assets folder from where you can access the animations. Find the one you want to use and make a note of where it is in the folder structure. You can preview the effects by double-clicking on one and hitting play in the window that opens up.

Once you have chosen, turn back to the Kill script. There are two steps to adding an effect.

First, we need to declare a code variable for the effect through which it can be accessed. Create a GameObject variable using the statement GameObject SmokeEffect. Add [SerializeField] in a line above the declaration so you can assign the effect from the Inspector.

```
[SerializeField]
GameObject SmokeEffect;
```

Next, write the code to instantiate the effect in the OnMouseDown method. Copy the following code into your script.

```
void OnMouseDown ()
//This method will determine what happens to the sprite once its clicked in-game
    {
    Destroy (gameObject);
    //This will destroy the gameObject this script is attached to
    Instantiate (SmokeEffect, transform.position, Quaternion.identity);
    //The effect object is instantiated and matched to the slime's position
    }
}
```

Let's break down this statement:

- "SmokeEffect" calls the name assigned to the effect variable
- "transform.position" grabs the position values of the sprite when it is clicked to instantiate the effect in the same position
- "Quaternion.identify" sets the effect's rotation to zero

Remember to save your script before returning to Unity. Lastly, select the sprite, and navigate to its script component. You will see a new serialized item called SmokeEffect. Drag the animation you want into this source.

Run the game and click on your sprite. Cool, right?

In the next chapter, we will add more complex game mechanics.

8

YOUR GAME PART 2—GAME MECHANICS

I n the previous chapter, we created a scene and added a background and sprite. We added components to the sprite to make it susceptible to physics and created code to destroy it. Lastly, we added an animation to its destruction.

But what happens if the sprite reaches the bottom without being clicked? As is, it simply slides off the screen. While that's fine and well, we want the sprite to disappear when it is no longer on the screen. If it is not destroyed through the click/tap, the object will continue to exist until the game stops running. As such, we need to make provision for what will happen once it reaches the bottom of the screen.

ADDING A BOTTOM/FALLING EFFECT

Basically, what we want to do is make it so that the game destroys the sprite once it reaches a certain point. Depending on your background image and sprite, you can get creative with this. Say your background is an image of a mountain and a lake. You can set it up to look like the sprite fell into the lake. You can create an entire game scenario just from this effect. Take the example scenario, there's a slime sprite on a galaxy background. The slime could easily be replaced with an alien or spaceship that can fly away to invade Earth if it wasn't destroyed. Take a second look at your background and sprite and consider the possibilities.

That said, in the example, the slime will poof out of existence with a slightly different animation. Normally, the sprite is destroyed when the player clicks on it. The click/tap is what triggers the destruction. To destroy the sprite when it reaches the bottom, we will need a trigger.

Create an empty GameObject and call it Bottom (or anything else suitable for your background), and add a Box Collider 2D component to it. Click on Edit Collider and manually drag the edges until it covers the length of the scene. Next, move the object so it and the Collider sit at the bottom of the screen. Manipulate it until it looks something like the example below:

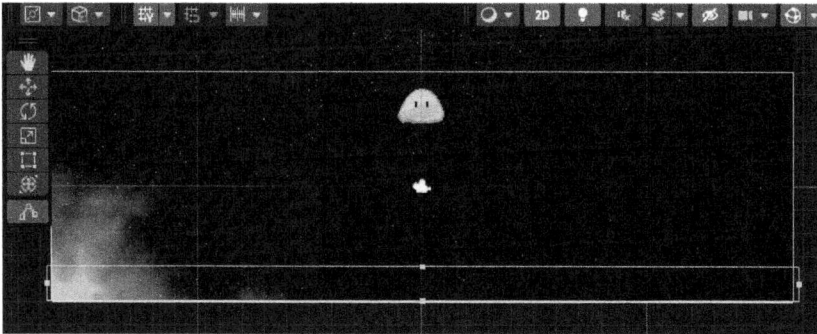

The green outline shows exactly where the Collider edges are and where the sprite will be destroyed. Once the sprite's Collider meets the bottom's Collider, it will trigger the destruction of the sprite.

Next, we can add the necessary code to destroy the sprite. In the Kill script, create a private void method named OnCollisionEnter2D with the parameters (Collisions2D collision). Inside it, reiterated the Destroy(gameObject) statement.

Save the file and run the game. You will see the sprite blink out of existence once it reaches the bottom. To make it more exciting, we can add another effect.

Choose a second, different effect that fits your scene. If, for example, you had the mountain and lake background, you could use a water splash effect. The example uses a simple poof effect that simulates the slime disappearing in a puff of smoke. Now add the effect by following the same steps taken to add the first animation.

First, in the Kill script, create a GameObject variable called BottomEffect.

```
[SerializeField]
GameObject SmokeEffect;

[SerializeField]
GameObject BottomEffect;
```

Next, instantiate the effect using the same code as before.

```
private void OnCollisionEnter2D (Collision2D collision)
//This method will determine what happens when the sprite hits another object with a collider
{
    Destroy (gameObject);
    Instantiate (BottomEffect, transform.position, Quaternion.identity);
}
/* Code sources from https://blog.sentry.io/2022/04/01/unity-tutorial-developing-
your-first-unity-game-part-1    and    https://blog.sentry.io/2022/04/01/unity-
tutorial-developing-your-first-unity-game-part-2  Retrieved Aug 2022 */
```

This could, however, cause a problem later down the line. As it is, the sprite will be destroyed if it collides with anything, including other sprites. When we later have multiple sprites on the screen, this code will destroy them if they collide with each other.

Therefore, we need to make provision for inter-sprite collision by defining which collision will trigger destruction.

Add a custom tag to the object containing the bottom collider to differentiate it from other objects.

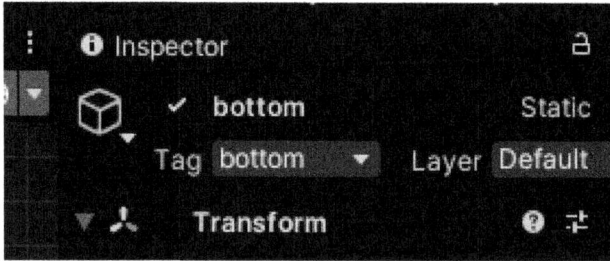

Make sure that it is set to the new tag. Back in the Kill script, add a conditional statement to the collision method. This will test if the collision was with an object tagged as "bottom" by referencing the object's tag.

```
private void OnCollisionEnter2D (Collision2D collision)
//This method will determine what happens when the sprite hits another object with a collider {

    if (collision.gameObject.tag == "bottom")
    //tests whether the sprite has hit something tagged with bottom    {

        Destroy (gameObject);
    }
        Instantiate (BottomEffect, transform.position, Quaternion.identity);
    }
}
/* Code sources from https://blog.sentry.io/2022/04/01/unity-tutorial-developing-your-first-unity-
game-part-1 and https://blog.sentry.io/2022/04/01/unity-tutorial-developing-your-first-
unity-game-part-2 Retrieved Aug 2022 */
```

If the other object in the collision has the bottom tag, the sprite will be destroyed. If it does not have the bottom tag, the sprite won't be destroyed. This way, when the sprite later starts colliding with other sprites, none of them will get destroyed.

Lastly, drag the effect you have chosen into the serialized item in the sprite's script component.

The sprite is now ready to be saved as a Prefab.

CREATING A SPRITE PREFAB

In order to spawn more sprites, we need to have a Prefab from which they can be instanced. If new sprites are created from the Prefab, they will all be linked to the necessary code and assets. Before saving it as a Prefab, double-check that it looks the way you want it to in-game. Confirm that it is the right size for the game.

If you will remember, Prefabs are saved configurations of an object's components. You can create a new Prefab by dragging the object whose configuration you want to save into the Project window. Once you are sure it has been saved, you can delete the sprite from the scene.

Now the game can be set up to spawn instances while the game is playing. We do it in this manner for two main reasons: ease and performance. We could, technically, create a few hundred of them and keep them deactivated or out of view until they are needed. It would, however, be a hassle to code and would drag down game performance to boot. This way, we do not have hundreds of sprites clogging up storage, and they also get destroyed immediately after the game stops running, freeing up performance.

CREATING SPRITES AT RANDOM

Something worth noting is that we do not want sprites spawning just anywhere. There's very little point to any of this if sprites are spawning outside of the camera's view. We need to ensure that they are only spawning within the screen's limits.

Before any of that, let me introduce you to Random. Random is a C# command that generates a number at random. Using Random.Range specifies a range within which that number is to be generated. For example, Random.Range (0,20) generates a random number between the values zero and twenty. Random can be used to provide a different X and Y value for the sprite's position property.

Normally, we'd be able to assign two random values to X and Y, but since we are restricted by the screen's dimensions, we cannot do that. We also cannot set a specific screen size to allow for device adaptability. By using the values of Screen.height and Screen.width, we can limit the range to the boundaries of the screen. Taking all that into consideration, we need to apply a combination of Random and the camera's perspective to generate the values needed for each spawn's position.

This is a complex snippet of code. Copy it over into your Spawn script and then we can break it down.

```
public class Spawn : MonoBehaviour {


    [SerializeField]
    GameObject slime;

    //Start is called before the first frame update
    void Start ()  {

        float posY = Random.Range (Camera.main.ScreenToWorldPoint
            (new Vector2 (0, 0)).y,Camera.main.ScreenToWorldPoint
            (new Vector2 (0, Screen.height)).y);
        //Generates a random number between the values 0 and the height of the screen
        float posX = Random.Range (Camera.main.ScreenToWorldPoint
            (new Vector2 (0, 0)).x,Camera.main.ScreenToWorldPoint
            (new Vector2 (Screen.width,0)).x);
        //Generates a random number between the values 0 and the width of the screen

        Vector2 spawnPos = new Vector2 (posX, posY);
        //Assigns the random number to the X and Y values of the instance object's position property
        Instantiate (slime, spawnPos, Quaternion.identity);
        //Creates a prefab instance at the position indicated by spawnPos
    }
    /*          https://blog.sentry.io/2022/04/01/unity-tutorial-developing-your-first-
    unity-game-part-2 Retrieved Aug 2022 */
```

First, declare a serialized GameObject variable to represent your sprite.

The rest of the code is better understood by working through the process backward. To get to the eventual Instantiate statement, we need to provide the value for spawnPos. This variable holds the value Vector2 (posX, posY). As you might guess, posX holds the X value of the position, and posY stores the Y value of the position.

Vector2 indicates that the value relates to the position property of the Transform component.

The variables posX and posY need to each generate values within a range. To estimate the range, we need to access the screen dimensions as viewed through the camera. For that, we need to call the camera and convert its view to a usable value. The statement Camera.main.ScreenToWorldPoint accomplishes this. This will convert the camera's perspective into a numerical value that relates to the world and will give us a value with which we can create a range.

In the case of posY, we first need to determine the minimum value within the range. This value will be zero but needs to be converted to match the max value so we use the Camera.main statement mentioned above. For this, we use Camera.main.ScreenToWorld-Point(new Vector2(0,0)). Similarly, for the second value, we need to find the max value of the range. We use the same statement but instead of (0,0) as the Vector2 parameter, we use (0, Screen.height). This finds the highest point of the screen's vertical height. Thus, we have a range between zero and the height of the screen.

For posX, we do basically the same thing with a small difference. The minimum value in the range is determined the same way as with posY. Instead of (0, Screen.height), we need to use (Screen.width, 0) as the second Vector2 parameter. The reason for the swap is simple. A position value is (X, Y). To determine the Y value, we need X to be zero and vice versa. Therefore, in the posX statement, the Screen.width needs to be in the X value of the parameter and the Y value needs to be zero.

If this is difficult to comprehend, you are not alone. This is a very complex piece of code. You are not the only one having a hard time wrapping their head around it. This is not only an amalgamation of programming and complex mathematics. This involves abstract geometrical mathematics nested in practical mathematics in relation to abstract object visualization. A tip for the future, save this snippet of code somewhere to use later on. There's not a single fixed value to be found in his code, and that means it will work in just about any 2D random spawn scenario.

Lastly, for this script to work, it needs to be attached to an object. Since there is no existing sprite until the game starts running, we attach it to the Main Camera object. Once attached, you will see a serialized item for the sprite in the script component. Drag your Prefab file into this source to assign that file to be spawned.

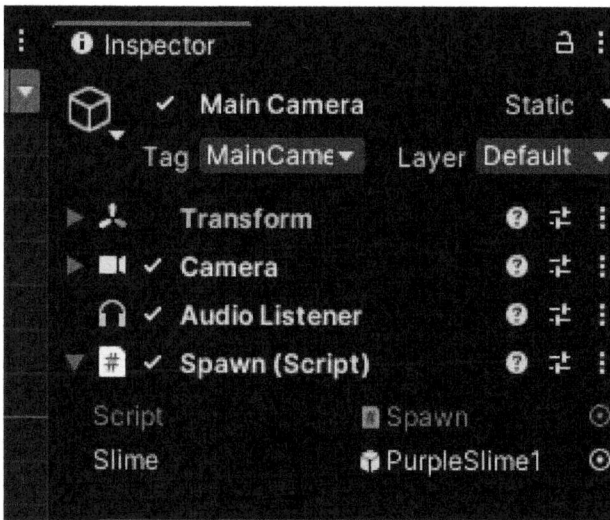

Save everything. Trust me, you do not want to lose progress now and have to redo this part. Run the game and see what happens. For now, one sprite will appear on the screen at a random position every time the game is run. The next time you run the game, it will spawn somewhere else.

INSTANCING MULTIPLE SPAWNS

Now that the code has been set for random spawn, we can adapt it to multiple random spawns.

There are several ways of achieving multiple instances. The first and easiest way is to put the Instantiate statement in the Update method. This will, however, cause problems. Update runs once per frame and the default frame rate is 60 frames per second. That means that 60 sprites will be created per second. Which is, quite frankly, an unholy amount of sprites in less than three seconds.

The second option is to create a For loop in the Start method. Using a For loop, we can determine a fixed number of spawns.

```
public class Spawn : MonoBehaviour {

    [SerializeField]
    GameObject slime;

    //Start is called before the first frame update  void Start ()
    {


        for (int i = 0; i < 10; i++)
        //for loop runs the code to generate a random position 10 times
        // 10 instances are created at run-time
        {
            float posY = Random.Range (Camera.main.ScreenToWorldPoint
                (new Vector2 (0, 0)).y,Camera.main.ScreenToWorldPoint
                (new Vector2 (0, Screen.height)).y);
            //Generates a random number between the values 0 and the height of the screen
            float posX = Random.Range (Camera.main.ScreenToWorldPoint
                (new Vector2 (0, 0)).x,Camera.main.ScreenToWorldPoint
                (new Vector2 (Screen.width,0)).x);
            //Generates a random number between the values 0 and the width of the screen

            Vector2 spawnPos = new Vector2 (posX, posY);
            //Assigns the random number to the X and Y values of the instance object's position property

            Instantiate (slime, spawnPos, Quaternion.identity);
            //Creates a prefab instance at the position indicated by spawnPos
        }
    }
    /* https://blog.sentry.io/2022/04/01/unity-tutorial-developing-your-first-unity-game-part-2 Retrieved Aug 2022 */
```

This is great for a scenario in which you need to spawn multiple instances at once, but not if they will be falling off the screen. The problem with this method in the current context is that Start only runs once. If we use this method, a set number of sprites will spawn all at once and then stop spawning until you exit and rerun the game.

The third and best method is to use an IEnumerated Coroutine. This is essentially a While loop with a delay timer between iterations. Using this method, sprites will keep spawning as long as the game is running. It will also mean that spawns are not occurring at the same time but in intervals. The method looks like this:

```
// Start is called before the first frame update
void Start ()   {

        StartCoroutine (spawningSlime ());
    }

IEnumerator spawngSlime ()    {

    while (true)
    {
        yield return new WaitForSeconds (1f);
// This delays each iteration of the loop by 1 second, causing a second's delay between each spawn

        float posY = Random.Range (Camera.main.ScreenToWorldPoint
            (new Vector2 (0, 0)).y,Camera.main.ScreenToWorldPoint
            (new Vector2 (0, Screen.height)).y);
        // Generates a random number between the values 0 and the height of the screen
        float posX = Random.Range (Camera.main.ScreenToWorldPoint
            (new Vector2 (0, 0)).x,Camera.main.ScreenToWorldPoint
            (new Vector2 (Screen.width,0)).x);
        // Generates a random number between the values 0 and the width of the screen

        Vector2 spawnPos = new Vector2 (posX, posY);
        /* Assigns the random number to the X and Y values of the instance object's position property

        Instantiate (slime, spawnPos, Quaternion.identity);
        // Creates a prefab instance at the position indicated by spawnPos
    }
}

/* https://blog.sentry.io/2022/04/01/unity-tutorial-developing-your-first-unity-game-part-2 Retrieved Aug 2022 */
```

First, create an IEnumerator method named spawnSprite. Inside it, create a While loop. For now, the loop condition will be (true), but we will come back to it later on. Yield return new WaitForSeconds lets us set a delay timer between spawns. The example value is 1f, which translates to one second. You can set this value to whatever you want.

Cut the code written for the random position generation and paste it into the yield return block. Lastly, call it in the Start method using StartCoroutine(spawnSprite()). Save the script and run the game as a test. You should now be able to see sprites spawning at random.

CREATE A SCORE COUNTER

The last of the game mechanics to create is a scoring system. To make this game truly functional, we need to keep track of the number of sprites killed and display that as a score.

All we need to achieve this is a counter to keep track of kills and a Text object in which to display the variable. This can be set up to reset and start from zero every time the game is opened, but for this game, we will keep track of the score consistently. Every time the game is started, it starts on the last session's score and keeps counting.

First, we need to create a public integer named TotalScore in the Kill script outside all methods. It must be public so that it can be accessed from other classes. This data will be stored in a built-in class called PlayerPrefs. This class stores all data that needs to be kept while the game is not running, like game settings and player preferences.

The following code increases TotalScore and saves its value to PlayerPrefs. In the method OnMouseDown, add this code.

```
void OnMouseDown ()
// This method will determine what happens to the sprite once it's clicked in-game

{
    TotalScore = PlayersPrefs.GetInt ("Score", 0);
    // Counter variable is assigned the retrieved value of a score object built-in class PlayerPrefs   TotalScore ++;
    // totalScore is increased
    PlayerPrefs.SetInt ("Score", TotalScore);
    // the score object is adjusted to the value of totalScore
    PlayerPrefs.Save();
    Debug.Log ("Score is " + TotalScore);
    Destroy (gameObject);
    Instantiate (SmokeEffect, transform.position, Quaternion.identity);

}

/* Code sourced from https://blog.sentry.io/2022/04/01/unity-tutorial-developing-your-first-unity-game-part-1   and   https://blog.sentry.io/2022/04/01/unity-tutorial-developing-your-first-unity-game-part-2 Retrieved Aug 2022 */
```

This code grabs the value of TotalScore from the PlayerPrefs class, increases it, and saves the new value. For the time being, we display this value in the Debug log to test that it works.

Save the code, and run the game to see if the score increases.

Creating a Score Display

To display the score, we need a Text object. Create a new UI Text and drag it into the canvas. Rename this object to ScoreText. Change its display to fit your game and anchor it in the upper left corner. You can change the color, font, and font size however you want.

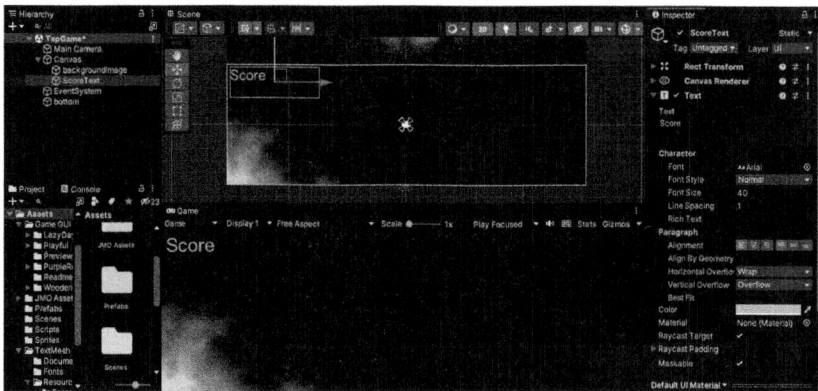

Next, we need to add code to change this display dynamically to update the score. In the Spawn script, add this to the using statements at the top: using UnityEngine.UI. This will give the script access to the UI elements. Create a new serializable Text object called scoreText and the public int TotalScore.

```
[SerializeField]
Text scoreText;

public int TotalScore;
```

In the Update method, call the value of TotalScore from the PlayerPrefs class and display it in the Text variable.

```
// Update is called once per frame

void Update ()
{
    TotalScore = PlayerPrefs.GetInt ("Score", 0);
    scoreText.text = "Score " + TotalScore.ToString();

    /* code sources from https://blog.sentry.io/2022/04/01/unity-tutorial-developing-
    your-first-unity-game-part-2 Retrieved Aug 2022 */
```

Finally, add the Text object to the Spawn script item in the camera's component.

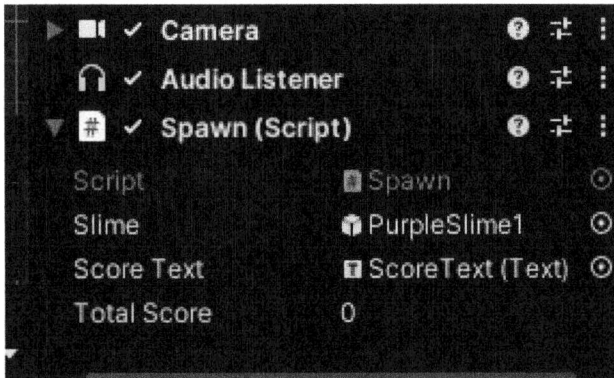

Save everything and run the game to see the display change dynamically.

That's it for the game mechanics. In the next chapter, we can change the game's UI to set up a menu and pause function.

9

YOUR GAME PART 3—ADDING A UI AND FINAL TOUCHES

CREATING A MENU SCREEN

E very game needs an interactive UI, and part of that UI is a starting screen. In other words, we need to create an opening Menu screen. To accomplish this, we must create a new scene called Menu or MainMenu.

Save TapGame, and copy the Canvas and EventSystem objects before creating a new scene. By copying the canvas, we do not have to redo the steps to set up the background. Be sure to also paste an Event System object or create one in the new scene. Without it, none of the features will respond to user interaction.

Delete the ScoreText object from the Menu scene. Open the canvas's Inspector and drag the new camera into the Render source. You should now have an empty scene with a Camera, Canvas, and Event System in the Hierarchy.

Title

There are two ways you can go about adding a title to the scene. The first is to import and add an image as a sprite. This is the easiest method since it doesn't have to be adjusted beyond scale and position. However, if you cannot find an appropriate image, you can use a Text object instead. Using a Text object, you can import a font that suits the game and adjust the text properties until it looks good.

Play Button

If you imported a UI package from the Unity Store, there will likely be some button images included. If not, you can source some from any of the art sources mentioned above or from a Unity package. In the example, the Purple Rock set found in the Game GUI Buttons package is used (Ashraf, 2017).

Add a button to the canvas and call it Play. Go to its Image component and drag the image you want to use into the Source Image property. Set the image to its native size and adjust it to fit the game.

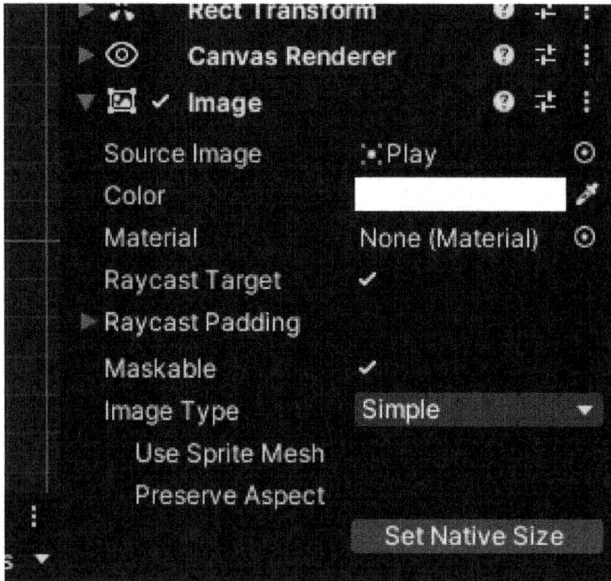

Delete the text object that comes with the button. Remember to check the Game View to ensure the scene looks good.

The Play button will have two functions. It will play a clicking animation and navigate to the TapGame scene.

ADDING AN ANIMATION

Under the Window tab in the menu bar, click on Animation and then Animations again. This will open an Animation window in the interface. Select the Play button in the Hierarchy, and click Create on the right side of the Animation window. It will ask you to create and save a new file. Name it playButton. Click Add Property, select Rect Transform, and then Scale.

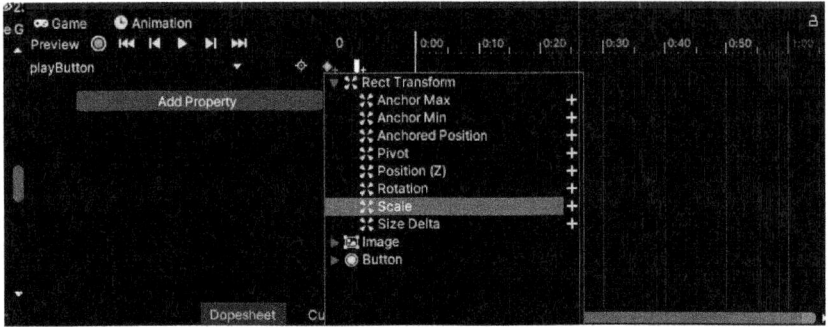

You will now see this:

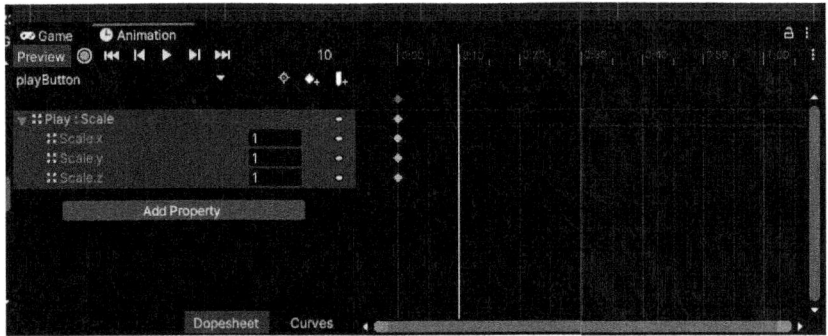

Move the line to 0.10 to set the animation time. Create two more sets of keyframes at 0.05 and 0.10 by double-clicking in the same row as the top keyframe. The animation will scale the button down to a smaller size at 0.05 and then return it to the original size at 0.10 to simulate the click. Select the keyframes at 0.05 and bring the line to them. Change the Scale x and Scale y values to something smaller, like 0.7 or 0.5.

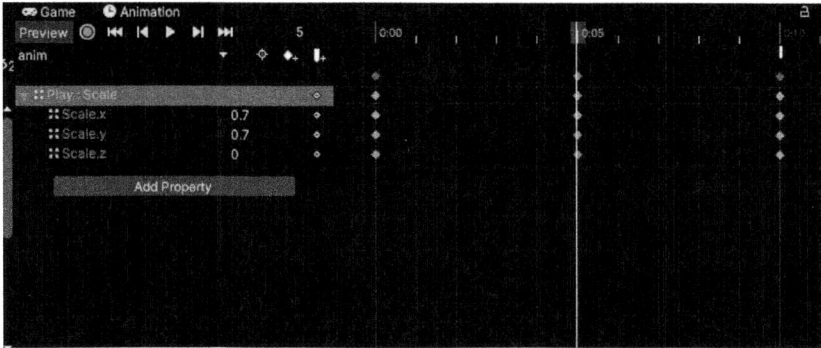

Repeat this process with the keyframes at 0.10 but change the values back to one. Click on the play icon next to preview to see the animation in the Scene View.

We want this animation to only play once when the button is clicked. An animation controller is needed to achieve that. The Animator component in the Play button's Inspector will have a property called Controller. Double-click on the source box to open the Animator window.

You will see a gray field with three colored rectangles. Right-click in the empty field and click Create State > Empty.

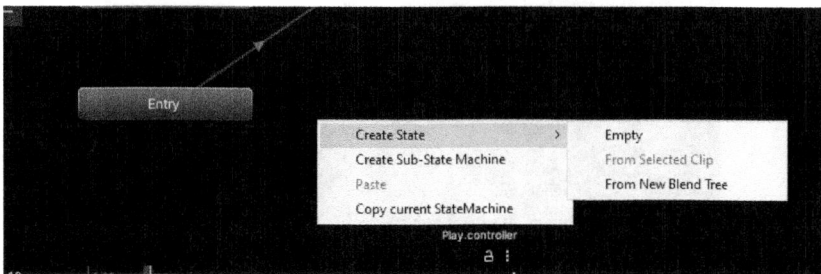

This will create a gray rectangle called New State. Right-click on that and set it to the default. Right-click on it again to make a new transition, and drag the cursor to the animation box. Repeat this to make a second transition between the animation state and the default state.

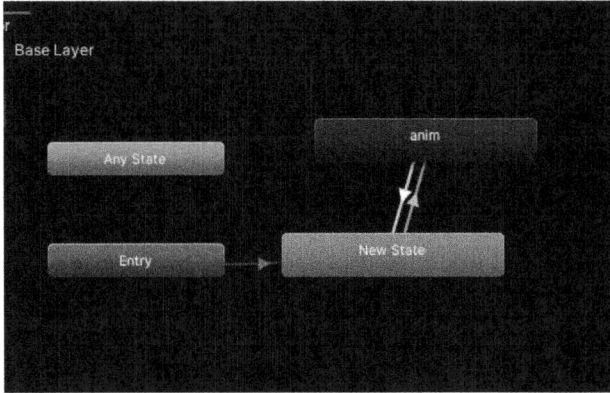

Next, we need to create a trigger to start the animation once the button is clicked. To the left of the field, there will be a window with a Layers and Parameters tab. Open Parameters, and create a trigger named Active.

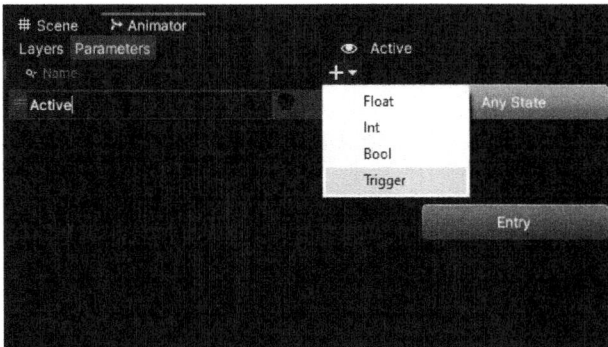

Select the arrow that shows the New State to animation transition. With it selected, uncheck the Has Exit Time in the Inspector, and add a new condition by clicking on the plus icon. It should look like this:

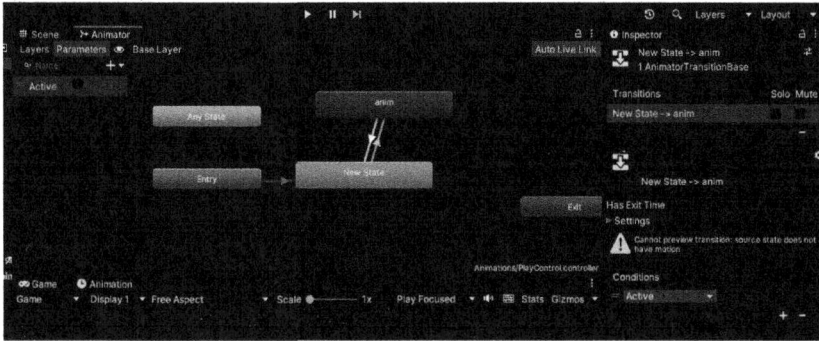

Save your work. In the Scripts folder, create a new script called Play, and attach it to the Play button.

Animation Script

First, declare an Animator variable called anim. In the start method, use the following statement to assign a value: anim = GetComponent<Animator> ( ). This will call the Animator component of the object to which the script is attached. Next, create a public void method called StartAnim to activate the trigger.

```
Animator Anim;
//private variable that will reference the animation

void Start ()
{
    anim = GetComponent<Animator> ();
}

public void StartAnim ()
//public function to trigger and call the animation from the button
{
    anim.SetTrigger("Active")
}
```

Save the script, and run the game to see the animations in effect.

Lastly, we need to construct code to allow the Play button to swap scenes.

Swapping Scenes

In the Play script, add the statement using UnityEngine.SceneManagement to the using statements at the top of the script. This will enable the object to navigate between scenes.

Create a new public void method called PlayGameScene, and add the statement SceneManagement.LoadScene("TapGame"). Make sure that you are using the same name as the one assigned to the game scene or it won't be able to call the correct file.

```
using System.Collections;
using System.Collections.Generic;
using UnityEngine;
using UnityEngine.SceneManagement;

public class Play : MonoBehaviour
{
    Animator anim;
    //private variable that will reference the animation

    void Start ()
    {
        anim = GetComponent<Animator> ();
    }

    public void StartAnim()
    //public function to trigger and call the animation from the button
    {
        anim.SetTrigger ("Active");
    }

    public void PlayGameScene ()
    //public method to load the scene tapGame        {

        SceneManager.LoadScene ("TapGame");
    }
/* code sourced from https://blog.sentry.io/2022.06/14/unity-tutorial-developing-your-first-
unity-game-part-3 Retrieved Aug 2022 */
```

Your Play script should look like the above example.

Finally, we need to add an event to the end of the animation to call the code that will swap the scenes. In the Animation window, select the 0.10 keyframes, and click Add Event. It is the most right icon in the image below.

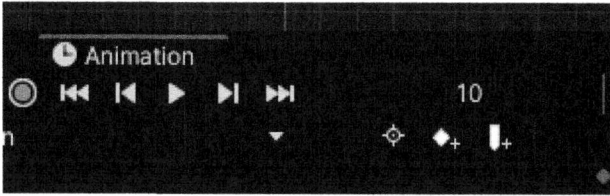

You will notice a similar icon appear under the 0.10 time just above the keyframes. Click on that to open the list of available methods. Scroll down to find PlayGameScene.

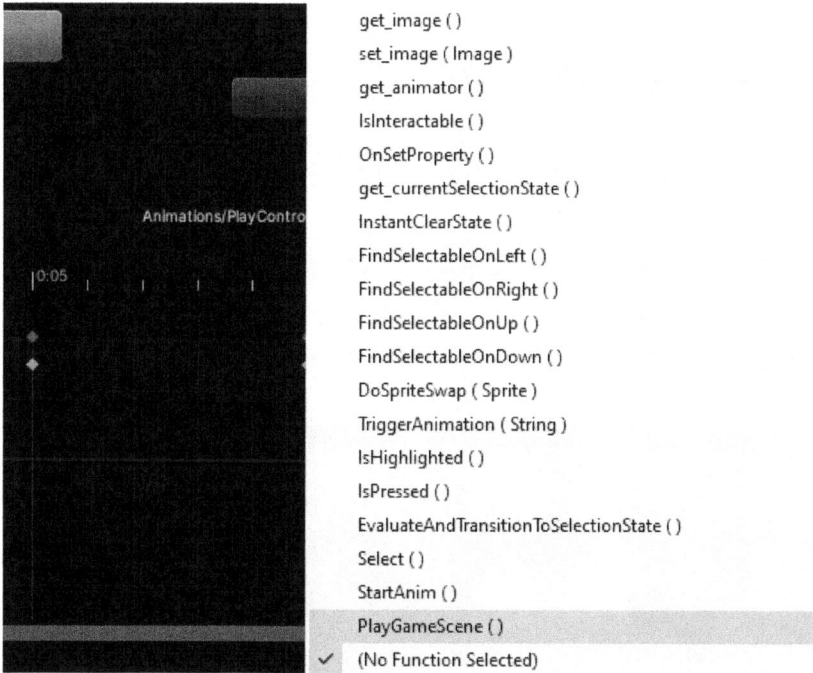

When you try to run the game now, it will produce an error. We need to add the scenes to the Build Settings. In the File tab of the menu bar, find Build Settings and open it. Right at the top of the window, you will see a box and an Add Open Scenes option. Click on that. If the TapGame scene doesn't appear on the list, open it from the Project window, and click Add Open Scenes again. Make sure the Menu scene has been saved before opening TapGame. You should now have both the Menu and TapGame scenes in the Build Settings.

Run the game and test it by clicking the Play button.

ADDING A PAUSE BUTTON TO THE GAME

If you are not already in the TapGame scene, go ahead and open it. A button is needed so the player can pause the game. This button will dim the background image and bring up a pause window. This window will feature buttons to resume gameplay, swap to the menu, and toggle sound on/off.

First, we need to add a Pause button in the same way we added a Play button to the previous scene. Create a button object, and drag it into the canvas. Find the image you want to use for the button, and drag it into the Image Source property. Set it to native size and adjust its scale to fit the object. Anchor it to the upper right corner, and delete the text object that came with it.

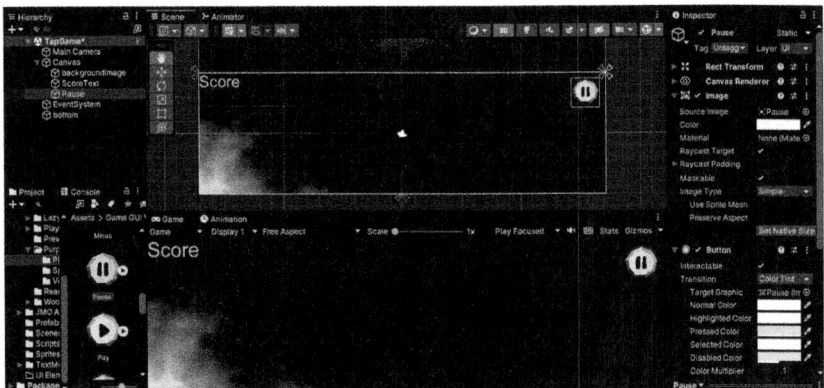

To distinguish the pause screen from the normal screen, we need to add another Image object. This will be either a plain dark image or a darker version of the same image. This image will be displayed over the background image and set to a lower opacity to create an overlay. We want to be able to see the background, but make it clear that the game is not in a playable state. In the example, we use a darker version of the background with a red tint to change its color to look more purple.

If you have not already, create a new Image object and rename it to darkScreen to distinguish it from backgroundImage. In the color option of the Image component, set the opacity to overlay the image. The example was set to around 75% opacity, but go with whatever looks good for your game.

Next, we need to add a frame for the pause window. Find and import a UI panel asset. If you cannot find one you like, go to opengameart.org and search for the UI Pack by Kenney (Kenney, 2014). Among those files are a gray panel that can be tinted to suit your game's look. This pack will also come with button images that can be adjusted in a similar manner. Make sure that the frame is added as an Image and not as a sprite. Add an Image object, and set the Image Source property instead of dragging the image asset into the Hierarchy. Rename it to pauseFrame.

Next, add a Text object and three buttons to the frame. Set them as children of the frame object in the Hierarchy. It is easier to deactivate only the frame than it is to deactivate each individual component. The Text object will act as the title for the pop-up and should be adjusted to read as such. Change the color, size, and font properties to suit your game. The first button will be the resume button, the second the exit button, and the third will toggle sounds. Set them up to look good as a cohesive unit, and name each object appropriately.

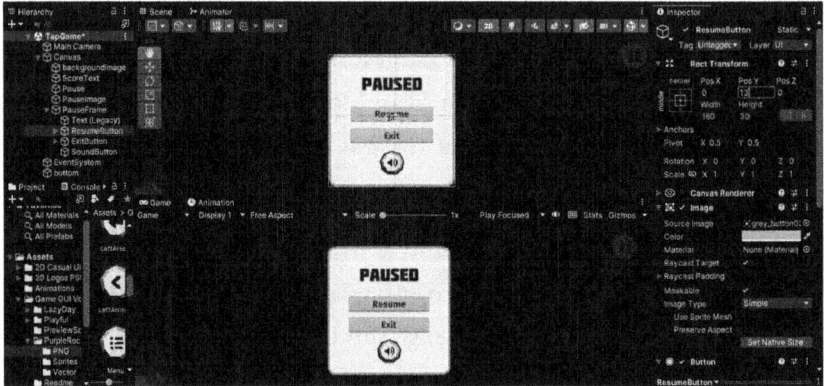

The next step is to add functionality to each of these buttons.

Pause Button

When the Pause button is clicked, the darkScreen and pauseFrame should become active. It should also stop all game mechanics. Remember the (true) condition of the Enumerator method in the Spawn script? This is where we change it.

In the Spawn script, create a public int variable called IsPaused. In the Start method, initialize that variable to the value of zero. While it has a value of zero, the game will be playing, and when its value is one, the game will be paused.

Replace the (true) condition of the While loop to (IsPaused == 0). This will test the value of the variable to determine if the game is in Play mode. While the value remains zero, the game will keep spawning sprites.

```
int IsPause;
//Variable to add to our condition to test whether or not to spawn objects void Start ()
{

    StartCoroutine (spawningSlime());   IsPause = 0;
    //initialize IsPause as 0


}

    IEnumerator spawningSlime ()   {

    while (IsPause == 0)
    //Condition that while IsPause remains 0, keep spawning. Onces it's 0, stop spawning
    {
            yield return new WaitForSeconds (1f);

            float posY = Random.Range (Camera.main.ScreenToWorldPoint
                            (new Vector2 (0, 0)).y,Camera.main.ScreenToWorldPoint
                            (new Vector2 (0, Screen.height)).y);

            float posX = Random.Range (Camera.main.ScreenToWorldPoint
                            (new Vector2 (0, 0)).x,Camera.main.ScreenToWorldPoint
                            (new Vector2 (Screen.width,0)).x);

            Vector2 spawnPos = new Vector2 (posX, posY);

            Instantiate (slime, spawnPos, Quaternion.identity);       }


    }
```

Next, provide code for what happens when the Pause button is clicked. Create a new public void method called PauseGame and copy the following code.

```
public void PauseGame ()
//Method that will provide instructions for what happens when the game is paused {

    IsPause = 1;
    //changes the value of IsPause to stop the spawning
darkScreen.SetActive(true);
    frame.SetActive (true);
    //Activates the pause screen and pause frame

}
/* code sourced from https://blog.sentry.io/2022.06/14/unity-tutorial-developing-your-first-unity-game-part-3 Retrieved
Aug 2022 */
```

This method changes the value of IsPaused to one and activates the darkScreen and pauseFrame. For this code to work, we need to create code objects to represent the darkScreen and pauseFrame. Add [SerializeField] to all of them so that they can be linked to the relevant objects from the Inspector.

```
[SerializeField]
GameObject darkScreen;
[SerializeField]
GameObject frame;
//Two new code objects are declared to represent the dark pause screen and the pause frame
```

While we are working with them, assign their counterparts in Unity.

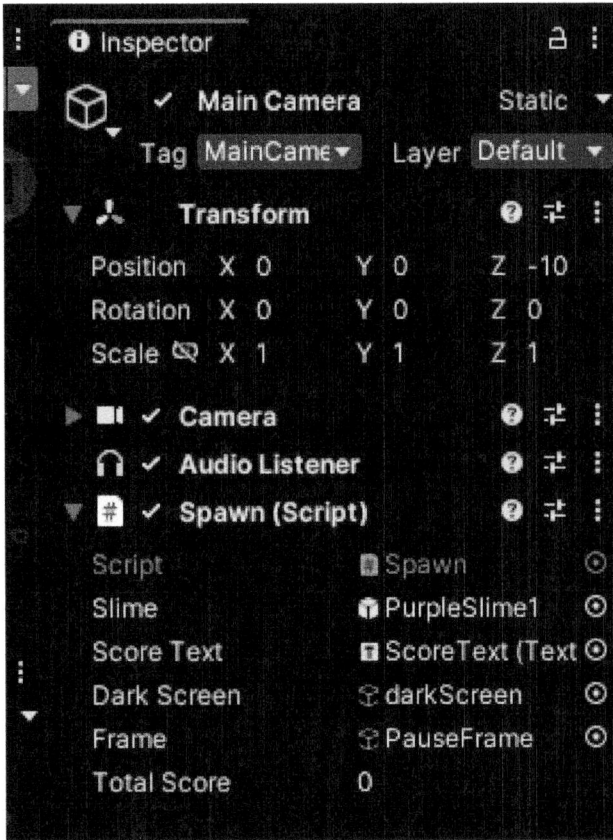

While in Unity, navigate to the Pause button's OnClick property, and click the plus icon. Drag the Camera into it and select the PauseGame method.

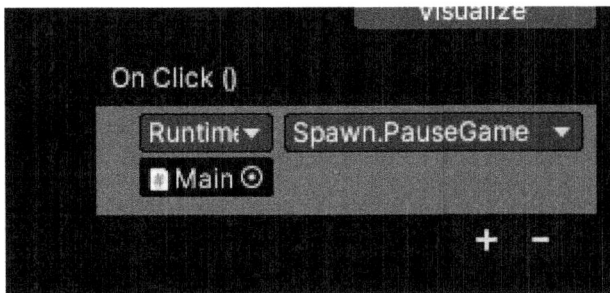

Lastly, the sprites that were in existence at the time the Pause button is clicked need to be destroyed. It is possible to set the game up so that they are not destroyed, but it is rather complex to make them stop falling and then resume falling again later. Go to the sprite prefab and adjust it to include a custom tag. The example sprite is given a slime tag to differentiate it from other objects. With the tag, we can add a feature that will destroy everything with that tag once the Pause button is clicked.

The simplest way to accomplish this is to create an array to catalog the existing sprites and then destroy them using a For loop. In the Spawn script, create a GameObject array called gameObjects using this statement: GameObject [ ] gameObjects.

```
GameObject [] gameObjects;
//Array used to store all instantiate slimes at the time of pause
```

Modify the Update method to look like this:

```
//Update is called once per frame void
Update ()
{
    totalScore = PlayerPrefs.GetInt ("Score", 0);

scoreText.text = "Score " + totalScore.ToString();
    if (IsPause == 1)
    //condition checks if game is paused
    {
gameObjects = GameObject.FindGameObjectsWithTag("slime");

//catalogues all the instantiated slimes on the screen at the time of pause
foreach (GameObject slime in gameObjects)
    {
        GameObject.Destroy (slime);
        //Code to destroy all the catalogued slimes
    }
  }
}
    /* code sourced from https://blog.sentry.io/2022.06/14/unity-tutorial-developing-your-first-unity-game-part-3 Retrieved Aug 2022 */
```

Save everything, and run the game to test the Pause feature.

Resume Button

For the Resume button, we need to do everything done for the Pause button but in reverse. That is to say, we need to change

IsPaused back to zero, deactivate the darkScreen and pauseFrame, and restart the spawn method.

In the Spawn script, create a public void method called ResumeGame and add the following code:

```
public void ResumeGame ()
// Method that will determine what happens when the resume button is clicked
{
    IsPause = 0;
    // Changes the IsPaused value back to 0 to restart the spawning
    darkScreen.SetActive (false);
    frame.SetActive (false);
    // Deactivates the pause screen and frame
    StartCoroutine (spawningSlime());
    // Restarts the spawn methods

    /* code sourced from https://blog.sentry.io/2022.06/14/unity-tutorial-developing-
    your-first-unity-game-part-3 Retrieved Aug 2022 */
```

Once again, drag the Main Camera into the Resume button's OnClick and select the ResumeGame method. Save everything, and run the game to test the Resume button.

Exit Button

The Exit button will need to navigate the player back to the Menu screen. This process is exactly the same as what we did with the initial scene change from the Play button. Add using Unity-Engine.SceneManagement to the top of the Spawn script.

Create a public void method called MenuScene, and add the code to make it swap back to the Menu scene. Again, be sure that you are referencing the name of the scene as it is saved in the Assets folder to ensure that the right file is called.

```
public void MenuScene () {

    SceneManager.LoadScene ("MainMenu");
    // Code to switch back to the menu
}

/* code sourced from https://blog.sentry.io/2022.06/14/unity-tutorial-developing-your-first-
unity-game-part-3 Retrieved Aug 2022 */
```

In Unity, select the Exit button and drag the Main Camera into its OnClick. Choose the MenuScene method from the drop-down.

Save everything, and run the game to test the Exit button.

ADDING SOUND FX

The last remaining element of functionality is to provide the necessary code for the sound on/off button. To do that, we need to add sound to the game. More specifically, we need to add a sound effect for when the sprite is destroyed.

If you do not already have a sound clip, you can find one at opengameart.org or sounds-resource.com. Once you have a sound you like, import it to the project.

Create an empty GameObject called SoundManagerObject. This object will act as a collection of available sounds to the game. Next, create a new script called SoundManager, and attach it to the empty object. In that script, add the statement using UnityEngine.UI.

First off, create all the necessary variables. We will need a variable for the AudioSource and another variable that will test whether or not the sound has been toggled on or off. We also need object variables for the soundOn and soundOff images and the button.

```
using System.Collections;
using System.Collections.Generic;
using UnityEngine;
using UnityEngine.UI;

public class SoundManager : MonoBehavior
{
    public AudioSource popSound;
    // Variable used to reference the sound

    int IsSound;
    // variable to check if sound is on or off

    public Sprite soundImage;
    public Sprite soundOffImage;
    public Sprite SoundButton;
    // Variables used to reference the sound images and button
```

The variable IsSound will be stored in the PlayerPrefs class. In Start initialize the variable by referencing PlayerPrefs. When IsSound has a value of one, the sound is considered on, and if it has a value of zero, the sound is considered off.

Next, we need to make provision for the different possibilities relating to the sound toggle. Create public void methods for PlaySound, MuteSound, and UnmuteSound. These will provide instructions that can later be called when the button is pushed.

```
public void PlaySound () {

    IsSound = PlayerPrefs.GetInt ("Sound", 1);

if (IsSound == 1)
    {
        popSound.Play ();
        //Play the sound
    }
}

public void MuteSound () {

    popSound.volume = 0;
    //Volume of the sound is reduced to zero
}

public void UnmuteSound () {

    popSound.volume = 1;
    //Increases the volume of the sound
}
```

Lastly, we need a method to determine what happens when the SoundButton is clicked. Create another public void method called ToggleSound and copy the following code.

```
public void ToggleSound ()
{
    if (IsSound == 1)
    //Check if the sound is on when button is presses
    {
        IsSound = 0;
        PlayerPrefs.SetInt ("Sound", IsSound);
        PlayerPrefs.Save();
        SoundButton.GetComponent<Image>().sprite = soundOffImage;
        MuteSound ();
    } else
    //what will happen if the sound was off when the button is pressed
    {
        IsSound = 1;
        PlayerPrefs.SetInt ("Sound", IsSound);
        PlayerPrefs.Save();
        SoundButton.GetComponent<Image>().sprite = soundOffImage;
        UnmuteSound ();
    }
}
```

CODE GAMERS DEVELOPMENT: ESSENTIALS | 173

This code contains a basic If-Else statement to test whether the sound was set to on or off when the button was clicked. If the sound was on before the click, the sound will be turned off. If the sound was off at the time of the click, the sound will be turned on.

Save this script and return to Unity. We need to now make the final connections to assign the variables created in this script. Select the SoundButton and head over to its OnClick. Add the sound object and select the ToggleSound method.

Next, we need to set up the sound that will be played. Select the empty object and add an AudioSource component. Drag the audio file into the AudioClip property and deselect Play on Awake. Turn back to its script component and assign the relevant assets to their serialized items. For the Audio Source object, drag the SoundManagerObject into its source. That will link the clip from the AudioSource component.

The only thing left to do is add the sound to the click action. In the Kill script, create a soundManager variable called SoundManager. In the Start method, reference the soundObjectManager object and its script component.

```
SoundManager soundManager;
//Reference to the sound manager
void Start ()
{
    soundManager = GameObject .Find ("SoundManagerObject").GetComponent
                <SoundManager>();
}
    //This code will reference the sound object and attached script

/* code sourced from https://blog.sentry.io/2022.06/14/unity-tutorial-developing-
your-first-unity-game-part-3 Retrieved Aug 2022 */
```

Add the statement soundManager.PlaySound ( ) to the OnMouseDown method.

```
void OnMouseDown ()
//This method will determine what happens to the sprite once it's done in-game {

    totalScore = PlayerPrefs.GetInt ("Score", 0);
   //Counter variable is assigned the retrieved value of a score object from built-in class PlayerPrefs
    totalScore++;
    //TotalScore is increased

    soundManager.PlaySound();
    //Code that will play the sound when the sprite is clicked

    PlayerPrefs.SetInt ("Score", totalScore);
    //The score object is adjusted to the value of totalScore

    PlayersPrefs.Save ();
    Debug.Log ("Score is " + totalScore);
    Destroy (gameObject);
   Instantiate (SmokeEffect, transform.position, Quaternion.identity);
```

Save everything for the last time, and run the game.

NOW YOU HAVE A GAME

There you have it, a fully functional tap game with a UI, sound FX, and a randomly spawning sprite. Show it off to your family and friends!

If you have any questions regarding the material discussed in this book, please feel free to contact me at codegamersdev@gmail.com. Add a short description of your project to the email's subject line, and share the code you are having trouble with. I'm always happy to help others who are willing to learn!

CONCLUSION

Congratulations on building your first game! How does it feel? If you made it this far, truly well done. Everyone starts somewhere, and you are now well on your way to becoming a full-fledged game developer. As someone who started out as a gamer wanting to make something great, let me tell you that this is only the beginning. From one self-taught game developer to another, never give up, and never stop learning. Learning is not just about expanding your knowledge. It is also about being the best person you could be. The purpose of this book is to help you achieve your goals and grow to your full potential as a prospective developer.

Game development is not only a profession but also an outlet for creativity and joy. Video games are a source of entertainment and pleasure for countless people. The developers behind them are the cause of that.

We learned a lot in this book. This book explored programming languages and game engines. It delved into the basics of C# and how to work with the Unity engine. It helped you build a game and gave you the tools you need to further explore the field of game development. Hopefully, it has shown you that you do not need a degree or the best equipment to be a game developer.

By now, you have the tools to attempt more complex projects. Take those tools and put them to good use. Try your hand at different types of games. Explore this field and keep growing as a developer. You are only just getting started.

If you enjoyed this book or found it helpful, please leave a review on Amazon and share your thoughts.

GLOSSARY

Array: A collection of values of a similar DataType.

Canvas: A GameObject in which UI elements are organized.

Class: An object in which data and methods are contained as per OOP. Classes serve as a grouping of members for the sake of organization and effectiveness.

Collider 2D: A component that determines the area of effect of the GameObject it is attached to.

Component: A property or value assigned to a GameObject.

Condition: An expression that can be tested to return a result.

Constructor: A method that is used to instantiate objects of the class in which it is declared.

Deconstructor: A method declared in a class that destroys instances of that class when the program closes.

Delegate: A DataType that is used to reference methods according to their signatures. They can act as EventHandlers.

Event: A means of communication between classes. An event is a program's response to something happening that requires action.

Event System: A GameObject that is needed to provide intractability.

Field: A variable declared with Class Level scope that represents a property of any instance of that class.

GameObject: A game element that contains components.

Gizmo: A visual representation of an object's geometry. Characterized by three colored arrows visible when an object is selected.

Initializer: A variable declared in the definition of a For loop. It is used to create the condition of the loop and acts as a counter for the number of loop iterations.

Instantiation: The act of creating an object from a class or Prefab.

Iterator: The third parameter of a For loop, wherein the initializer's value is changed.

Method: A collection of statements aimed at the completion of a specific task.

Namespace: A code structure that contains classes and their members.

Object-Oriented Programming (OOP): A programming method where code is structured by objects.

Operand: The subject upon which an operation is executed.

Operator: A symbol associated with a pre-defined operation.

Parameter: Also known as an argument. A value that forms part of the signature of a method that defines the condition of operation. Can be used to convey data to a method.

Polymorphism: A feature of OOP that provides objects the ability to have multiple forms.

Prefab: A saved object configuration. Can be found in the Project Window.

- **Instance:** Objects made from a Prefab.
- **Variant:** Objects made from a Prefab with adjustments.

Primitive Object: Simple, automatically available objects found under the GameObjects tab.

Rigidbody: An object component that subjects the object to Unity Engine physics.

Signature: The means by which a compiler can recognize a method. Includes the method type, name, and order of parameters.

Sprite: A 2D image that exists in the game as a Gameobject.

Statement: A single line of code that serves to convey instruction. Ends in a semi-colon (;).

Static: A C# keyword that indicates that only one copy of the relevant information is allowed.

Variables: Containers for data of a defined type that can store data or act as a placeholder for data.

Void: A programming keyword that indicates a method's return type. It signifies that there is no returnable value.

REFERENCES

[Unity] coding guidelines & basic best practices. (2020, January 9). Avangarde-Software. https://avangarde-software.com/unity-coding-guidelines-basic-best-practices/

Adding a C# script to our Unity game project. (n.d.). Www.studytonight.com. Retrieved August 16, 2022, from https://www.studytonight.com/game-devel opment-in-2D/basics-of-unity-script

Aggarwal, A. (2019, January 19). *Scope of variables in C#.* GeeksforGeeks. https:// www.geeksforgeeks.org/scope-of-variables-in-c-sharp/

Aggarwal, A. (2021, June 11). *C# | Types of variables.* GeeksforGeeks. https://www. geeksforgeeks.org/c-sharp-types-of-variables/

Amlin, J. (2022, April 11). *Classes in C# using Unity.* Medium. https://levelup.gitcon nected.com/classes-in-c-using-unity-4325f2080353

Anbazhagan, G. (2017, June 24). *Creating and calling methods in Unity.* www.c-Sharpcorner.com. https://www.c-sharpcorner.com/blogs/creating-and-call ing-methods-in-unity

Anbazhagan, G. (2020, June 25). *Create 3D game objects In Unity.* Www.c-Sharpcorner.com. https://www.c-sharpcorner.com/article/create-3d-game-objects-in-unity3d/

Arm Ltd. (n.d.). *What is a gaming engine?* Arm | the Architecture for the Digital World. Retrieved August 5, 2022, from https://www.arm.com/glossary/gaming-engines

Ashraf, R. (2017). *Game GUI buttons - Purple rock.* https://assetstore.unity.com/packages/2d/gui/icons/game-gui-buttons-96277

Bird, M. (2021a, October 29). *How to use Prefabs in Unity.* TurboFuture. https:// turbofuture.com/computers/How-to-Create-a-Prefab-in-Unity

Bird, M. (2021b, December 6). *How to create and use scripts in Unity.* LevelSkip. https://levelskip.com/how-to/How-to-Create-and-Use-Scripts-in-Unity

Bite Sized Tech. (2021, August 24). *Classes, objects & constructors in C# | Unity game development tutorial | how to make a game.* Bite Sized Tech. https://bitesizedtech. com/post/how-to-make-a-game-classes-objects-constructors/

Blackwell, A. (2002). *What is programming?* PPIG, 14, 204–218. https://citeseerx.ist. psu.edu/viewdoc/download?doi=10.1.1.58.1345&rep=rep1&type=pdf

Bullock, J. (2021, January 14). *Why should I use Unity: Top 8 reasons.* TurboFuture.

https://turbofuture.com/computers/Why-Should-I-Use-Unity-Top-8-Reasons

C# - events. (n.d.). Www.tutorialspoint.com. Retrieved August 13, 2022, from https://www.tutorialspoint.com/csharp/csharp_events.htm

C# - loops. (n.d.). Www.tutorialspoint.com. Retrieved August 12, 2022, from https://www.tutorialspoint.com/csharp/csharp_loops.htm

C# - variables. (n.d.). Www.tutorialspoint.com. Retrieved August 10, 2022, from https://www.tutorialspoint.com/csharp/csharp_variables.htm

C# arrays (with easy examples). (2020, May 10). Www.tutorialsteacher.com. https://www.tutorialsteacher.com/csharp/array-csharp

C# arrays (with examples). (n.d.). Www.programiz.com. Retrieved August 11, 2022, from https://www.programiz.com/csharp-programming/arrays

C# comments: How to use them and why? (n.d.). Www.programiz.com. Retrieved August 9, 2022, from https://www.programiz.com/csharp-programming/comments

C# Curator. (2018, November 26). Comments in C#. Www.c-Sharpcorner.com. https://www.c-sharpcorner.com/UploadFile/puranindia/comments-in-C-Sharp/

C# Curator. (2019, March 20). What are access modifiers In C#. Www.c-Sharpcorner.com. https://www.c-sharpcorner.com/uploadfile/puranindia/what-are-access-modifiers-in-C-Sharp/

C# Destructor (With Examples). (n.d.). Www.programiz.com. Retrieved August 13, 2022, from https://www.programiz.com/csharp-programming/destructor

C# expressions, statements and blocks (with examples). (n.d.). Www.programiz.com. Retrieved August 9, 2022, from https://www.programiz.com/csharp-program ming/expressions-statements-blocks

C# for loop (with examples). (n.d.). Www.programiz.com. Retrieved August 12, 2022, from https://www.programiz.com/csharp-programming/for-loop

C# in Unity - constructors. (n.d.). Kybernetik.com.au. Retrieved August 13, 2022, from https://kybernetik.com.au/cs-unity/docs/introduction/methods/constructors

C# inheritance. (n.d.-a). Www.w3schools.com. Retrieved August 13, 2022, from https://www.w3schools.com/cs/cs_inheritance.php

C# inheritance. (n.d.-b). Www.javatpoint.com. Retrieved August 13, 2022, from https://www.javatpoint.com/c-sharp-inheritance

C# method (with examples). (n.d.). Www.programiz.com. Retrieved August 13, 2022, from https://www.programiz.com/csharp-programming/methods

C# methods. (n.d.). Www.w3schools.com. Retrieved August 13, 2022, from https://www.w3schools.com/cs/cs_methods.php

C# methods - functions with examples. (n.d.). Www.tutlane.com. Retrieved August 13,

2022, from https://www.tutlane.com/tutorial/csharp/csharp-methods-func tions-with-examples

C# operators. (n.d.). Tutorialsteacher.com. Retrieved August 11, 2022, from https://www.tutorialsteacher.com/csharp/csharp-operators

C# operators: Arithmetic, comparison, logical and more. (n.d.). Www.programiz.com. Retrieved August 11, 2022, from https://www.programiz.com/csharp-programming/operators

C# polymorphism. (n.d.). Www.w3schools.com. Retrieved August 14, 2022, from https://www.w3schools.com/cs/cs_polymorphism.php

C# polymorphism with examples. (n.d.). Tutlane.com. Retrieved August 14, 2022, from https://www.tutlane.com/tutorial/csharp/csharp-polymorphism

C# variable scope (with examples). (n.d.). Www.programiz.com. Retrieved August 13, 2022, from https://www.programiz.com/csharp-programming/variable-scope

C# variables. (n.d.). Tutorialsteacher.com. Retrieved August 10, 2022, from https://www.tutorialsteacher.com/csharp/csharp-variable

CG Cookie. (2022, February 21). *30 things every Unity developer should know.* Cgcookie.com. https://cgcookie.com/posts/30-things-every-unity-developer-should-know

Chand, M. (2022, August 3). *Working with C# arrays.* Www.c-Sharpcorner.com. https://www.c-sharpcorner.com/article/working-with-arrays-in-C-Sharp/

Coding guidelines. (n.d.). Www.mono-Project.com. Retrieved August 17, 2022, from https://www.mono-project.com/community/contributing/coding-guidelines/

Collins Dictionary. (n.d.). *Programming.* In Collins Dictionary. Retrieved August 5, 2022, from https://www.collinsdictionary.com/dictionary/english/programming

Cwalina, K. (2021, September 15). *Naming guidelines - framework design guidelines.* Docs.microsoft.com. https://docs.microsoft.com/en-us/dotnet/standard/design-guidelines/naming-guidelines?redirectedfrom=MSDN

Dane, M. (2017, November 8). *Methods | C#.* Mike Dane. https://www.mikedane.com/programming-languages/csharp/methods/

Dasel. (n.d.). *How do I interpret a compiler error?* Unity Support. Retrieved August 19, 2022, from https://support.unity.com/hc/en-us/articles/205930539-How-do-I-interpret-a-compiler-error-

Dave, A. (2022, April 6). *What makes Unity the best game development platform?* MindInventory. https://www.mindinventory.com/blog/unity-3d-game-development/

De Byl, P. (n.d.). *How to avoid noob errors when learning Unity.* Penny de Byl. Retrieved August 19, 2022, from https://www.h3dlearn.com/blog/unity-problems

Default constructor. (n.d.). Unitycontainer.org. Retrieved August 13, 2022, from http://unitycontainer.org/tutorials/registration/Type/Constructor/param_none.html

Evans, J. (2021, June 19). *What are classes in Unity.* Nerd for Tech. https://medium.com/nerd-for-tech/what-are-classes-in-unity-620e467fd4f

Events in C#. (n.d.). Www.tutorialsteacher.com. Retrieved August 13, 2022, from https://www.tutorialsteacher.com/csharp/csharp-event

Fahir. (2021, October 8). *C# programming with Unity - static classes.* Awesome Tuts | Learn How to Make Games. https://awesometuts.com/blog/c-sharp-static-class/

Friendly Frog. (2020, September 30). *How to access the method in other class in C# code example.* Codegrepper.com. https://www.codegrepper.com/code-examples/csharp/how+to+access+the+method+in+other+class+in+c%23

GameDevTraum. (2019, November 22). *{ CLASSES in PROGRAMMING } - description, video and examples in C#.* GameDevTraum. https://gamedevtraum.com/en/programming/object-oriented-programming/classes-in-programming-examples-in-unity/

Gasjek, D. (2022, April 19). *Beginner's guide to Unity - how to download and install Unity and visual studio.* 3D Development Bootcamp & XR Courses | Circuit Stream. https://circuitstream.com/blog/beginners-guide-to-unity-how-to-download-and-install-unity-and-visual-studio/

GeeksforGeeks. (2018a, May 22). *C# | Data types.* GeeksforGeeks. https://www.geeksforgeeks.org/c-sharp-data-types/?ref=rp

GeeksforGeeks. (2018b, June 8). *C# | Arrays.* GeeksforGeeks. https://www.geeksforgeeks.org/c-sharp-arrays/

GeeksforGeeks. (2019a, January 12). *Introduction to C#.* GeeksforGeeks. https://www.geeksforgeeks.org/introduction-to-c-sharp/

GeeksforGeeks. (2019b, July 9). *C# | Operators.* GeeksforGeeks. https://www.geeksforgeeks.org/c-sharp-operators/

Haynes, R. (2021, May 12). *Creating a new project in Unity.* Medium. https://rhetthaynes66.medium.com/creating-a-new-project-in-unity-c2d936e133ae

Hoppman, R. (2015, March 31). *Slime.* OpenGameArt.org. https://opengameart.org/content/slime-0

In-depth tutorial on C# conditional statements. (2022, August 7). Software Testing Help. https://www.softwaretestinghelp.com/c-sharp/csharp-conditional-and-decision-statements/

Juegoadmin. (2021, January 21). *7 ways to keep Unity project organized: Unity3d best practices.* Juego Studio. https://www.juegostudio.com/blog/7-ways-to-keep-unity-project-organized-unity3d-best-practices

Karia, R. (2020a, June 17). *C# for loop.* Www.tutorialsteacher.com. https://www.tutorialsteacher.com/csharp/csharp-for-loop

Karia, R. (2020b, June 28). *C# static class, methods, constructors, fields.* Www.tutorial-steacher.com. https://www.tutorialsteacher.com/csharp/csharp-static

Kean, K. (2022, February 5). *The 5 best game engines for beginners in video game development.* MUO. https://www.makeuseof.com/best-free-game-engine-for-beginners/

Kenney. (2014). *UI pack.* https://opengameart.org/content/ui-pack

keshav_786. (2021, August 16). *C# | Methods.* GeeksforGeeks. https://www.geeks forgeeks.org/c-sharp-methods/

Knowledgehut. (2019, March 1). *Learn introduction to C# (CSharp) programming language from scratch.* Www.knowledgehut.com. https://www.knowledgehut.com/tutorials/csharp/csharp-introduction

Lastbitcoder. (2021, December 16). *How to install Unity Hub on Windows?* GeeksforGeeks. https://www.geeksforgeeks.org/how-to-install-unity-hub-on-windows/

Lithmee. (2019, May 30). *What is the difference between static and dynamic polymorphism in Java.* Pediaa.com. https://pediaa.com/what-is-the-difference-between-static-and-dynamic-polymorphism-in-java/

Loops in C# tutorial [with examples]. (n.d.). Www.knowledgehut.com. Retrieved August 12, 2022, from https://www.knowledgehut.com/tutorials/csharp/csharp-loops

Lukosek, G. (2016). *Object, a container with variables and methods.* In Learning C# by Developing Games with Unity 5.x. Packt. https://subscription.packtpub.com/book/game-development/9781785287596/7/ch07lvl1sec66/custom-constructors

Macek, T. (2016, May 23). *The 10 most common mistakes that Unity developers make.* Toptal Engineering Blog. https://www.toptal.com/unity-unity3d/top-unity-development-mistakes

ManasiKirloskar. (2019, February 1). *Destructors in C#.* GeeksforGeeks. https://www.geeksforgeeks.org/destructors-in-c-sharp/

ManasiKirloskar. (2021, September 20). *Access modifiers in C#.* GeeksforGeeks. https://www.geeksforgeeks.org/access-modifiers-in-c-sharp/

Mangal, K. (2019, January 23). *C# | inheritance.* GeeksforGeeks. https://www.geeks forgeeks.org/c-sharp-inheritance/

Mangal, K. (2022, February 23). *C# | Class and Object.* GeeksforGeeks. https://www.geeksforgeeks.org/c-sharp-class-and-object/

MasterClass Staff. (2020, November 8). *Gaming 101: Guide to video game programming languages.* https://www.masterclass.com/articles/guide-to-video-game-programming-languages#what-is-a-video-game-programming-language

McMillan, T. (2021, October 25). *5 common mistakes in Unity (and how to fix them).*

Taryn Writes Code. https://blog.tarynmcmillan.com/5-common-mistakes-in-unity-and-how-to-fix-them

Methods in C# | Unity tutorial. (n.d.). Mammoth Interactive. Retrieved August 19, 2022, from https://mammothinteractive.com/methods-in-c-unity-tutorial/

Michael, H. (n.d.). *What are C# conditionals?* Educative: Interactive Courses for Software Developers. Retrieved August 11, 2022, from https://www.educative.io/answers/what-are-c-sharp-conditionals

Moakley, B. (2019, March 26). *Introduction to Unity: Getting Started – part 1/2.* Raywenderlich.com; raywenderlich.com. https://www.raywenderlich.com/7514-introduction-to-unity-getting-started-part-1-2

Momin, I. (2021, April 22). *Defining classes & structs — understanding reference and value types — Unity C#.* Medium. https://imran-momin.medium.com/defining-classes-structs-understanding-reference-and-value-types-unity-c-495b20144af2

MOOC Blog Team. (2021, December 13). *Best programming languages for game development.* Www.mooc.org. https://www.mooc.org/blog/best-programming-languages-for-game-development

Moreno, J. (2019). *Cartoon FX free.* https://assetstore.unity.com/packages/vfx/particles/cartoon-fx-free-109565

Mr. Unity Buddy. (2021, March 14). *How to make a simple game with Unity: For absolute beginners.* DEV Community. https://dev.to/unitybuddy/how-to-make-a-simple-game-with-unity-for-absolute-beginners-ei2

Nayan, V. (2011, March 2). *Understanding static & dynamic polymorphism.* Www.c-Sharpcorner.com. https://www.c-sharpcorner.com/uploadfile/37db1d/understanding-static-dynamic-polymorphism/

Nour, R. (2022a, March 21). *Unity tutorial: What you need to know before developing your first Unity game.* Product Blog • Sentry. https://blog.sentry.io/2022/03/21/unity-tutorial-what-you-need-to-know-before-developing-your-first-unity-game#game-objects

Nour, R. (2022b, April 1). *Unity tutorial: Developing your first Unity game - part 1.* Product Blog • Sentry. https://blog.sentry.io/2022/04/01/unity-tutorial-developing-your-first-unity-game-part-1#adding-a-new-scene

Nour, R. (2022c, May 9). *Unity tutorial: Developing your first Unity game - part 2.* Product Blog • Sentry. https://blog.sentry.io/2022/05/09/unity-tutorial-developing-your-first-unity-game-part-2#how-to-add-the-falling-effect-to-your-unity-game

Nour, R. (2022d, June 14). *Unity tutorial: Developing your first Unity game - part 3.* Product Blog • Sentry. https://blog.sentry.io/2022/06/14/unity-tutorial-developing-your-first-unity-game-part-3#how-to-create-a-main-menu

Padilla, J. A. (2018, May 15). *2019 video game industry statistics, trends & data*. WePC.com; WePC.com. https://www.wepc.com/news/video-game-statistics/

Pandit, D. (2016, June 19). *Type of methods in C#*. Www.c-Sharpcorner.com. https://www.c-sharpcorner.com/article/type-of-methods-in-c-sharp/

Pandit, N. (2019, September 4). *Different types of method in C#*. Tutorials Link. https://tutorialslink.com/Articles/Different-types-of-method-in-c/1164

Parrot, P. (2020). *20 Logo Templates with customizable PSD vector sources*. https://asset store.unity.com/packages/2d/gui/icons/20-logo-templates-with-customizable-psd-vector-sources-174999

Patil, A. (2022, April 25). *Conditional statements in C#*. Www.c-Sharpcorner.com. https://www.c-sharpcorner.com/UploadFile/8af593/conditional-statement-in-C-Sharp/

Patrick. (2017, October 26). *5 common coding errors in C# and Unity and how to solve them*. Learn to Create Games. http://learntocreategames.com/10-common-coding-errors-and-how-to-solve-them/

Pecanac, V. (2022, March 2). *Events in C#*. Code Maze. https://code-maze.com/csharp-events/

Raouf, O. A. (2020, June 1). *How to create Prefabs in Unity?* Medium. https://ouzani abdraouf.medium.com/how-to-create-prefabs-in-unity-8d2ff87bdad6

Rawat, R. (2019, March 13). *Difference between static and dynamic polymorphism*. ProgrammerBay. https://programmerbay.com/difference-between-static-and-runtime-polymorphism/

Ribeiro, A., & Gajsek, D. (2021, March 24). *Learn C# for Unity — objects and classes*. 3D Development Bootcamp & XR Courses | Circuit Stream. https://circuit stream.com/blog/learn-c-for-unity-lesson-5-objects-and-classes/

Rivello, S. A. (2021, July 11). *Unity — C# coding standards*. Medium. https://sam-16930.medium.com/coding-standards-in-c-39aefee92db8

Saluja, N. (2020, March 7). *Constructors In C#*. Www.c-Sharpcorner.com. https://www.c-sharpcorner.com/article/constructors-in-C-Sharp/

Sam, S. (2020a, June 20). *Scope of variables in C#*. Www.tutorialspoint.com. https://www.tutorialspoint.com/scope-of-variables-in-chash#

Sam, S. (2020b, June 20). *What are static members of a C# class?* Www.tutorialspoint.com. https://www.tutorialspoint.com/What-are-static-members-of-a-Chash-Class

Sam007. (2022, April 22). *Loops in C#*. GeeksforGeeks. https://www.geeks forgeeks.org/loops-in-c-sharp/

Schardon, L. (2022, February 22). *What is Unity? – A guide for one of the top game engines*. GameDev Academy. https://gamedevacademy.org/what-is-unity/

Scope of variables in C#. (n.d.). Tutorialspoint.Dev. Retrieved August 13, 2022, from https://tutorialspoint.dev/language/c-sharp/scope-of-variables-in-c-2

Shekhar, G. (2017, August 20). *Learning transform tools – Unity tutorial*. Gyanendu Shekhar's Blog. http://gyanendushekhar.com/2017/08/20/learning-trans form-tools-unity-tutorial/

Spasojevic, M. (2019, December 16). *Operators in C# (types of operators and usage examples)*. Code Maze. https://code-maze.com/csharp-operators/

Spasojevic, M. (2021, December 20). *Access modifiers in C# - differences and how to use them*. Code Maze. https://code-maze.com/csharp-access-modifiers/

Static members - The complete C# tutorial. (n.d.). Csharp.net-Tutorials.com. Retrieved August 13, 2022, from https://csharp.net-tutorials.com/classes/static-members/

Studytonight. (n.d.). *Creating first project with Unity 3D*. Www.studytonight.com. Retrieved August 7, 2022, from https://www.studytonight.com/game-develop ment-in-2D/hello-unity

StumpyStrust. (2014). *Space background*. https://opengameart.org/content/space-background-2

The Dev Codes. (n.d.). *C# destructor*. Thedeveloperblog.com. Retrieved August 13, 2022, from https://thedeveloperblog.com/c-sharp/destructor

Thompson, B. (2021, June 25). *C# if, switch, for, while loop statements tutorial [examples]*. Www.guru99.com. https://www.guru99.com/c-sharp-conditional-statements.html

Trivedi, J. (2019, March 27). *Understanding polymorphism in C#*. Www.c-Sharpcorner.com. https://www.c-sharpcorner.com/UploadFile/ff2f08/under standing-polymorphism-in-C-Sharp/

Tuliper, A. (2015, July 1). Unity: *Developing your first game with Unity and C#*. MSDN Magazine. https://docs.microsoft.com/en-us/archive/msdn-maga zine/2014/august/unity-developing-your-first-game-with-unity-and-csharp

TutorialsTeacher. (2021, August 19). *Variable scopes in C#*. Www.tutorialsteacher.-com. https://www.tutorialsteacher.com/articles/variable-scopes-in-csharp

Tyler, D. (2022a, July 19). *How to choose the best video game engine*. The Ultimate Resource for Video Game Design. https://www.gamedesigning.org/career/video-game-engines/

Tyler, D. (2022b, July 19). *Top 10 game programming languages: The beginner's guide*. The Ultimate Resource for Video Game Design. https://www.gamedesigning.org/career/programming-languages/

Unity classes. (n.d.). Www.javatpoint.com. Retrieved August 12, 2022, from https://www.javatpoint.com/unity-classes

Unity components. (n.d.). Www.javatpoint.com. Retrieved August 7, 2022, from https://www.javatpoint.com/unity-components

Unity GameObjects. (n.d.). Www.javatpoint.com. Retrieved August 7, 2022, from https://www.javatpoint.com/unity-gameobjects

Unity Technologies. (n.d.-a). *Prefab workflow.* Unity.com. Retrieved August 8, 2022, from https://unity.com/prefabs

Unity Technologies. (n.d.-b). *Working with scripts.* Unity Learn. Retrieved August 16, 2022, from https://learn.unity.com/tutorial/working-with-scripts#5f68b18eedbc2a001fbffd10

Unity Technologies. (2017, May 22). *Unity Manual: Getting started.* Docs.unity3d.com. https://docs.unity3d.com/560/Documentation/Manual/GettingStarted.html

Unity Technologies. (2018a, March 7). *Script compilation and assembly definition files - Unity manual.* Docs.unity3d.com. https://docs.unity3d.com/2018.4/Documentation/Manual/ScriptCompilationAssemblyDefinitionFiles.html

Unity Technologies. (2018b, March 19). *Unity manual: Creating and using scripts.* Unity3d.com. https://docs.unity3d.com/Manual/CreatingAndUsingScripts.html

Unity Technologies. (2020, July 7). *Creating new projects. Unity Learn.* https://learn.unity.com/tutorial/creating-new-projects?signup=true#5d92399bedbc2a05c1835459

Unity Technologies. (2022a, July 30). *2D primitive GameObjects.* Docs.unity3d.com. https://docs.unity3d.com/Manual/2DPrimitiveObjects.html

Unity Technologies. (2022b, July 30). *GameObjects.* Docs.unity3d.com. https://docs.unity3d.com/Manual/GameObjects.html

Unity Technologies. (2022c, July 30). *Position GameObjects.* Docs.unity3d.com. https://docs.unity3d.com/Manual/PositioningGameObjects.html

Unity Technologies. (2022d, July 30). *Use components.* Docs.unity3d.com. https://docs.unity3d.com/Manual/UsingComponents.html

Unity Technologies. (2022e, August 3). *Unity manual: Assembly definitions.* Docs.unity3d.com. https://docs.unity3d.com/Manual/ScriptCompilationAssemblyDefinitionFiles.html#:

Unity Technologies. (2022f, August 13). *Unity manual: Conditional compilation.* Docs.unity3d.com. https://docs.unity3d.com/Manual/PlatformDependentCompilation.html

Unity Technologies. (2022g, August 13). *Unity manual: Special folders and script compilation order.* Docs.unity3d.com. https://docs.unity3d.com/Manual/ScriptCompileOrderFolders.html

Wagner, B. (2021a, June 11). *Polymorphism.* Docs.microsoft.com. https://docs.microsoft.com/en-us/dotnet/csharp/fundamentals/object-oriented/polymorphism

Wagner, B. (2021b, September 12). *Methods - C# programming guide.* Microsoft.com.

https://docs.microsoft.com/en-us/dotnet/csharp/programming-guide/classes-and-structs/methods

Wagner, B. (2022a, January 12). *Statements (C# programming guide).* Docs.microsoft.com. https://docs.microsoft.com/en-us/dotnet/csharp/programming-guide/statements-expressions-operators/statements

Wagner, B. (2022b, January 25). *Events - C# programming guide.* Microsoft.com. https://docs.microsoft.com/en-us/dotnet/csharp/programming-guide/events/

Wagner, B. (2022c, February 16). *Inheritance.* Docs.microsoft.com. https://docs.microsoft.com/en-us/dotnet/csharp/fundamentals/object-oriented/inheritance

Wagner, B. (2022d, June 18). *Access modifiers - C# programming guide.* Microsoft.com. https://docs.microsoft.com/en-us/dotnet/csharp/programming-guide/classes-and-structs/access-modifiers

Wagner, B. (2022e, June 21). *Static classes and static class members - C# programming guide.* Docs.microsoft.com. https://docs.microsoft.com/en-us/dotnet/csharp/programming-guide/classes-and-structs/static-classes-and-static-class-members

Wood, D. (2015, October 4). *Creating and using methods (functions) in C#.* CodeMahal. https://www.codemahal.com/video/creating-and-using-methods-functions-in-c/

Wubitog. (2014). *3 pop sounds* [Sound]. https://opengameart.org/content/3-pop-sounds

Zuno, L. (2015, February 8). *Forest Background.* OpenGameArt.org. https://opengameart.org/content/forest-background

CODE GAMERS DEVELOPMENT: LUA ESSENTIALS

A STEP-BY-STEP BEGINNERS GUIDE TO START DEVELOPING GAMES WITH LUA

A.E. COLONNA

INTRODUCTION

" *Roblox gives builders the tools and freedom to put their imaginations into action.*

— DAVID BASZUCKI

The video game industry is ever-growing and constantly evolving. With the development of technology comes an evolution in games. Nowadays, more people have access to personal computers and consoles. As a result, the gaming industry expanded to match that accessibility. Gone are the days when you needed to visit a store to buy a new game. Now, we have online platforms where we have access to a variety of options at the click of a button.

Among these platforms is Roblox. Roblox is one of the biggest gaming hubs, and it's accumulated a staggering 29 million potential experiences. Roblox saw an average of 56 million daily users in 2022, and that number grows by 23% each year. It's no surprise, then, that it has seen more than 40 billion hours of engagement since 2008. With these numbers, you can see why 12 million designers and developers consider Roblox their platform of choice.

Roblox has created a space to build games and publish them with minimal effort. On top of this, it takes the pressure of finding an audience for your product out of your hands by hosting it on a platform that already draws millions of users. Perhaps most importantly, Roblox creates a space to learn and explore. It's free to use and lets inexperienced creators develop their skills and knowledge.

If you're reading this book, you clearly recognize it as the opportunity it is. Maybe you want to learn how to develop games and picked Roblox as a starting point; maybe you want to expand your skill set and diversify your options. Either way, welcome to *Code Gamers Development: Roblox Essentials*. Here, we will discuss Roblox as a platform and explore your career potential with it. We will take a tour of Roblox Studio and use it in practical examples you can follow along with. Together, we'll explore some programming basics and the logical processes of game development with Roblox.

Learning how to make games can be intimidating. With so much information out there on the topic, it can be hard to know where to begin. The programming aspect of game development is perhaps the most daunting of them all, but you don't need formal education or extensive experience to achieve success. All you need is some time, the willingness to learn, and the determination to see it through. With those qualities, you'll be able to learn everything you need to know.

Lastly, know that mistakes are normal. Even the best developers make mistakes. They're part of the process and largely unavoidable. As humans, we don't like making mistakes, but they're not something you need to avoid at all costs. Part of being a successful developer is learning not to fear errors and instead learning to work with them. I'll include some tips on problem-solving as we go and point out some common mistakes and errors you might encounter.

With all that said, let's begin!

1

ROBLOX DEVELOPMENT

B efore we can get into practical development, let's take a look at Roblox as a platform, what it means to be a Roblox developer, and what you can expect from it.

WHAT IS ROBLOX?

Roblox is an online platform that hosts a variety of gaming experiences. Despite often being described as such, Roblox worlds aren't games in the way you might expect. It's a collection of virtual worlds where users can collectively share an experience. For that reason, we call them experiences instead of games.

Many experiences are game-like in that they employ game mechanics to fulfill objectives while others are nothing more than a virtual place where people can meet and interact. The truth is that the content on Roblox is so diverse that it's difficult to qualify them as anything other than experiences.

Unlike many other gaming platforms, Roblox doesn't provide individual game files for users to download and install. Instead, it lets you build a 3D world in its virtual environment and then gives users access to that world through its servers and player software.

BEING A ROBLOX DEVELOPER

A Roblox developer is anyone who makes, designs, or contributes to the creation of an experience. Anyone with a browser can become a Roblox developer; it's as simple as heading to roblox.com and clicking on Create. This will give you access to all the tools you need to become a developer (more on this in Chapter 2).

Most people come to Roblox to have fun and experience something interesting. Many users eventually turn to development out of curiosity. Roblox is not only aware of this but encourages it. The founder of Roblox made it with the intention of creating an environment in which users could explore their creativity and interest. As such, it has become a popular learning tool for growing developers.

Being a Roblox developer has many benefits. For starters, it provides you with all the tools and resources you need. Its software is free to download, and you can find a lot of information in its documentation and forums to help you on your way. On top of that, being a Roblox developer lets you practice your coding skills, learn how to solve problems, and express yourself creatively.

Roblox has been shown to promote the skills needed for careers in science, technology, engineering, and mathematics. The things you learn with Roblox can open the door to a future career in making games, web development, software engineering, and even graphic design.

ROBLOX AS A LEARNING TOOL

It's undeniable that our world is largely influenced by technology. As such, computer literacy has become as essential as being able to read. At the same time, coding has become more relevant, too. Many people think of coding as a programmer's skill, something that has no application beyond a career in IT. However, it's an invaluable skill. Without coding, we wouldn't have artificial intelligence, complex websites, or interactable computer systems.

Roblox recognizes this. It combines the creative aspects of building worlds and creating experiences with the technical skills of game design and programming. With Roblox, people as young as seven years old have been able to learn these skills. It's well-known that younger brains are more adept at learning. While they're still developing, our brains are more pliable, making it easier to learn new skills. However, that doesn't mean it's only kids who can learn using Roblox; anyone can benefit from it regardless of their age.

FINANCIAL OPPORTUNITIES AS A ROBLOX DEVELOPER

While Roblox is mostly a tool for learning and creative expression, many developers use Roblox to earn an income. In 2021, Roblox paid more than 500 million USD to developers, proving that there is money to be made here (Landsberg, 2022).

Know, however, that not every developer manages to make a successful living from Roblox. The platform is largely free, and most of its users are children with restricted access to money. This means that consumers are less likely to spend money unless they really want to. The developers who succeed in earning money have been around for years, and their experiences reflect that. Don't go into this expecting an easy income.

Roblox uses a virtual currency called Robux. A person can get Robux by purchasing it through the platform using real-world money or by earning it through sales. If you earn money through your content, your account will receive Robux. There are a couple of ways you can earn with Roblox's monetization setup:

- **Paid access:** A simple way to make money with your experience is to place it behind a paywall. With this, users will make a once-off payment to gain access to your product. Note, however, that this will affect the number of users willing to give your game a try. Most users won't want to pay for something they haven't tried yet. Instead of using it as a tool for financial gain, many developers use this to restrict access to the experience for testing purposes or to create an early access system for loyal users.
- **Game passes:** A game pass is an in-game item that will give users special access or privileges for a fee. With this game pass, the user will be able to enjoy additional content like restricted areas, game buffs, or special items. Instead of restricting access to the experience as a whole, game passes allow you to limit who can access certain parts of it. Once the game pass has been purchased, those parts become available to the person who bought it.
- **Developer products:** These are items that are available for repeat purchase in your experience. Think in-game coins, energy refills, special equipment, etc. These items are usually related to the experience itself and would give users the option to spend money to enhance it.
- **Private servers:** Roblox hosts experiences on multiple public servers. As users join in, they are added into

available servers with other players. You can give players the option to create private servers and control who gets to be in that server. This is helpful when players want to share an experience with friends or for streamers who want to create content without the risk of unknown players. Private servers can be offered at no cost, but many developers charge a monthly fee to reserve a private server as an easy means of monetization.

- **Avatar items:** A big part of being on Roblox is creating an avatar that will represent you in experiences. Many users put a lot of effort into creating the perfect avatar. Roblox does offer free items, but people are more willing to spend Robux on custom pieces like clothing and character assets. As such, creating catalog items is one of the most lucrative means of monetization. If you submit an item to the catalog and it is approved, the item will be available for users to purchase. You then receive a share of the profits from each sale.

- **Premium payouts:** Roblox offers user memberships. Premium members pay a monthly subscription fee and receive a monthly Robux stipend in return. With premium payouts, you can earn Robux just by having a premium member engage in your experience. The payout you receive will depend on the amount of time members spend in your experience. It happens automatically regardless of any other means of monetization you have but will not occur in experiences that have paid access.

- **Plugins:** Unlike the other items on this list, this one relates to other developers. If you create a plugin that adds functionality to Roblox Studio or its tools, you can publish that plugin on the creator marketplace. There, other developers can buy the plugin for their own use.

Developer Economics

Roblox has a well-thought-out economic structure. In 2022, statistics showed that more than three million developers earned money through Roblox and that they earned roughly 29 cents for each dollar of sales (*Developer Economics | Roblox creator documentation*, n.d.). This statistic is an average and might not accurately reflect everyone's earnings.

To incentivize developer growth, Roblox does not charge any fees to creators who do not monetize their experiences. That means that you won't be responsible for paying any platform fees as long as you aren't earning Robux. Once you monetize your experience, a share of your profit will go to Roblox itself to cover overhead costs and other expenses.

On top of the share that goes to Roblox, there are also other fees associated with monetization, like transaction fees, hosting fees, and marketing costs. In total, you can expect to walk away with roughly 29% of your total profit.

This might seem a little unfair to you. At the end of the day, you lose about 70% of your earnings, but consider this: Roblox is not a site that's meant for making money. It aims to give budding developers the chance to gain experience and hone their skills. They offer free software, the platform to host creations, and the servers and networks that let your products reach consumers. Once developers start earning money from it, Roblox takes a portion of that money to ensure the platform's stability.

The share of profits you receive can vary somewhat depending on how you earn. If, for example, you make sales through the avatar catalog, Roblox would take a larger cut of the profit. This is because the platform divvies up profit between the creator and seller. In the case of catalog sales, you're the creator while Roblox itself is the seller. In the case of in-experience sales, on the other hand, you're both creator and seller and will accordingly receive both cuts.

Converting Robux into Real Money

If you're a member of the Development Exchange (DevEx) program, you'll be able to exchange Robux for real-world currencies. To become a DevEx member, you must satisfy a few requirements. You must

- have earned at least 30,000 Robux. (Roblox differentiates between earned and purchased Robux; purchased Robux will not count toward the 30,000.)
- have a verified email linked to your account.
- be 13 or older.
- be a community member who is in good standing and who has not violated terms of service.
- have a viable DevEx account. (First-time users will be invited to create an account once their application has been approved and they meet all the above criteria.)

If you're not a member of DevEx, you will still be able to earn Robux; you just won't be able to transfer it to another bank account.

TYPES OF ROBLOX DEVELOPERS

While some developers are able to handle entire projects on their own, most are not. As you move beyond the basics, you'll likely find yourself working with other developers on different projects. Each individual brings their own specialties and skills to the table. Based on this, developers fulfill different roles depending on what they do for the project.

The most common types of developers you'll encounter on Roblox include the following:

- **Graphic designer:** This is often the easiest field to get into and the hardest to master. There's a lot that goes into being a graphic designer for a project. It's not just a matter of making sure everything looks pretty. It involves knowledge of color theory, the ability to create an atmosphere with visual elements, logo design, and rendering. Graphic designers are often the ones responsible for creating the right impression since logos and banners are some of the first things users will see when looking at an experience.

- **Scripter:** These developers are responsible for handling the code of the experience and providing functionality to it. This can be intimidating, and as such, many people steer clear of it. While it can be difficult, it's one of the most rewarding roles. Without scripters, we'd be limited in what we can create. It's not as hard as it seems; Roblox uses Lua, a powerful but simple coding language that's easy to learn and master. There are tons of resources for scripters, including support forums and educational material.

- **3D modeler:** Also known as asset creators, 3D modelers create visual meshes to add dimension to your experiences. These meshes can be applied to game items, decorations, or any other visual objects to change the way they look.

- **Builder:** A builder creates the environment of the experience and makes the world in which it takes place. If your experience is set in a forest, the person who creates the forest itself will be the builder.

- **UI designer:** These developers handle the user interface (UI) and create the menus, toolbars, and any other interactable screens. Players use the UI to interact with the experience, and a UI designer is responsible for ensuring that it works properly and effectively while also looking good.

For this book, we'll do a little something of everything. As we move through the practical examples, you'll get a taste for each of these different roles. A well-rounded developer is invaluable. Having the ability to do more than one thing makes you an asset to any team and will let you handle a solo project if you want to. At the same time, being exposed to all the different aspects of development lets you explore your options. As you gain more experience, you'll be able to figure out where your talents lie and find where you fit best. Use this book as an opportunity to try out all these different roles. Feel them out, and you might just surprise yourself with what you discover.

2

ROBLOX STUDIO

WHAT IS ROBLOX STUDIO?

The platform has its own unique development software called Roblox Studio. It comes equipped with all the tools you'll need, including a code editor. It's been described as intuitive and easy to use while still having the power and versatility of any other game engine. Its ease of use is one of its main benefits and the main reason why it's such an effective learning tool.

On top of this, it makes publishing your game super easy. All you need to do is open the File tab, and click Publish to Roblox As. It will then prompt you to fill in the necessary details. Studio makes updating preexisting experiences just as easy. Again, select File and Publish to Roblox. Instead of filling in new game details, click the Update Existing Games option. This will display all your published experiences. Choose the one you want to update, and it will do the rest.

Another benefit is its expansive community of developers. Roblox is first and foremost a social platform; players meet up with others to share experiences. When you join the community, you join both gamers and developers. With as many developers as the platform has, you'll always find someone willing to share your struggles, give advice, or help where needed.

Beyond the support of a community, you'll also find other resources. If you head over to Roblox's documentation and support sections, you'll find all the information you could ever need.

SETTING UP ROBLOX STUDIO

Before we get started to develop experiences, you need to install the necessary software. In your browser, go to www.roblox.com. If you don't have an account, you'll need to register. When signing up, you'll be asked to provide your date of birth, a username, and account password. If you already have an account, you can sign in. Once this has been done, turn your attention to the menu bar at the top of the screen.

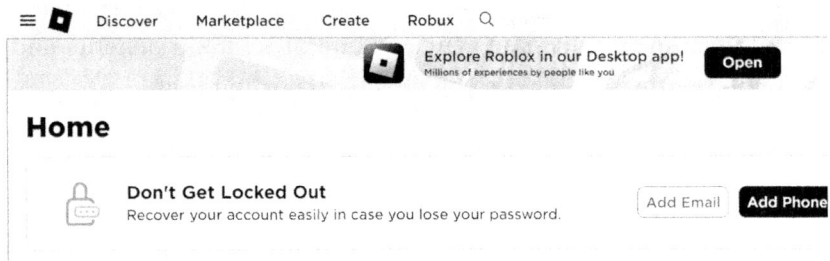

Click on Create, where you'll see a welcome screen with a button that reads "Start Creating" in the middle.

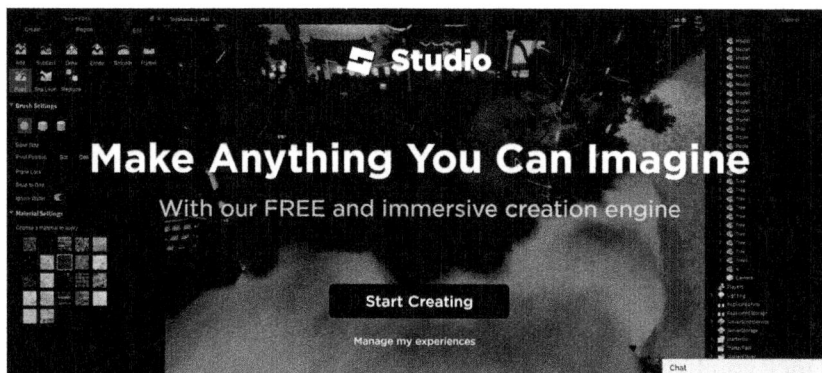

Click on it to launch the program. If you do not already have it installed, you'll see this:

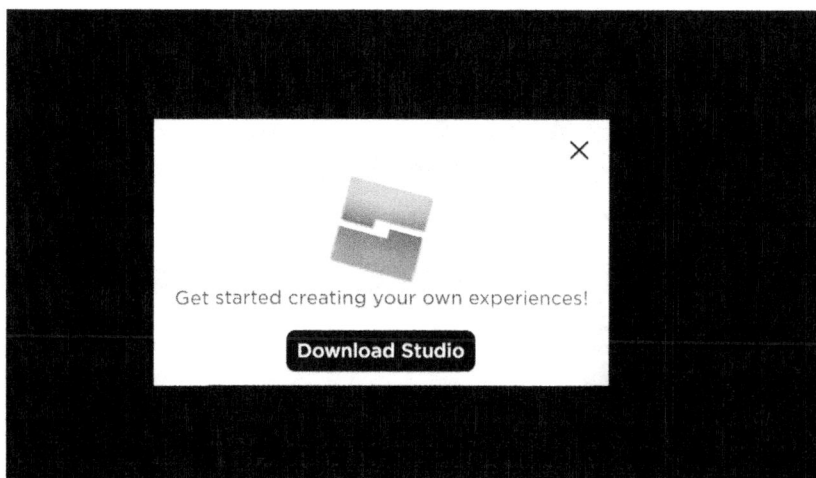

Click "Download Studio" to download the installer. Once it's completed, you can launch it from your file manager.

There are a few system requirements, so make sure your computer meets these before trying to install it. Studio is supported by both Windows and macOS. For Windows, you need to have Windows 7 or higher and Internet Explorer version 11. (If you use Windows 10 or higher, IE will have been replaced by Edge and you don't have to worry about this.) For Mac, you need macOS version 10.11 or higher.

There are also a few hardware requirements. Your computer needs to have at least 1 GB of free RAM, a 1.6 GHz processor, and an internet connection. The last one isn't strictly required, but it helps to ensure that the program stays up to date and lets you back up your progress to your Roblox account.

Once you have Studio installed, go ahead, and launch it.

STUDIO TOUR

When you first open Roblox Studio, you'll see this:

Here you can see the various templates you can use when creating a new experience. The first three are flat, open spaces, while the rest have prebuilt environments. For now, click on Baseplate (the first one) to create a blank project and see the Studio interface.

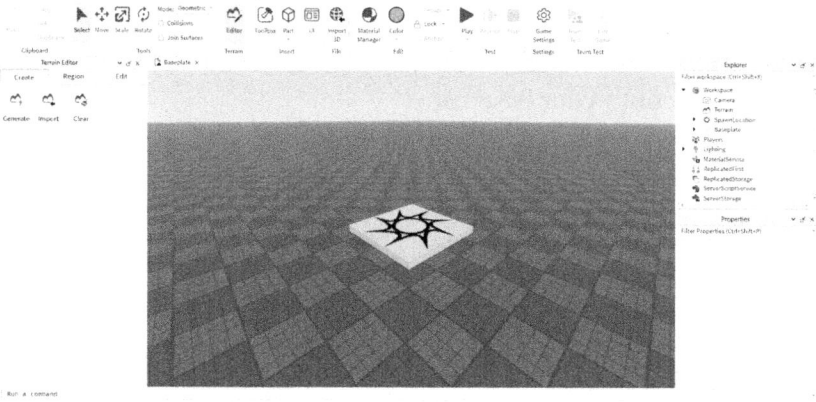

The object in the center is a spawn locator. For now, you can delete it or just ignore it.

This is the basic layout; you can change it at any time by dragging windows around, closing the ones you don't want in your workspace, or opening others.

In the middle of the screen, you'll see the viewport. This shows you what your players will see when they enter the experience. You can look around by holding down right-click and dragging your mouse in any direction. Make sure that your cursor is in the viewport or else this won't work. To move through the environment, use WASD or your directional keys like you would if you were a player.

Tools

At the top of your workspace, you'll find the menu bar. Here you'll find all your tools and various options. We won't cover them all right now, only the important ones.

To demonstrate how the tools work, let's add a part into the experience. In the Home tab, select Part, and then Block. This will add a basic brick onto your baseplate.

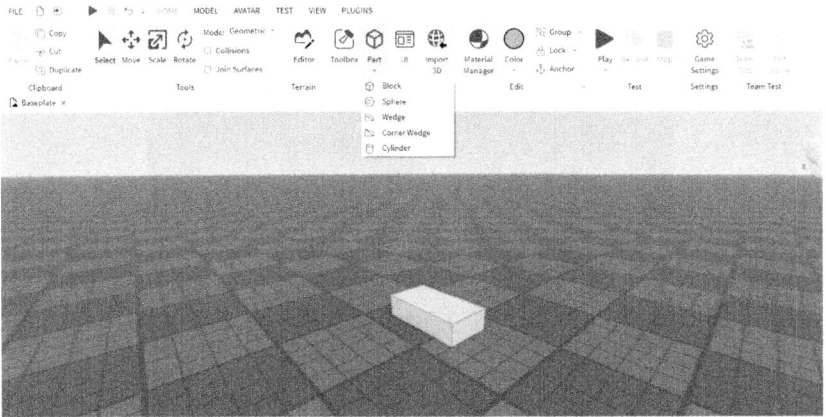

Your first important tool is **Select**. This is the default tool and is used to select parts. When a part is selected (like above), it is highlighted by a blue outline.

The second is **Move**. Like the name suggests, it lets you move a part around. Select the tool from the menu bar, and then click on your block. You'll see this:

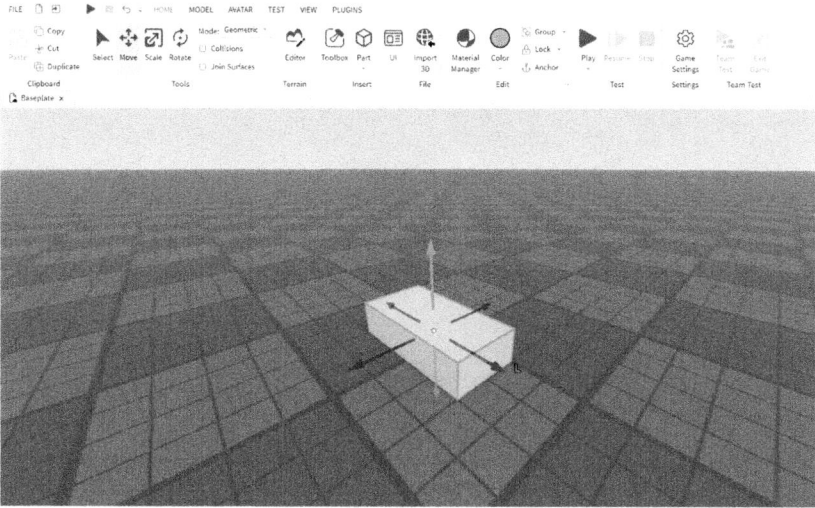

The colored arrows indicate the axes along which you can move an object. Each represents a dimension (x, y, and z). Parts move according to these dimensions. Click and hold the block and then drag your mouse along one of the colored lines to make the part move.

Third, we have **Scale**. Scale refers to an object's size in relation to its environment. Again, select Scale and then click on your block.

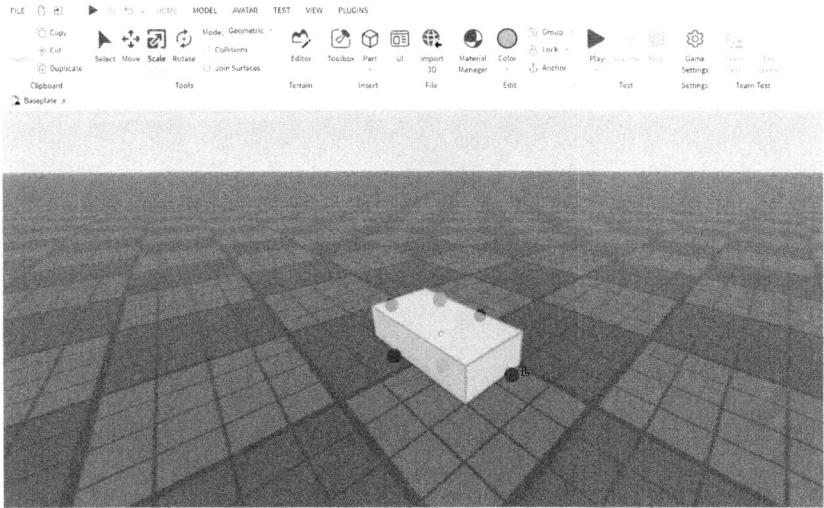

The colored markers indicate the dimensions along which you can scale the part, much like with Move. If you click and hold the green marker and drag your mouse upward, the block will become taller. Likewise, if you click and hold one of the red markers and drag your mouse, the block will lengthen.

Lastly, there is **Rotate**. This tool lets you rotate the part. Like with the others, select Rotate and click on the block to show the visual markers you can use to rotate it.

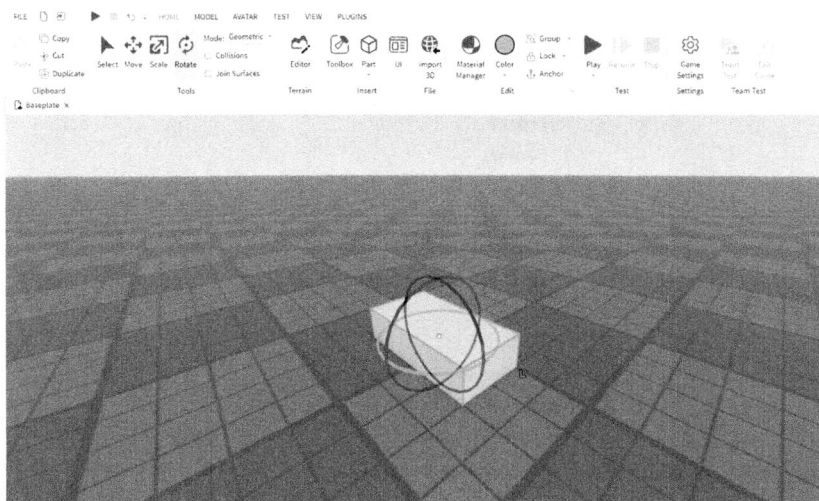

Take some time to play around with these tools. Learn how they work and familiarize yourself with how they affect the block. You can also test them out on other parts since each shape has a slightly different geometry. The best way to learn is to try it out for yourself, so test out the mechanics.

Windows

On the right of the default layout, you'll see your two most important windows aside from the viewport. The first is the **Explorer**. Here you will see everything in a file tree. This window lets you see your project files and structures them into a more convenient setup. As your project grows, this file tree will expand. Instead of combing through your environment to find individual parts, you can instead scroll through the explorer.

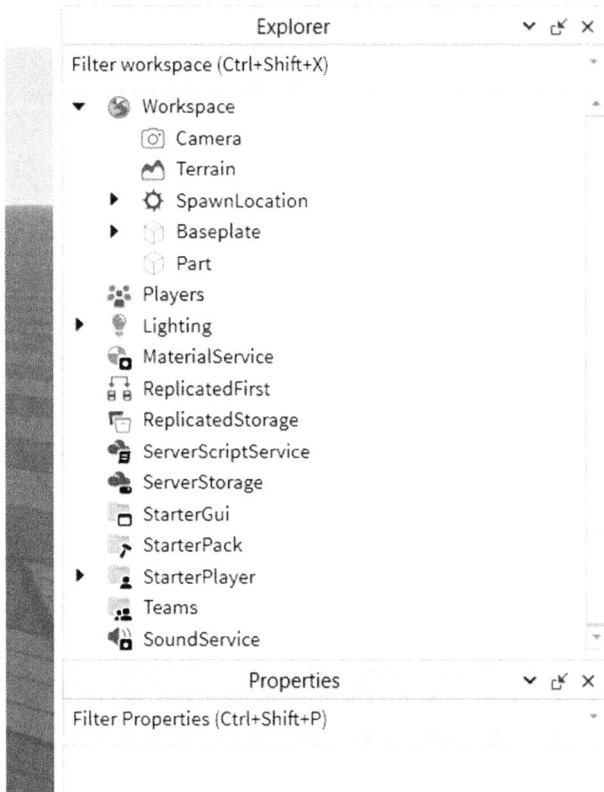

The other one is the **Properties** window. Here you will be able to see the different characteristics of a selected part. If you want to change the color, transparency, weight, or any other detail of an object, you can do it here. If you have a part selected, the window will look like the image below. If not, it remains blank.

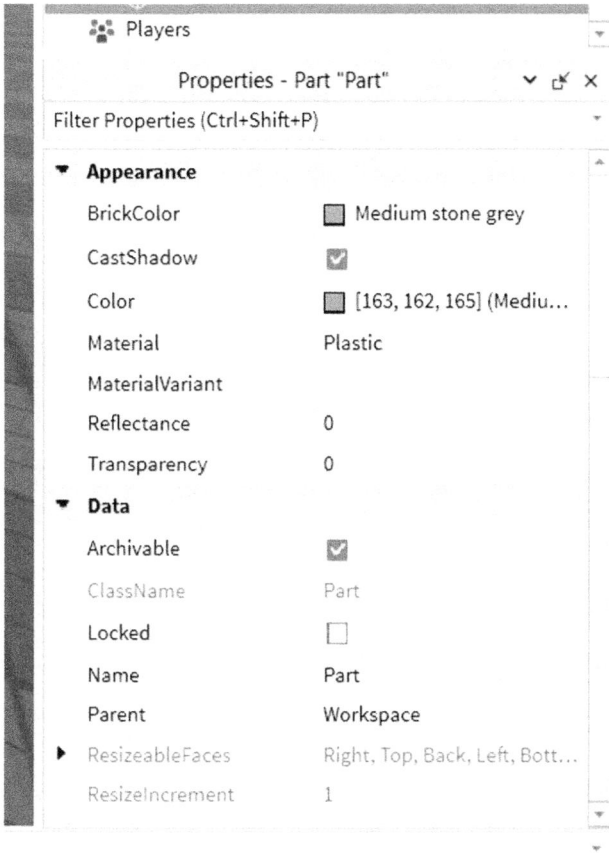

There are also other windows you can open as needed. The **Terrain Editor** is open when you first create a new project, but most developers close it while they're not using it. You can reopen it under the Home tab by selecting Editor.

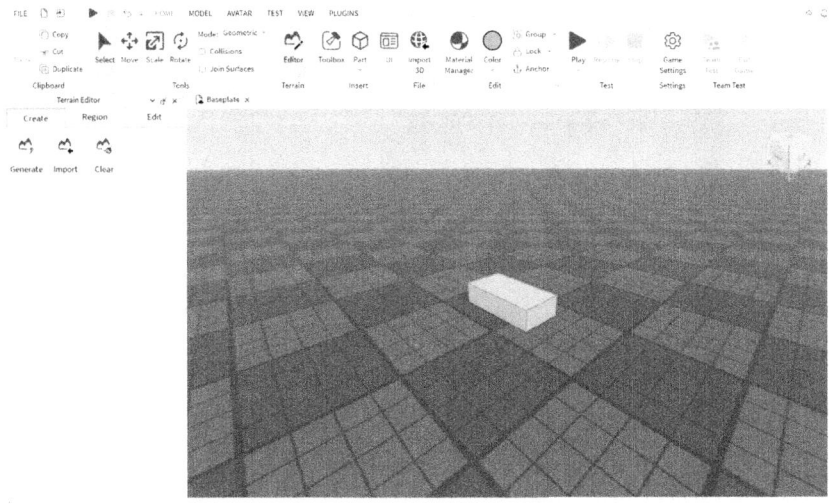

Another optional window you'll encounter a lot is the **Toolbox**. Under Home, click on Toolbox. This will open a catalog of premade assets you can add into your experience.

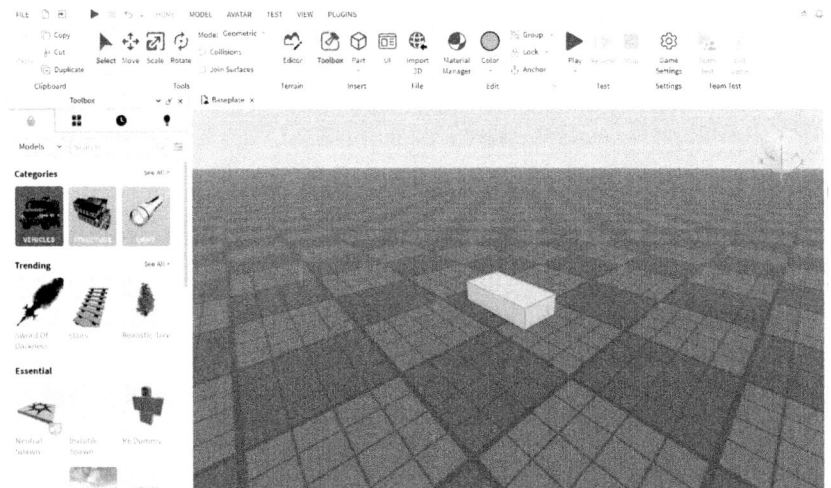

LUA

Roblox uses Lua, a powerful and lightweight programming language, to manage game behavior and mechanics. As a language, it offers simple syntax and easy integration. It was created to extend the functionality of other languages and systems. As such, it's rarely used as a stand-alone language and is instead used in scripting, customizing existing software, and creating or expanding game systems. Unlike many other languages, this one does not create its own forms and applications. Instead, it's embedded into applications created by other systems. In this context, Roblox Studio creates the experience; i.e., the application. We then use code to enhance it and provide functionality that Studio cannot.

Lua needs to be compiled, a process in which code is translated into machine language before it's run by a computer. It uses a C compiler and shares many similarities with other C-based languages. As such, it's highly compatible with most other programming languages and systems. At the same time, it is much simpler and has a significantly smaller learning curve.

What Makes Lua Great?

There are many coding languages, each with its own unique features. So what sets Lua apart from other languages?

1. **Speed:** A language's speed relates to how quickly it can complete tasks, and Lua is considered one of the fastest. It can process complex tasks in short amounts of time, both during testing and at run time.
2. **Size:** Since it's designed to be integrated into other systems, it takes up very little space. In game development, there's a constant battle for storage. Everything that adds

to the game takes up space. The more storage it takes up, the more you'll struggle with performance. In total, its source code and documentation only occupy around 1.3 MB of space.

3. **Portability and embeddability:** Since the language is so compact, it can be imported just about anywhere. It's highly compatible with most systems and rarely requires complex adjustments to work with other languages.

4. **Simplicity:** This is an incredibly simple language. It has limited syntax and is easy to read and comprehend, even if you don't have a lot of experience.

5. **License:** Lua comes with a free-use license. It's part of an open-source distribution package, meaning that users don't have to worry about any licensing fees or infringements.

Pros and Cons

Some of Lua's benefits are that it

- is easy to integrate with preexisting apps and projects.
- is flexible and lightweight.
- has simple syntax, making it an easier language to learn than other more syntax-heavy languages.
- uses a standard C compiler, meaning it can run virtually anywhere.
- uses dynamic variable creation. (We'll discuss variables and what this means in a later chapter.)
- has an active community of developers, meaning there are plenty of documentation, tutorials, and support.

Some of its drawbacks include

- having limited libraries. It might take longer to debug a Lua script than others.
- creating only global variables.
- offering limited pattern-matching support. Pattern matching is a tool used in programming to recognize patterns in data. This is useful for finding errors and filtering large amounts of code. It does not identify patterns but instead finds those it can already identify to increase productivity.

Areas of Use

We mostly use Lua in game development due to its portability and small storage footprint. This is mostly because it is compatible with more powerful languages like C++ (the language used in the Unreal game engine). It can also be added into existing code to optimize the productivity of other languages without risking the integrity of the code that's already there. Furthermore, it reduces the impact of performance on less lightweight languages.

So, other than games, what can you make with Lua? It can be used to develop web applications, developer tools, and extensions. It has even been used as a programming language for industrial programs like *Adobe Lightroom* (an image manipulation app) and *MySQL* (a database manager). Lastly, it can be used by end users to create plugins and extensions for existing software or games. For example, players of *World of Warcraft* use Lua to create extensions that customize their gameplay.

How Does Lua Compare to Other Languages?

Languages like Python and Java are coding giants. They have so many applications and uses, and they've each amassed a following of dedicated users. While Lua is not strictly a programming language (it's a scripting language), it's still mentioned in the same breath as these giants because it's used alongside them. While it is very different, it still measures up and compares to other languages.

For starters, Lua accepts a variety of coding styles—including object-oriented, data-driven, and procedural programming—while languages like Java are limited to one or two.

Lua and Python share their simplicity of syntax, compatibility with multiple styles, and multi-platform applicability. Python is the slower of the two since it's not a compiled language. Python is an interpreted language, meaning that its code is interpreted on the fly rather than compiled before running.

Lua is similar to Javascript (a web-based language) in that it cannot be used for general-purpose programming. However, it's not limited to web-based platforms and can still be integrated into other products.

3

YOUR FIRST EXPERIENCE – CREATE AN OBBY

An obby, short for obstacle course, describes a game in which players traverse a series of hurdles to progress from level to level. This often takes the form of interconnected platforms and floating objects the user has to jump across. It usually has check-points at regular intervals to save player progress and sometimes features a leaderboard to track which players have gone the furthest. They can be pretty comprehensive, with some having thousands of levels.

Obbies are a Roblox classic since they're fairly easy to create and grow. Players enjoy them since they're a great way to pass the time and show off your skills.

In this chapter, we will build a short, classic obby that features a handful of floating parts as obstacles. I will explain each step of the process with images. Follow along and build your own. Use whichever shapes, colors, and layouts you want.

CREATE THE OBBY

Open Roblox Studio and create a new project with the Baseplate template.

Make sure that you have the Explorer and Properties windows open in your workspace. If they aren't, click over to the View tab in your menu bar and select Explorer and Properties to open them up. You can close the Terrain Editor if it is open.

In the examples below, you'll notice that my Explorer is situated to the left of the viewport. Yours will be on the right, above Properties, by default. It can stay there if you so prefer.

Next, turn your attention to the Explorer. In it, you'll see an entry titled Workspace. This represents what you see in the viewport. Click on the little arrow next to it to view everything that's currently in it. In a brand-new project, you'll see four items:

camera, terrain, spawn location, and baseplate. Select the Baseplate and delete it.

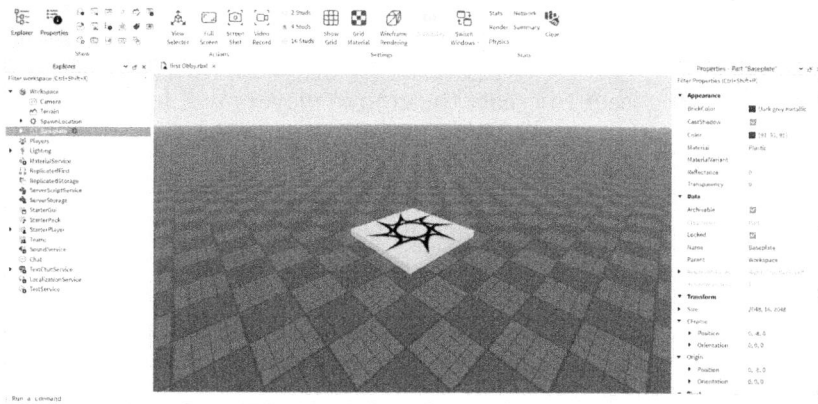

The baseplate acts as a stage on which you can build a world. For this obby, we are going to create a series of floating obstacles and won't need it. Once you have removed the baseplate, you'll see the SpawnLocation floating in empty space.

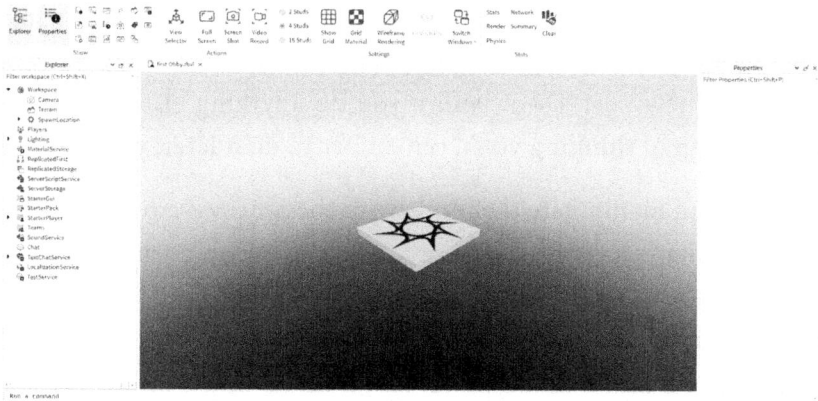

The SpawnLocation object determines where players will end up when they join an experience. It will act as the first platform and starting point for our obby. Once a player has spawned onto it, they can jump from it onto the first object.

CREATING PARTS

Each new obstacle consists of a separate part. These individual parts work together to create the course players will follow. In the Home tab, click on Part and then Block as you did in Chapter 2. The block will appear on or near your SpawnLocation. Once a part is created, you need to anchor it. Select the block and find the Anchor option.

Without a baseplate, parts will fall away as soon as you hit play; anchoring stops this. It essentially keeps them in place so that players can jump across them. Get into the habit of anchoring parts as soon as you've created them. Make it the first thing you do with each new part. Do it before you do anything else. Don't fall into the trap of thinking you'll remember to do it later; you won't.

Now we can manipulate the block with the tools we covered in the previous chapter. Scale it to the size of your choice and move it into position next to the spawn point. It should be close and big enough for a player to jump onto. Mine looks like this:

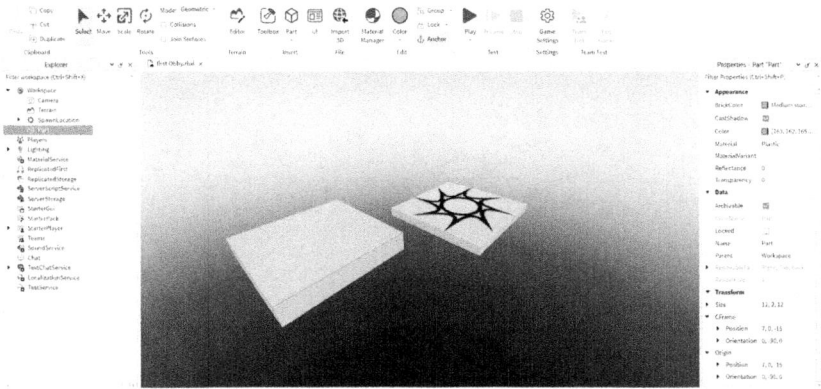

Next, use the Properties window to change how it looks. Select the block to access its properties. Under Appearance, find the BrickColor property.

Changing this will change the base color of the part. Click on the area next to it and choose the color you like. I chose the color Bright blue. Next, scroll down a little to find the Material property. This will let you change the texture of the block.

Parts have a default material of plastic. If you open the drop-down, you'll see a variety of options. Take your time to go through them all and see how they look. I went with Slate, and my block now looks like this:

If you look at the other properties, you'll notice that it has a variety of customizable characteristics. Among them are the Transform values.

Filter Properties (Ctrl+Shift+P)

▶ **Appearance**

▶ **Data**

▼ **Transform**

▼ Size   22, 2, 19

       X   22

       Y   2

       Z   19

▼ CFrame

    ▶ Position   9.5, 0, -22

    ▶ Orientation   0, -90, 0

▼ Origin

    ▶ Position   9.5, 0, -22

    ▶ Orientation   0, -90, 0

▶ **Pivot**

▶ **Collision**

▶ **Part**

▶ **Assembly**

▼ **Attributes**

    No Attribute has been added yet

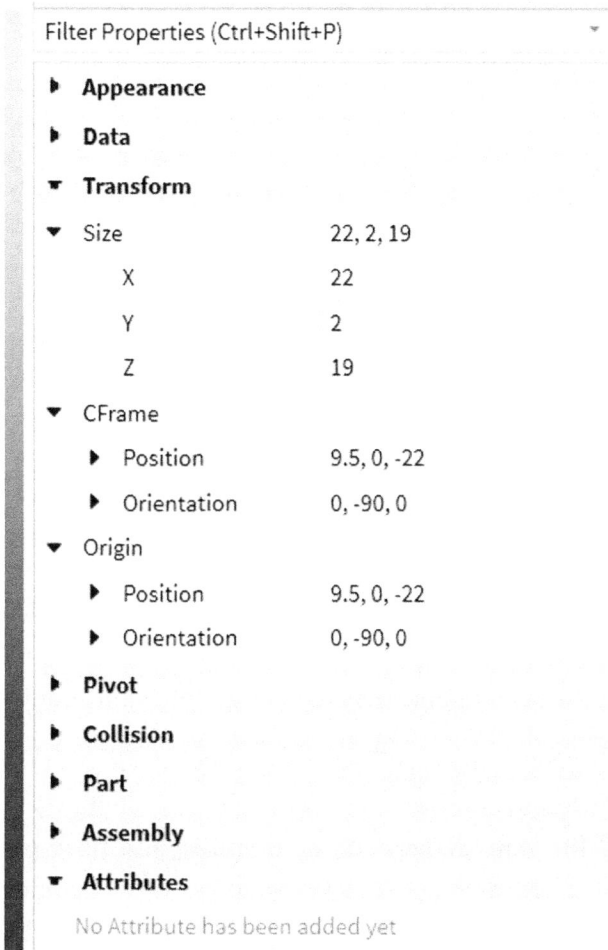

When you used tools to resize and move the block, these values changed accordingly. They represent the part's position and size through numbers. You can move, scale, and rotate the part by entering new numbers into the corresponding values. However, it's tricky to know exactly which numbers to use to get the transformation you want. It's a lot easier to simply use the tools to visually adjust parts through the viewport.

Once you're happy with the first part, repeat the process with a second one. I added a red block with the same material.

This one is a different size and is angled slightly. This is to show you that similar objects can differ from each other depending on how they are transformed and customized. Even though these blocks are the same shape, they look completely different.

Keep adding new parts until you have an obstacle course you like. Remember to anchor your parts as you create them. Use a combination of different shapes, colors, textures, and positions to add variety. How you arrange objects will affect the outcome, and you can use this to your advantage. Add angles and turns to the course to make it more challenging or keep your objects in a straight line to make it easier. You can, of course, lay a series of blocks right next to each other to create a continuous path, but that wouldn't be much of an obstacle course.

As your obby grows, it will get harder to see what you're doing. Use the built-in controls to change how you see the world. Holding right click and dragging your mouse will let you look around without moving. WASD will let you physically move around the environment. You can also use Q and E to move up and down. To zoom in and out, use your mouse's scroll wheel. These mechanics are mostly the same if you're using a trackpad instead of a mouse.

It's helpful to view your experiences from different perspectives. Experiences are 3D worlds; what looks good from one angle might not work from another. Use these controls to move around and inspect your project from all sides.

Once you have enough obstacles, add a final block, and turn it into a flat platform. Change its color to any color of your choice and then select neon as its material. This will create a shining end goal for your players to land on once they have finished the course.

This is what my obby looks like after a few more parts and pieces:

PLAYTESTING

A game isn't fun if it's impossible to beat or too easy. To ensure that an experience is playable, we need to test it. Planning can only take you so far, and it's important to take the time to make sure everything works the way it should. Studio has a play feature that will let you spawn in as a player to test things from the perspective of an end user. To do this, find one of the two play buttons and click it.

During testing, make sure that your obstacles are within jumping distance of each other, that they're the right size to land on, and that they're all anchored. Any objects that weren't anchored will fall away as soon as the game is run, so this is a great way to double-check that everything is where it should be. Once you're satisfied, you can stop playing by clicking a Stop button, which you'll find near the Play buttons.

PROPER PRACTICE

This is a good place to give you a few tips and pointers for learning good developer habits. The first and most important tip is to save regularly. There are few things as demoralizing as spending hours working on something and then losing all your progress due to some unforeseen circumstances. A lot of things can lead to lost data: the power can go out, your computer can shut down, or another person can interfere. To avoid losing a chunk of progress, get into the habit of saving regularly. When you first create a new project, save it immediately, even if you haven't done anything yet. After that, make sure to save periodically; don't just leave it for when you're done.

Always name your files appropriately. It's easy to tell experiences apart when you only have one or two, but as you grow and learn, you'll start accumulating project files. As they pile up, it will become harder to tell which is which. Good file management is essential, even if you only do this as a hobby. Create a separate folder for your experiences and save each project in a new subfolder within it. Any other file that relates to a specific project can go into the same folder. This way, you keep everything in one place, making it easier to find things like notes, ideas, or plans. Don't just name them "Project1" or "Game2," either. Name them something that describes what the experience relates to. For example, "FirstObby" or "TribeSimulator." Choose a name that will tell you exactly what it is at first glance.

On the topic of naming, name your parts. Each part is a unique object and, as such, should have a unique identifier. Roblox automatically names them "Part." This becomes problematic when you want to use a specific object in code. If they are all called the same thing, you won't be able to reference the correct one in a script. Furthermore, appropriate naming makes it easier to manage your experience through the Explorer. It's very difficult to identify specific objects on sight when they all have the same name or have nonspecific names. Take a look at my Explorer for the obby we have just built.

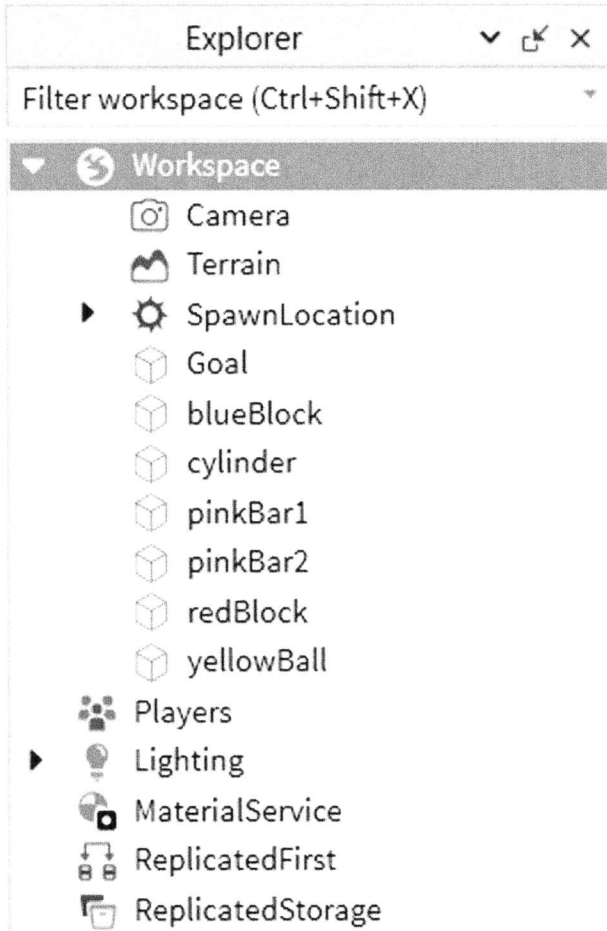

Just by looking at the parts listed, you can immediately tell which object is which. In small projects like this one, file organization isn't as important since we can see the entire experience all at once in the viewport and Explorer. Bigger undertakings, however, aren't as easily managed.

To change an object's name, select the part and scroll down to the Data section in the Properties window. There you'll find the property called Name.

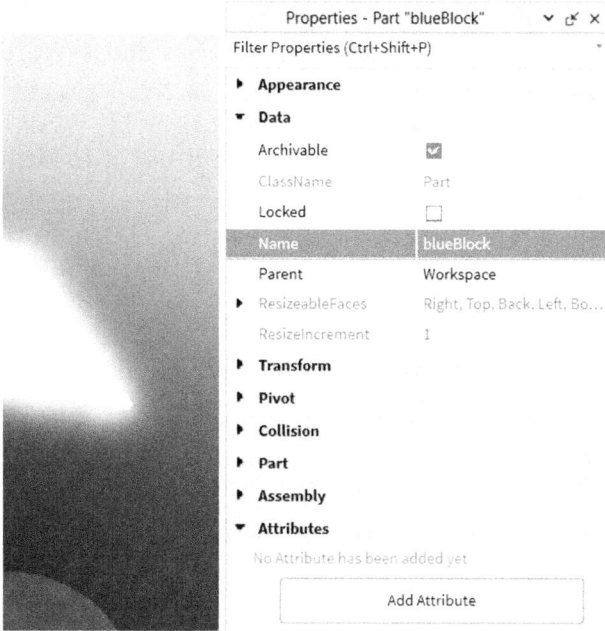

Click in the space next to it and type in an appropriate descriptor. Again, use names that are descriptive.

Of course, no one can force you to use proper practices. Know, however, that we have them for a reason and that they exist to make your life as a developer as easy as possible. Once you start working on more complex projects, these practices will help you optimize your work and productivity. It's a lot easier to form good habits from the start than it is to have to unlearn improper habits and replace them with better ones. Proper practice might not make much of a difference to you right now, but it will begin to matter later in your career—so stick with them for the time being.

UP NEXT

You now have a functional experience. Obbies don't need any fancy functions or features, but you can add a few extra things to make them more fun. To do that, you'll need code. In the next chapter, we'll dive into a few coding basics and explore how to create scripts.

For the time being, save your obby; we'll use it to demonstrate how code works and add onto it as we go.

VARIABLES AND OBJECTS

CREATE A SCRIPT

S cripts are files in which we write code to provide instructions for how experiences should behave. They can be used to make provision for things like:

- handling player stats, like health and energy
- item drops
- enemy spawns
- NPC behavior
- environmental changes.

Adding a script to your project is easy. In the Explorer, find the item called ServerScriptService. This is a container for scripts and script-related assets. All objects contained in it will apply to the experience and run if they aren't disabled. In short, this is a convenient place to store general scripts you want to add to your project.

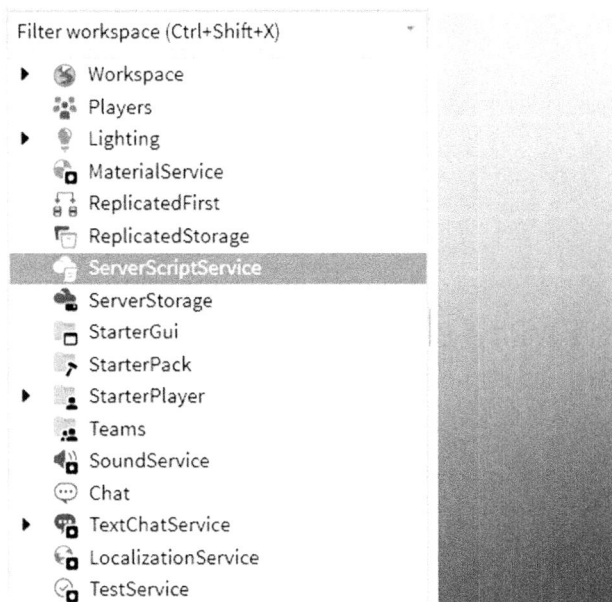

When you hover your cursor over it, a little + will appear next to it. Click on this and, from the drop-down list, find and click Script. You can also use the search bar if you can't find the right option.

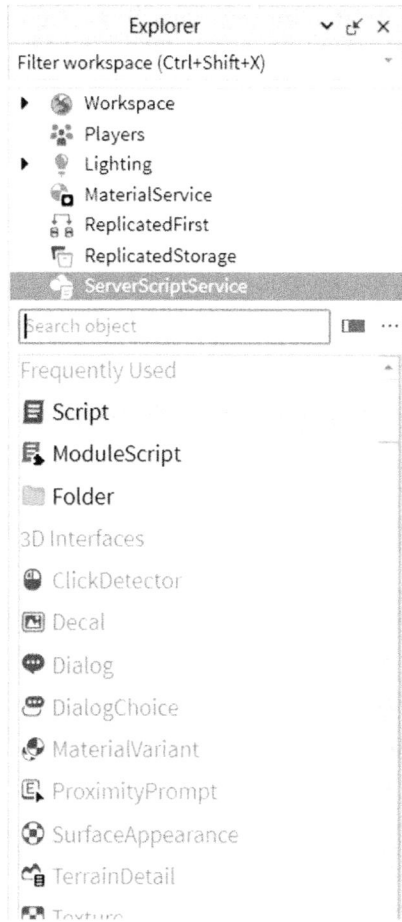

A new script will be added and opened. Rename it "TestingScript." I know it's easier to just leave them as is or name them Script1 and Script2, but that's a recipe for disaster. It's not unusual to have multiple scripts, even in smaller projects. Avoid wasting time having to open and look through all of them to find something by renaming them consistently.

In this new script, you'll see a line of code. It reads: print("Hello world!"). This is a basic line of output code. *Print* is a built-in command that tells the computer to display the value contained in brackets to the Output window. This line of code will thus print "Hello world!" into your experience's output when you play it.

To open the Output window, go to the View tab and select Output as below:

This is a great window to have open in your workspace, especially as you learn how to code. I recommend docking it in the bottom of the screen below the viewport. When you're not using it to check output, you can collapse it using the controls in the top right-hand corner of the window.

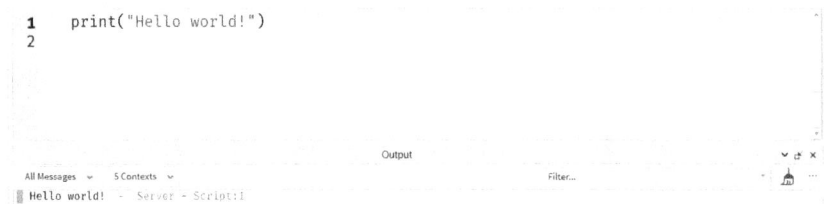

The Output window lets us test code by displaying values and messages. This is incredibly helpful if you aren't sure code is working correctly and need a way to see what it's doing. The displays in it do not affect gameplay at all, so we can use it to see things for ourselves when the experience is run. You'll see in some of the examples below that each output will refer back to the relevant line of code, making it easy to see where errors occur and where to go looking for inconsistencies in values.

CODE STRUCTURE

Before we get into the technical things, let's talk about coding structure.

First, a code compiler does not concern itself with empty lines and white space. You can have multiple blank lines between code and it won't change how it is interpreted. The computer doesn't care about the blank spaces, but it's often easier for people to read code when everything is spaced out rather than crammed together. Add empty lines and blank spaces in your code as needed to make it easier to follow for others and yourself.

Secondly, most characters and symbols used in code have the same meaning in Lua as they do beyond it. These symbols are called operators, and Lua uses them to dictate code behavior. For example, when it sees "+" it will know to add things together. When it sees "=" it knows that the things on either side of the operator are equal. Most operators can be interpreted the same way in code as they are in normal life.

Lastly, code often contains comments. Comments are lines of code that we do not want the compiler to execute. We use them to make notes and explain lines of code to others. You'll see me use them a lot to explain certain parts of the examples.

To make a comment, use two dashes (--) to preface the statement you want to make. Everything that follows the dashes will be ignored by the computer. This works for single-line comments. If you want your comment to span multiple lines, use two dashes followed by two square brackets to open the comment and then two square brackets to close it (--[[...]]).

```
 1    -- this is a single line comment
 2
 3  --[[ this is
 4    a
 5   multi-line
 6   comment ]]
 7
 8   print("This is not a comment")
 9
10
```

Output

All Messages ⌄   5 Contexts ⌄   Filter...

This is not a comment   Server - Comments:8

In the example above, the lines in green are comments. If I placed a command like print in comments, nothing would be displayed since the computer would ignore it.

DATA TYPES

Values and objects have assigned data types. This is because we do different things with different kinds of information. For example, we use numbers in math, whereas we use words in reading. The same is true for programming. The type of data we work with is determined by what we do with it.

In Lua, there are eight main data types, and they are:

- **String:** a combination of characters put together. Strings are often words or sentences but can also include special characters and numbers. They are always placed in double quotation marks (i.e., "..."). Thus, if you put something in quotes, it will be regarded as having the data type string.
- **Number:** any number character we usually use in mathematics; for example, 1 or 13. Note that it has to be the number and not the fully written-out word. One is not

a number, but 1 is. Numbers can include both whole and decimal numbers.

- **Nil:** represents the absence of data and value. It's not the same as zero and is closer to the concept of nothing. The nil data type is applied when there is no value.
- **Boolean:** true or false. It can only ever be one of these two values. We mostly use them to test conditions or check if requirements have been met.
- **Table:** a collection of independent values characterized by an index number or key. We use tables to collect different, unique values that are related to each other.
- **Userdata:** represents a chunk of storage in which UserData is kept.
- **Function:** a unit of code that completes a task. Using functions, we can group lines of code together under one name or identifier. The name then becomes the function, and we can use it to refer to the group as a whole.
- **Thread:** a data type that refers to individual threads of execution.

The last three aren't something you need to break your head over just yet. They do not represent values or data we work with. Instead, they are code objects. For now, it's enough to know that they exist and that they are different from other data types.

The other five, however, are important to know before we get into the next sections. They are the types you'll encounter as values, i.e., the data your game will need to handle. It's important to at least have a basic understanding of the differences between them.

VARIABLES

Variables in programming are placeholders in code for data that you do not have. Think of them as empty boxes that can store information and values. When we want to make provision for data we don't have at the time of coding or data that might change, we use variables to stand in their place.

We do the same thing in mathematics, where we use a variable (often x or y) to represent an undetermined number in an equation until we can calculate what that value is. Programming variables are the same as mathematical variables in that we use them as placeholders for data.

Think about this: You don't know who is going to play your game until they themselves decide to do it. You also don't know what they'll do once they begin playing. Despite that, you still need to make provisions for those things so that your game can handle any players or behaviors it encounters. You cannot explicitly code for every possibility, so we use variables instead.

Declaring and Initializing Variables

To create a variable, we declare it. Declare in this context means to create a name for the variable and use it for the first time. Initialization is when we assign a value to it. Most of the time, these two things happen at the same time, but they can also occur separately.

Each variable has a unique name. This name acts as its identifier in code and is what we use to reference its value. A name can include any combination of letters, numbers, or special characters. Note, however, that a variable name cannot begin with a number and cannot contain any spaces.

Lua reserves the use of certain words. These words have preas-signed meanings and cannot be used for other things like names. A few examples of reserved words are:

- and
- if
- or
- then
- else
- for
- function
- repeat
- return

Names and identifiers are case-sensitive. For example, freshWater, FreshWater, and freshwater are three different names. Take note of how you spell and capitalize the names of your variables since you'll have to repeat them exactly when you want to use them again.

For this reason, we use certain case styles when assigning names. There are two main styles you need to be aware of. The first is Pascal Case (hereafter PascalCase). In this style, we capitalize the first letter of each word in a compound name. A compound name is where we use two or more words together; for example, FirstName, BlueBlock, and PascalCase. If the name is only a singular word, it will be capitalized; for example, Block or Calculate. This style is usually used for naming classes, events, and system functions.

The second is Camel Case (hereafter camelCase). The first letter or the first word in a compound name remains lowercase while the first letter of every subsequent word is capitalized. For example, firstName, blueBlock, and camelCase. If there is only one word, it

244 | A.E. COLONNA

will be entirely lowercase; for example, block or calculate. This style is the one you'll use for most variables and functions.

When you want to assign a value to a variable, use the following formula: name = value. For example:

```
1
2    x = 32 --this is a number
3    welcomeMessage = "Welcome to Code Gamers" --this is a string
4    testBoolean = true --this is a boolean
5
6    print (x)
7    print (welcomeMessage)
8    print (testBoolean)
9
10
```

Output   ⌄ ⊡ ✕

All Messages ⌄   5 Contexts ⌄   Filter...   ⌄   ⚲ ⋯

32   Server - Variables:6
Welcome to Code Gamers   Server - Variables:7
true   Server - Variables:8

If you want to change a variable's value, you can do so with the same code as you used to initialize it: i.e., name = value. This will override the value that was previously assigned. Using the above example, if I added a line of code to say x = 65 and then printed it, the output would reflect this:

```
1
2    x = 32
3    welcomeMessage = "Welcome to Code Gamers"
4    testBoolean = true
5
6    print (x) --this will print 32
7    print (welcomeMessage)
8    print (testBoolean)
9
10   x = 65
11
12   print (x) --this will print 65
13
14
```

Output   ⌄ ⊡ ✕

All Messages ⌄   5 Contexts ⌄   Filter...   ⌄   ⚲ ⋯

32   Server - Variables:6
Welcome to Code Gamers   Server - Variables:7
true   Server - Variables:8
65   Server - Variables:12

Scope of Variables

The scope of a variable determines where it can be used or altered.

Global variables can be used throughout the entire project, regardless of where they were declared. Unless otherwise specified, a variable will be global by default. With global variables, you don't have to worry about where you can use them or where they were created. If it has been declared, it can be used.

Local variables are accessible only to certain functions and classes. It's almost always better to use local variables since they are quicker to access and more secure. While global variables can be used everywhere, they can also be changed anywhere, meaning there's a higher risk to their integrity.

To declare a local variable, simply preface the declaration with the word "local." Using the example variables from above, I can turn welcomeMessage and testBoolean into local variables while leaving x as the default global.

```
1
2    x = 32
3    local welcomeMessage = "Welcome to Code Gamers"
4    local testBoolean = true
5
6    print (x)
7    print (welcomeMessage)
8    print (testBoolean)
9
10
```

Variables and Data Types

Lua is known as a dynamically typed language, meaning that you don't have to specify a data type for each variable. The variables themselves do not have an inherent data type but instead assume the data type of their values.

The main data types for variable values are strings, numbers, nils, and booleans. Each value is automatically typed based on how it is described in code. When the value is described with quotation marks, like in welcomeMessage, it's a string. If it has a numerical value, it takes the type number, like x. If the value is either true or false, it is a boolean.

If there is no assigned value, it will automatically take the type nil. If you try to display a variable with no value, you'll get an error.

```
9
10    emptyVariable
11    print (emptyVariable)
12
13
```

Output   ⌄ ⎚ ✕

4 Types   All Contexts   Filter...   ⏷   ⋯

ServerScriptService.Variables:10: Incomplete statement: expected assignment or a function call   Studio - Variables:10

See how the variable declaration is underlined in red? That indicates that there's something wrong. If you look at the output and the red error message in it, you'll see that an assignment or function call was expected. Since the variable was never initialized, it does not have a value, meaning there's nothing to display.

CHANGING PROPERTIES IN CODE

When you first add a part to an experience, it's easiest to modify it using the Studio tools and Properties window. This is because we can see the part and how it fits into the environment. Some parts aren't affected by gameplay and don't need any code. Things like trees and background buildings, for example, can be created and then left as is.

If a part needs to change during the course of gameplay, you'll need to use code to change its properties. This can include visual properties like color and material, transform values like size and position, and others like mass and whether it's anchored. The same properties found in the Properties window can also be accessed and altered in code.

Use the following formula to construct code to change a property:

game.Workspace.Name.Property = PropertyValue.

First, we need the object's location. Before the program can do anything, it needs to know which object the change will apply to. For this, we use the object's location within the Explorer; this is called its path. Parts are contained in the Workspace, and the Workspace is located in the game. Each location is separated by a full stop. Thus, your path begins with "game.Workspace." Add the name of the object you're referencing; hence, "game.Work-space.Name."

Next, identify which property you want to change and add it onto the path. If I wanted to change the Color property, I would add ".Color" to the object's path. If I wanted to change its material, I would add ".Material" instead.

After the operator "=" we need to define the new value of the property. To change the object's color, we use the built-in function Color3.fromRGB( ). This function uses three numerical values between 0 and 255 to describe the red, green, and blue balance of a color. Bright blue (the color I originally chose for this block) has the RGB value (13, 105, 172). You can manually type these values as parameters for the function, but I'd recommend using the built-in color selector that pops up when you type the function.

```
2    game.Workspace.blueBlock.Color = Color3.fromRGB()
3
4
```

Click on either of the colored squares to open the color selector. From here, you can choose one, and its RGB values will automatically be added into the function.

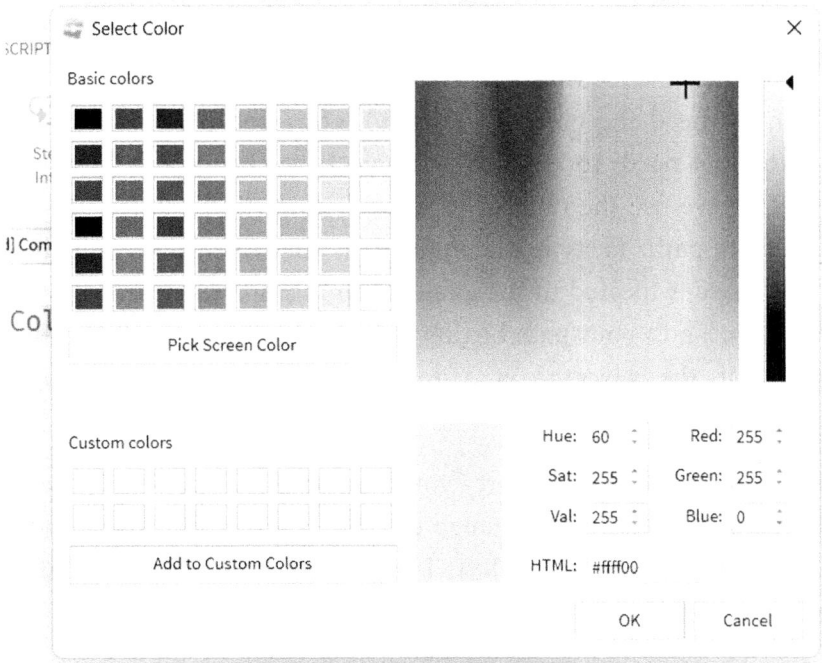

Cool, right?

If I wanted to change blueBlock from my obby into a yellow block, the code would look like this:

```
1
2   game.Workspace.blueBlock.Color = Color3.fromRGB(255, 255, 0)
3   |
4
```

Once I hit play with this script enabled, you will see that the block has changed color.

Note that each property has a corresponding value and data type. For this example with Color, the value is the Color3.fromRGB function. For Material, the value would be a string like "Slate" or "Ice." Other properties might have number values, booleans, or other functions. As you type, the code editor will give you possible options as a pop-up. Use them to guide you.

Troubleshooting

There are multiple reasons why your property changing code might not work. The first thing you can check is whether you're using the correct object name. The one used in code has to match the Name property exactly. The same goes for the property identifier. If the property is called Material, you need to type "Material" into your code; "material" or typos would cause an error.

The next thing you can check is the path. Make sure that you have included all relevant locations. You can use the Explorer to check.

Your best bet when it comes to troubleshooting is to run the game and see which error messages you get. This will give you a hint as to what you're looking for. If you don't know how to fix it, copy and paste it into Google and see what you can find out about it online. You can also look for code that's underlined. If you hover your cursor over the underlined errors, a dialogue box will tell you what's wrong.

OBJECT RELATIONSHIPS

Objects in this case refer to everything added into your experience. It can also refer to code objects.

Every part and object in your game exist in relation to others. More often than not, they also exist in a hierarchy. You can see this in the way the Explorer organizes things into folders and subfolders. Take Workspace as an example. It exists as an object within the project itself. Inside it, there are various other objects, like the parts that make up your obby. This is a parent-child relationship. Every object that contains something else is a parent, while everything that is contained in something is a child. In this case, Workspace is the parent, while the objects in it are children of it.

This relationship is mostly organizational, but we use it to our advantage to create reusable code. Take a moment to imagine an obby with thousands of obstacles. Now imagine having to manually code things for every individual part in it. That's a lot of coding, and we don't have the time or patience for that. So instead of providing code for each individual object, we create reusable scripts. But how can we create reusable code for different objects when that code needs unique names? That is where object relationships come in.

Generally, we add scripts under ServerScriptService. While the scripts are attached there, we need each object's unique name to reference it. If we attach a script directly to an object, however, we don't have to specify a unique name. Once attached, the script becomes a child object to the parent part, creating a parent-child relationship between them.

Remember how we can use variables in place of specific information? We can do the same thing here with names. By attaching a script directly to an object, we can use script.Parent instead of an object name or path. If we then create a variable and store "script.Parent" as its value, we can use that variable as a stand-in for the name in code.

To demonstrate, in your obby, click the plus next to any of your obstacles and select script. This will create a child script for that part. I added one to blueBlock and renamed it ColorChange. In that script, create a variable called partName and assign it the value script.Parent to let it take the part's name. Now this variable can replace the part's path from the property change code.

```
1    partName = script.Parent
2    --this creates a variable and assigns its value to be the name of the part
3    --in this case, partName = blueBlock
4
5    partName.Color = Color3.fromRGB(85, 255, 127)
6    --the variable can be used intead of a path to change the part's color
7
8    |
```

For this example, I changed the block's color to green. Note that it never once mentions the part by name. This is what my obby looks like after I run the game with this script attached to blueBlock.

We can see that the script works, so let's duplicate it. Right-click the script in Explorer, click duplicate, and then drag the copy to any of the other objects to attach it. I added it onto pinkBar2.

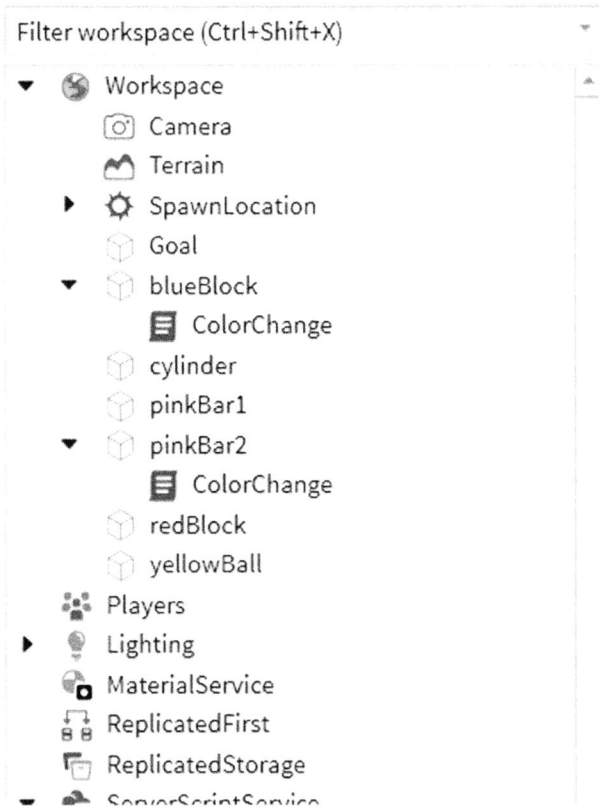

If you open it, you'll see that it's the exact same code. If I run the game, both blueBlock and pinkBar2 are now green.

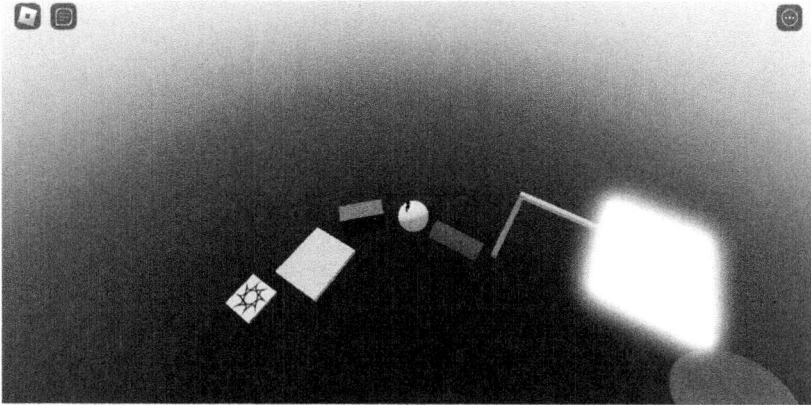

This means that you can use that script regardless of what the object itself is named. This isn't game-changing for an experience like the one we've been building, but it's incredibly valuable in others. With this relationship, we can create duplicable parts and reusable code.

This also only affects the parts to which the scripts are attached. Only those objects change color, meaning that the child scripts aren't affecting the rest of the experience. At the same time, I can still change other objects by using the paths as we did previously.

This method has tons of applications. Let's say you want to create an obby where all the parts change colors together at random. Without object relationships, you would write the property change code for each unique name. Of course, you can still copy and paste it, but you'll have to go through and change the names. With the relationship, you can write it once, duplicate the script, and attach it to each object without needing to change anything about it. This can save a lot of time and effort by giving us the ability to minimize repetitive work.

FUNCTIONS AND EVENTS

WHAT ARE FUNCTIONS?

Functions, also sometimes called procedures or subroutines, are units of code grouped together under a single name or identifier. Code can easily become complex and multidimensional. To make it easier to manage, we use functions.

Take a moment to think of an average, everyday task you do often, like brushing your teeth. Think about all the steps involved in it. First, you have to go to the bathroom. Then you have to pick up your toothbrush, open the toothpaste, squeeze some of it out, close it again, and so on. Despite it being a simple task, there are a lot of things that go into doing it. And yet, we can tell someone "I brushed my teeth," and they'll immediately know what it involves.

This is, in essence, what a function is. We can group individual lines of code aimed at performing a single action within a descriptor or name. That name then invokes the various steps and code associated with it whenever it is referenced. On their own, functions cannot execute code. They need to be called for their code to run. To call a function, you use the name you assigned to it.

This makes functions useful for creating reusable code and minimizing repetition. They can be used for a variety of things, like performing calculations, displaying output, and creating objects. Roblox has tons of predefined functions, and you've already used them. Print, for example, is one of them.

There are two main types of functions. One is used to perform actions based on data given to it. These functions are used to do things like display output or change colors. The other is used to take data, process it, and return a value. You can use these to perform calculations, test conditions, manipulate data, etc.

The first step in creating a function is defining it.

Defining Functions

To create a function, you follow these basic steps:

1. Define its scope.
2. State the keyword "function" to indicate its data type.
3. Assign a name (usually in camelCase).
4. Define the function parameters or arguments in brackets.
5. Set up the block of executable code.
6. State the keyword "end" to indicate the end of the function block.

```
1
2   local function functionName (parameters)
3       --code
4       --code
5       --code
6   end
7
8
9
```

Like any other code object, if you want it to have local scope, preface the definition with the word "local" or it will take the default global scope. The keyword "end" is usually automatically filled in once you hit enter after the second bracket, but it's always good to make sure it is there. If your code isn't doing what it should, one of the first things to check is whether or not the "end" is in the right place. Everything between it and the definition is considered part of the function. Everything after it is not.

This particular function will receive data via the parameters and use it to execute code.

Parameters

Also known as arguments, parameters are function-specific variables that store data. These variables are local to the function and cannot be used elsewhere. When a function is called, the parameters store the data provided to the function in these variables.

For example, here is a function that performs some simple math. It takes three numbers (given as parameters), adds them together, and then prints the result.

```
1
2   local function doMath (a, b, c)
3       local result = a + b + c
4       --[[the function takes three numbers, adds them together
5       and then displays the result]]
6       print(result)
7   end
8
9
10
```

To use this function, I call it in code. Calling a function involves typing its name and then providing values to each corresponding parameter.

```
1
2   ▾ local function doMath (a, b, c)
3         local result = a + b + c
4         --[[the function takes three numbers, adds them together
5         and then displays the result]]
6         print(result)
7     end
8
9
10    doMath (1, 6, 5) --the function is called and values sent as parameters
11
12    |
```

Output

All Messages ∨   5 Contexts ∨   Filter...

12   Server - functions:6

The parameters a, b, and c are used to store the numbers given to the function when it is called; in this example, a = 1, b = 6, and c = 5. The function takes those numbers and adds them together. The sum is assigned to a local variable called "result" and then printed. As you can see, the result is 12. If I changed the numbers I gave the function as arguments, the result would change accordingly.

If you provide more data than expected when you call the function, it will ignore any extra values. On the other hand, if you do not provide enough values, the unassigned parameters will be nil.

Functions do not need to have arguments. If, say, your function gathers data from somewhere else, you can simply leave the brackets empty. Parameters are useful when you want them to process specific information like the numbers above.

You can also use variables as parameters in call statements. For example:

```
1
2   - local function doMath (a, b, c)
3         local result = a + b + c
4         --[[the function takes three numbers, adds them together
5         and then displays the result]]
6         print(result)
7   end
8
9     aa = 1
10    bb = 6
11    cc = 5
12    doMath (aa, bb, cc) --the function is called and values sent as parameters
13
```

Output

All Messages ∨ 5 Contexts ∨   Filter...

12   - Server - functions:6

In this case, the same values are still being sent to the function, they are just contained in a variable. This allows us to use data that we do not have yet or data that changes subject to player behavior. In the above example, if the values of aa, bb, and cc change, the function's result will also change accordingly.

Return

The previous example used a function that only executes code. If we want to use a function that processes information and returns a value, its setup would look slightly different.

```
1
2   - local function functionName (parameters)
3         --code
4         --code
5         --code
6         return --value
7   end
8
9
10
11
```

A return function takes information, processes it, and returns its result as a value. Unlike the previous example, it will not print the value as part of the function but rather send that result to the code in which it was called.

```
1    ▾ local function calculateSum (x, y, z)
2          return x + y + z
3              --function adds the three numbers when called and returns the sum value
4      end
5
6
7      print(calculateSum (8, 2, 6))
8      --the function is called and the result is given and printed
9
```
Output
All Messages   5 Contexts
16   Server - Functions 2:7

This is useful for when that returned value is necessary for other code. Let's say you have a function that calculates a player's health after taking damage from an enemy. By using a return function, you can now use the result for other things like further damage calculations, updated player stats, and displaying it in the UI.

Since it returns a value, we can assign a variable to hold that value and then call the function as part of its initialization.

```
1    ▾ local function calculateSum (x, y, z)
2          return x + y + z
3              --function adds the three numbers when called and returns the sum value
4      end
5
6
7      sumValue = calculateSum (8, 2, 6)
8      --variable sumValue is declared and assigned the return value
9
10     print(sumValue) --sumValue is used to display the function's return
11
12
```
Output
All Messages   5 Contexts
16   Server - Functions 2:10

Like above, it uses local variables as parameters to store arguments given to it. It can also take values as variables when called.

Methods

In Lua, functions are considered a unique data type. This means that we can use them as members of other objects like classes and tables. When a function is part of another object, it becomes a method. Methods differ from other functions in that they require the object they are contained in to be called as a parameter—much like how we need to reference an object's parent in a path. A method declaration looks the same as any other function, except that it always takes "self" as the first parameter. Essentially: function functionName (self, other parameters).

This is particularly relevant when it comes to Roblox's built-in functions relating to parts and game objects. Whenever a new part is created, it inherits its members from the Instance class. This lets us access all the functions built into this class and is why we can do things like create objects in code, change their properties, or duplicate them. Most of these functions exist as members of each specific part. Therefore, we need to go through the part object to access them.

For example, Destroy() is a predefined method we can use to code the destruction of an object in-game. Each part has an inherent Destroy method, and to access it, we need to path through the part itself. At the same time, we need to supply the part as a parameter for Destroy so that it can know which part to act on. To use it, the code will look like this: partName.Destroy(partName).

This is what sets methods apart from other functions. Methods exist as members of objects and can only be accessed through those objects. At the same time, they take those objects as a parameter.

Lua has a special notation for methods. Normally, we use a dot notation where each object and member are separated by full stops. For example, partName.Destroy(partName).

```
1   local partName = Instance.new("Part")
2   --a new part object has been created
3
4   --[[code that does somethign with the part]]
5
6   partName.Destroy(partName)
7   --dot notation
8
9
```

With methods, we can also use the colon notation to avoid the repetitive use of the object name. For example, partName:Destroy(). The colon essentially tells the computer to infer that the method (i.e., Destroy) should be applied to the object (i.e., partName).

```
1   local partName = Instance.new("Part")
2   --a new part object has been created
3
4   --[[code that does somethign with the part]]
5
6   partName:Destroy()
7   --[[colon notation.
8      automatically fills in Destroy(partName)]]
9
```

Whenever you see this colon notation in a script or code example, you can thus infer that it is a method that applies to the object named in it.

Methods as Table Members

We haven't covered tables much as of yet, so let's take a quick look at them. Tables are collections of multiple values. Each individual value is a table member and is characterized by a key or index value. The key acts as that entry's identifier. It will look something like this:

```lua
1   tableName = {
2       --[[members are characterized by an identifying key and corresponding value
3           basically key = value
4           entries are seperated by commas after each value]]
5       member1 = "I am entry #1",
6       member2 = "I am entry #2",
7       member3 = "I am entry #3"
8   }
9   --[[everything inside the { } is part of the table.
10  wherever the computer sees {} it will know that the obejct is a table]]
11
```

Tables let us group related data into one object instead of managing multiple variables. We can also put functions into tables where they become method since they are members of the table object. When you add a function as a table member, its definition takes a different form. Normally, a function definition looks like function functionName (parameters) end. In tables, however, the name becomes the key, and the rest of the definition becomes its value. Since it is a method, it also takes "self" as a parameter. Altogether, the entry will look something like this: methodName = function (self, other parameters) end.

Now, when you want to call the method, you use its parent object and then the name of the method; i.e., tableName.method-name(tableName, parameters) or tableName:methodName(parameters).

```lua
1   tableName = {
2       --entry1 = value,
3       --entry2 = value,
4       methodName = function (self, randomNum)
5           print(randomNum)
6       end,
7   }
8   --to call the method
9   tableName:methodName(5)
10
```

Callbacks

When we use functions as parameters for other functions, it's known as a callback. Callbacks are no different from other functions. The only distinction is that they are also used as parameters.

Callbacks can become quite complex. They essentially provide called functions with the ability to access other functions (the callbacks) to tell them what to do. This gives the main function access to the callback's code and instructions. It's a little like a game of telephone, so let's break it down step by step. First, a regular function (FunctionA) is called in code. It receives another function (the callback) as one of its parameters. Through that, FunctionA calls the callback. The callback executes its code and returns a value to FunctionA that it then uses to execute its code. By using the callback, FunctionA can thus do what it was called to do.

Callbacks have very few uses in Roblox, but they are one of Lua's most powerful tools. They exist in most other programming languages, but the syntax for them is complex enough that most people don't bother using them. Lua, however, simplifies them enough that they can be used effectively. In general programming, callbacks have a lot of applications, but in Roblox, we mostly just use it to instance new objects. Let's look at callbacks in this context.

Roblox has a built-in object class called BindableFunctions that lets us create functions that can be used across other scripts throughout the server. Unlike regular functions, these exist as objects in the experience and not just as code or data objects. Creating them through the BindableFunctions class also lets us use its members like Invoke. Invoke is a predefined method that lets us dictate what should happen when this bindable function is called.

Let's say you have a function that creates new objects for the game. This function lets you instance a new object with all of its built-in members, assigns a name to it, sets its size, adds it into the Workspace, and anchors it.

First, we create a function called createPart through the BindableFunction class. It needs to be an instance of BindableFunction so that we can access its Invoke member.

```
1    local createPart = Instance.new("BindableFunction")
2    --creates a new function
3
```

Next, create a function definition for it with the OnInvoke method. This will let us provide code for what should happen when a new part is created and this function is called. We can also create the code block for the createPart function.

```
1    local createPart = Instance.new("BindableFunction")
2    --creates a new function
3
4  ▸ createPart.OnInvoke = function(name, size)
5        --[[defines the new function that was created and provides
6        what it should do when called]]
7        local part = Instance.new("Part", Workspace)
8        --creates a new object in the game
9        part.Name = name
10       part.Size = size
11       part.Anchored = true
12       --assigns properties based on information received through parameters
13   end
```

When the createPart is called, it instances a new object. It receives two parameters; namely, name and size. These parameters will contain the values that will be added into a new object's proper-ties. In the code, we assign the value in name to its Name property and assign the size value to its Size property. We also anchor the part like we did for all other obstacles in the obby.

Finally, we invoke the createPart function object by typing create-Part:Invoke() and passing it the values needed for the new. Altogether, the entire code looks like this:

```
1   local createPart = Instance.new("BindableFunction")
2   --Step 1: create a new function
3
4   createPart.OnInvoke = function(name, size)
5     --[[Step 2: define the new function that was created and provide
6       what it should do when called]]
7     local part = Instance.new("Part", Workspace)
8       --creates a new object in the game
9     part.Name = name
10    part.Size = size
11    part.Anchored = true
12      --assigns properties based on information received through parameters
13  end
14
15    --Step 3: call the function to create the part with its properties
16  createPart:Invoke("Brick", Vector3.new(5,5,5))
17
18    --[[example sourced from https://roblox.fandom.com/wiki/Callback
19      retrieved in March 2023]]
20
```

When I run the experience, there's a new brick added into the Workspace.

Invoke is a method and can thus use the colon notation. Without it, the call statement would be: createPart.Invoke(createPart("Brick", Vector3.new(5,5,5)). The createPart function is used as a parameter for Invoke() and becomes a callback for it. Remember that Invoke is a member of createPart due to it being an instance of BindableFunction. As such, Invoke needs to be pathed through createPart.

If you have trouble following this part, you're not alone. Callbacks are hard. Copy this code into a text file somewhere and keep it on hand as a reference for creating new objects through a function. The fact that it includes a callback isn't all that relevant since this is one of the only ways we use them in Roblox.

OTHER FUNCTIONS TECHNIQUES

Anonymous Functions

Functions can be named or unnamed. Unnamed or anonymous functions do not have unique names of their own, and they are usually used as callbacks or event handlers. Like their named counterparts, anonymous functions still require the keywords "function" and "end." The definition of an anonymous function looks the same as a regular function, except without the identifier. In other words, it will look like: function (parameters) [code] end.

The function we defined after createPart.OnInvoke is technically an anonymous function. In that case, there was no need to name it since it was bound to the Invoke method and wouldn't be called on its own.

Functions in ModuleScript

The whole point of using functions is to make code more efficient and organized. Instead of weaving them into general code blocks, we can define them somewhere else. ModuleScripts are special scripts in which we can place different functions. This allows us to keep all our functions in one convenient place and then import them into other scripts. This makes them easier to find if we want to check what's in them or change them. This is also an easy way of making sure that important functions are accessible to other scripts.

You create a ModuleScript the same way you would an ordinary script. Select ServerScriptService, click the +, and find ModuleScript.

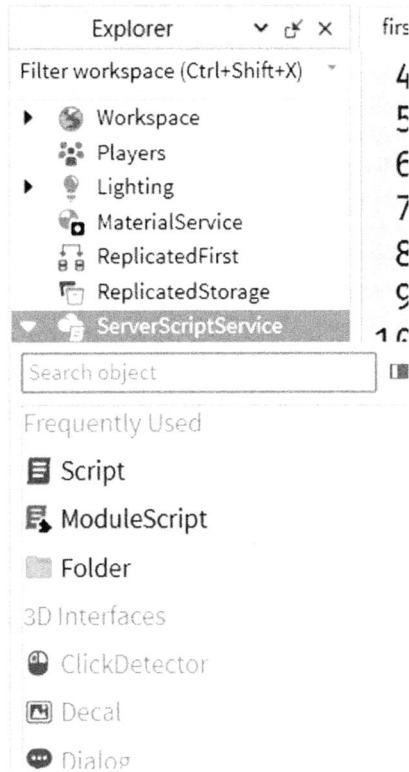

ModuleScripts group functions into a table. As such, they always open with a table declaration. In fact, this declaration will already be in your ModuleScript when you open it. All you have to do is replace "module" with an appropriate name. You can then add your functions into it. To add functions to it, see the *Methods as Table Members* section.

```
1    local moduleName = {
2         --function 1
3
4         --function 2
5
6         --function 3
7    }
8
9    return moduleName
10
```

ModuleScripts cannot run code on their own. They only define the object in which functions are contained. As such, they need to be imported into other scripts. To do this, create a local variable in your regular script and assign the module to it using "require()." This typically looks like: local moduleVariable = require(Server-ScriptService.ModuleScriptName). The parameter for require is the location of the ModuleScript and its name. In this case, it is attached to ServerScriptService. It can also be attached to ReplicatedStorage if it is meant to be used for server-client communication.

If you have a particularly complex experience, you can create multiple modules and then sort functions by purpose. This way, you can group related functions together and keep unrelated functions away from each other. Doing this also means that scripts aren't accessing functions that aren't related to them. For example, if you have a survival game that includes mechanics for farming, fishing, and combat, you can group functions related to each one in separate modules. That way, scripts related to fishing won't access functions related to combat.

Variadic Functions

Normally, functions have a set number of parameters. This doesn't have to be the case. Some functions, like print, can take any number of arguments. Lua also lets you create functions with undetermined or varying numbers of parameters.

To create a variadic function, define it like normal but place an ellipse (...) where you would normally define parameters. In other words: function functionName (...) end. In the code block of the function, you then create a table to index all the values given as arguments when called.

```
1   local function functionName(...)
2     --function is declared and ... is used to imply an uncertain number of parameters
3         local args = {...}
4         --[[here a table is created to store all possible data
5         that might be sent as parameters when the function is called]]
6   end
7
```

EVENTS

Events are data types that represent the occurrence of something in the experience. Think of things like a player interacting with the game through keystrokes, objects colliding, or anything else that requires a response from your code. Roblox scripting is largely event-based, as is most game development since the whole point of video games is having an experience you can interact with.

Roblox already has a variety of predefined events like PlayerAdded for when new users join the experience or Touched for when objects come into contact with each other. You can also create custom events.

Event Handlers and Connecting Them to Events

When an event occurs (or fires), we use functions known as event handlers to manage them. These functions tell the game what to do when the event fires. The only difference between regular functions and event handlers is that we use the latter for the specific purpose of managing events. We use the predefined method Connect to link a function to an event, thus making it the event handler.

To illustrate this, let's create an event handler for when a new player is added to the experience. This function will get the name of the player and then display it with the message ". . . joined the game."

```
1    local Players = game:GetService("Players")
2
3  - local function onPlayerAdded(player)
4        --function that displays the name of the player that's been added
5        print(player.Name, " joined the game!")
6    end
7
8    Players.PlayerAdded:Connect(onPlayerAdded)
9    --the function onPlayerAdded is connected to the PlayerAdded event
10
11   --[[code sourced from https://create.roblox.com/docs/scripting/events/using-events
12       retrieved in March 2023]]
13
```

Event handlers are largely named to match the event they will manage. We take the name of the event (e.g., PlayerAdded) and add "on" to it (e.g., onPlayerAdded). This name describes its purpose as an event handler for that event. This is standard practice and makes it easier to identify event handlers on sight. For example, if there's an event called RoundStarted, its event handler will be called onRoundStarted.

Disconnecting Functions from Events

You can also disconnect functions from events. In the case of PlayerAdded, the function connected to it is automatically disconnected when the player leaves the game. This is because a new Player object is created for every user that joins. It is through this object that the connection is made. When the user leaves, the object is destroyed, and the function is disconnected.

We can replicate this effect in other events and functions. If you do not want the same event handler managing an event more than once or want to stop it from responding to the event, you can disconnect them using the Disconnect method.

Let's say your code has to manage an event that occurs when two parts touch. When this happens, we want a function to test whether this other part was the target. If it was the target, the function will display "You hit the target!" and then disconnect that function from the event. If it was not the target, the function should stay connected to keep testing Touched events until the target has been hit.

```lua
local part = workspace.Part
local targetPart = workspace.TargetPart
--objects that represent the parts

local connection
--[[declare a variable that will represent the connection so that we can disconnect
    it within the function itself]]

local function onPartTouched(otherPart)
    if otherPart == targetPart then
        --condition that tests whether collision was with the targetPart
        print("You hit the target!")
        connection:Disconnect()
    end
    --[[after the message has been displayed,
    we can disconnect the function from the event]]
end

connection = part.Touched:Connect(onPartTouched())
--variable is initialized with the value of the connection between event and function

--[[code sourced from https://create.roblox.com/docs/scripting/events/using-events
    retrieved in March 2023]]
```

Note that this script is intended to be attached to an object. It will then test any other part that comes into contact with it.

BindableEvents

Like BindableFunctions, BindableEvents is a built-in Roblox class with predefined members we can use to create custom events. In the above example, part.Touched is a built-in event. As such, we don't have to provide code to determine when it should be triggered or what it's named. It also comes pre-equipped with methods like Connect and Disconnect.

If we create events from scratch, we have to make provisions for all these things. Creating events as instances of BindableEvents lets us access its members. That means we can use methods like

Connect and Disconnect to assign event handlers, and methods like Fire to indicate when the event occurs. Using BindableEvents also gives us the ability to use this event in other scripts.

There are two ways to create a new event with this. The first is to add one the way you would a new script. Find the object you want to bind it to, most likely ServerScriptService or ReplicatedStorage, click the + and then find BindableEvent. You might have to search for it. This creates an event object whose properties you can change.

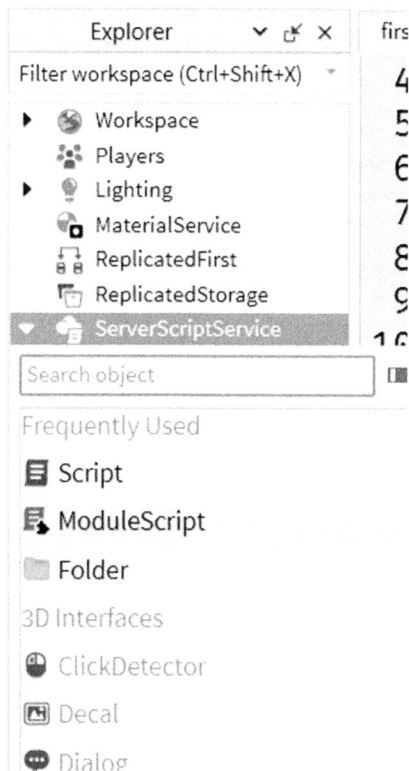

The other way is to instance it through code. We do this the same way we create a new object through Instance or add a new function through BindableFunction. Start by declaring a new event variable and initialize it as an instance of BindableEvents. Once the object has been instanced, set its Name and Parent properties.

```
1    local newEvent = Instance.new("BindableEvent")
2    --create the object for the new event
3    newEvent.Name = "RoundStarted"
4    --give it a name
5    newEvent.Parent = "ServerScriptService"
6    --place it within the ServerScriptService
7
```

Now that the event is defined, let's write a function to manage it. This function should print a message. Then, connect the function to the event. Since this event is an instance of BindableEvent, we need to add ".Event" to access event-related methods. Finally, define when the event occurs by using ":Fire()."

```
1    local roundStarted = Instance.new("BindableEvent")
2    --create the object for the new event
3    roundStarted.Name = "RoundStarted"
4    --give it a name
5    roundStarted.Parent = game:GetService("ServerScriptService")
6    --place it within the ServerScriptService
7
8  · local function onRoundStarted ()
9        print("Round has started!")
10   end
11
12   roundStarted.Event:Connect(onRoundStarted)
13   --connect function to the event
14   roundStarted:Fire()
15   --fire the event
16
```
```
                                   Output                              ∨ ⊘ ×
 4 Types  ∨    All Contexts ∨                       Filter...              ⚖ ⋯
 ▌ Round has started!    — Server - bindable event:9
```

Since this is all in one script, I use the local variable in which I created the event to connect and fire it. If you fire it from another script, you can use its assigned name instead. Note that event names are written in PascalCase while variables are written in camelCase.

Remote Events and Functions

Most interactive programs run on a client-server communication system. The server refers to the program itself while the client refers to the user's computer. When a user interacts with the program, the client communicates with the server. The server then processes it through inter-server communication and then responds to the client with output. We usually don't want server-side communication to cross over the boundary to clients, and so we limit the interaction between servers and clients.

Thus far, we've been using ServerScriptService for our scripts, functions, and events. This allows scripts to communicate with each other on the server side of the barrier without crossing over to the client. However, sometimes there is a need for server-client communication. This is especially relevant to events since events are what manage player interactions. For example, when a player presses W, their character needs to move forward. To do this, the client (i.e., the player's computer) needs to communicate the keypress to the server so that the player object can move.

Events that manage interactions like this are called remote events, and Roblox makes provisions for many of them. If you want to create custom remote events and functions, you can do so by attaching scripts and event objects to ReplicatedStorage. If you want to manage them through code, you access the RemoteFunctions and RemoteEvents classes. This comes with its own code techniques.

For more information on this, head over to create.roblox.-com/docs and search for remote events.

DEBOUNCE

Some events, like part.Touched, will keep firing. To stop them from doing this, we use debounce to act as a trigger manager. This is a technique that lets us limit the number of times an event can execute code. With it, we can basically put events on a cooldown.

To use debounce in code, we create a boolean variable and initialize it to be false. The first time an event fires, we change debounce to true. While it is true, the event cannot fire again. When enough time has passed, we revert it to false to enable the event to be triggered again.

Let's put it into practice. First, attach a new script to the first object in your obby and create a basic Touched event and onTouched function for it.

```
1   local part = script.Parent
2   --create a variable to reference the part to which the script is attached
3
4   local function onPartTouched ()
5       --function that displays "part was touched"
6       print("part was touched")
7   end
8
9   part.Touched:Connect(onPartTouched)
10
```

If you run it as is, you'll notice in your output that the display message gets repeated for every time your character touches the block. Every step will fire it again. In the time it took my character to move from one end to another, this event fired four times as shown below.

```
                              Output                              v  x  x
  All Messages  v    All Contexts  v          Filter...
  ▌ ▶ part was touched (x4)    Server - Script
```

I want to make it so that this event won't fire multiple times but will still be available if I want to return to this block. For this, I use debounce. First, create a local variable called debounce and assign it the value false.

```
1   local part = script.Parent
2   --create a variable to reference the part to which the script is attached
3   local debounce = false
4   --boolean variable created and set to false.
5
```

It's important that this variable be local. While it can take other names, it's standard practice to name it "debounce" to make it clear what it does. However, we'll likely have multiple debounce variables per project, and making them local means we can use the name "debounce" for them all.

Next, we create a basic conditional to test the value of debounce. This will check whether debounce is false. If it is false, the code will execute. If it isn't, the test will fail, and the code won't execute. The following code prints the message "part was touched," sets debounce to true, waits for five seconds, and then sets debounce back to false.

```
1    local part = script.Parent
2    --create a variable to reference the part to which the script is attached
3    local debounce = false
4    --boolean variable created and set to false.
5
6    local function onPartTouched ()
7        --function that displays "part was touched"
8        if debounce == false then
9            --[[conditional that tests whether debounce is false
10               if it is false, the code will execute. if it is true, the event will not fire]]
11           debounce = true
12           print("part was touched")
13           wait(5)
14           debounce = false
15       end --end of conditional
16   end --end of function
17
18   part.Touched:Connect(onPartTouched)
19
20   --[[code adapted from https://www.youtube.com/watch?v=HoZkuvd6RPA
21        retrieved in March 2023]]
22
```

As long as debounce is true, the code won't run. Wait is a built-in function that basically tells the program to wait for how many seconds is indicated in the parameter. In this case, "wait(5)" tells the game to wait for five seconds. Once that time has passed, debounce returns to false, meaning the code can run again.

If you want an event to fire only once, all you need to do is set debounce to true and leave out the rest. That means that debounce will stay true and the condition will fail every time. You can also disconnect the event handler at this point. We'll cover conditionals in more detail in the next chapter.

278 | A.E. COLONNA

If you run it now, the message will only pop up once every five seconds if you're moving around. Note that debounce does not mean the part stops being touched. The event technically still triggers. The game just isn't executing the event handler code. This technique helps manage things like weapons' cooldowns, damage mechanics, or spawns.

PRACTICAL EXERCISE – CREATE A BUTTON-ACTIVATED BRIDGE

For this exercise, you want to create a feature in your obby that works as a bridge between two objects. This bridge starts out half invisible and impassable. The idea is to make something players can't walk across until a button has been pressed.

All parts added into an experience have a CanCollide property which means they can collide with other parts. If this is turned off, the player will not be able to stand on it and will instead fall through it.

Add a part somewhere in your obby that will become your bridge object. In the Properties windows, disable the CanCollide property and set its Transparency to 0.5. Transparency lets you enter any value between 0 and 1 where 1 is invisible and 0 is opaque. The higher the value, the more transparent it will be. Make sure it's anchored.

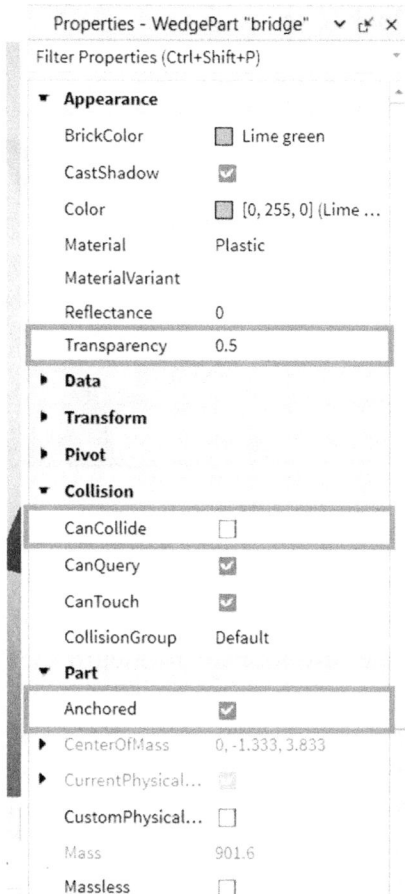

To make this bridge traversable, the player will have to touch a button. Just before the bridge, add a floating brick that will act as a button. Make sure that it is somewhere they can reach and set it to float above everything else. It shouldn't touch any other object. You can also make it red to show that it hasn't been touched yet.

Here's what mine looks like:

Attach a new script to the button object. In this script, create two variables to represent the button and bridge and initialize them. Since the script is attached to the button, you can use script.Parent for it. For the bridge, use its path to identify it (i.e., game.Workspace.bridge).

To make the button work, you will use the part.Touched event. Go ahead and create a function that will do the following when the button is touched:

1. Change the color of the button to green to show it's been touched.
2. Set the bridge's transparency to 0.
3. Activate the bridge's CanCollide so the player can walk across.

Lastly, add a debounce to optimize the function and make it run only once.

Try this on your own first before looking at the answer below.

```
1    local button = script.Parent
2    local bridge = game.Workspace.bridge
3    --variables for the button and bridge
4    local debounce = false
5
6  ▾ local function onButtonPress ()
7  ▾      if debounce == false then
8              --function for making the bridge accessible and turning button green
9              debounce = true --makes it so fucntion can only run once
10             button.Color = Color3.fromRGB(0, 255, 0)
11             bridge.Transparency = 0
12             bridge.CanCollide = true
13             print("button pressed, bridge available")
14         end
15     end
16
17     button.Touched:Connect(onButtonPress)
18     --connecting function to the Touched event
19
20  ▾ --[[code adapted from
21         https://create.roblox.com/docs/education/coding-2/parameters-practice-buttons
22         retrieved in March 2023]]
```

Our Generation Has a Unique Opportunity That No Other Generation Has Been Able to Benefit from to the Same Extent – Gaming!

"Failure doesn't mean the game is over, it means try again with experience." Unknown

It's true that there have been some exceptions in the years prior to Gen Z. Steve Jobs and Bill Gates changed the world of computing forever. In the gaming world, no one should forget the contributions made by legends such as Ralph Bear, Jerry Lawson, and Sid Meier.

Thanks to the foundations laid by these heroes, we have the chance to develop code, create games, and even earn money by doing something we love.

The first stages of understanding Roblox were daunting, even terrifying. Despite feeling overwhelmed, you have had a chance to explore this online platform and get confident with the tools it has to offer. You may have even created your first Obby! Kudos to you!

But the learning journey isn't over yet and there are many ways you can still improve your game development and programming skills. Mistakes will be inevitable but the game is far from over. And with some extra help and practice overcoming your coding challenges, the world of opportunities will continue to grow for you.

That's not the only thing that grows! Have you noticed an increase in your confidence? Do you hold your head a little higher after spending time with a community of people that get you?

Think back to a short time ago when you were that student who was constantly told your future depended on your academic performance, just adding to your pressure. Or those days when you keep going to work with no clear vision of your career. Now think of all the hundreds and thousands of young people who feel the same way you did.

All it takes is a few minutes to share your experience developing games to help other young adults achieve the same things that you are.

The great thing about Roblox is that these people aren't going to 'steal' your opportunities. The more people there are learning and enjoying Roblox, the stronger everyone becomes!

Scan the QR code for a quick review.

CONDITIONALS

Programs can only be interactive if they have the ability to react to player behavior. Even the simplest games run into scenarios where they need to weigh options to respond appropriately.

WHAT ARE CONDITIONALS?

Conditionals are code statements that let us give programs the ability to make decisions about how to react to certain circumstances. They let us add features like power-ups, rewards, or special events. In other words, conditionals let us tell computers to run certain code if and when specific circumstances are met.

We use conditionals for many things and for many reasons. If something involves some element of cause and effect, odds are there's a conditional attached to it. It's also a very commonly used programming technique—common enough that every language uses them. Like many others, Lua uses an if-statement.

INTRO TO IF-STATEMENTS

A basic if-statement follows very simple logic; namely, if something is true, do this. Its code structure reflects that. It reads: if [condition] then [code] end. Everything contained between "then" and "end" forms the code block and will be executed only if the provided condition is true. If the condition is not met, the code in the block is ignored.

Conditions

The hardest part of handling if-statements is setting up the condition. A condition is any statement where one value is compared to another. For example, debounce == false or number == 10.

Regardless of what the condition is, it always returns the value true or false. In essence, the computer checks the condition and asks itself "Is this true?" A condition succeeds if the comparison is true. For example, 1 + 1 = 2 will be true because one plus one is in fact two. On the other hand, 2 + 2 = 5 will be false because two plus two does not equal five.

We use comparison operators to define conditions. They tell the computer how to compare the values it was given. The most common comparison operators are:

- == (equal to)
- ~= (not equal to)
- < (less than)
- > (greater than)
- <= (less than or equal to)
- >= (greater than or equal to)

For example, if I wanted to check whether a number had a value greater than 10, the condition would be "number > 10." In this case, the condition would be true if the number's value was 11 or more. If I wanted to check if the number's value was equal to 10, I'd use "number == 10."

To illustrate, create a new script and create a variable called score with the value zero (0). Now, code an if-statement to test if this score is less than 10. Add an appropriate display message to check if the code works.

```
1    --basic if statement
2    local score = 0
3    --variable used in condition
4
5    if score < 10 then
6        print("score is less than 10")
7    end
8
9
10
```

Output

All Messages   5 Contexts   Filter...

score is less than 10   Server - Script:6

Go ahead and change score's value to something greater than 10 and see what happens.

We can also use multiple variables in one comparison. Say, for instance, you want to compare a player's current and past scores. Create two variables, one for each score value, and create a conditional that will compare them. The goal is to see if their current result is better than the previous one. Provide an appropriate message to display if their current score is higher.

```
1    --basic if statement
2    local currentScore = 33
3    local prevScore = 25
4
5    if currentScore > prevScore then
6        print("congratulations! you have a new high score!")
7    end
8
9
```

Output

All Messages   5 Contexts   Filter...

congratulations! you have a new high score!   Server - Script:6

Now let's add something new. If-statements should almost always have a corresponding else statement. Else is a keyword that tells the program what to do if the condition was not met. Simply add else and the code you want to execute before "end" to provide an alternative option.

```
1    --basic if statement
2    local currentScore = 33
3    local prevScore = 25
4
5    if currentScore > prevScore then
6        print("congratulations! you have a new high score!")
7    else print("try again")
8    end
9
```

Now, if the currentScore is lower than the prevScore, the else statement will execute since the condition failed.

Multiple Conditions

While the most basic if-statement has one condition, you can add two or more. This is for when your program needs to weigh more than one condition at the same time or when it needs to test two different values. By using certain keywords, you can add as many conditions as you want into a single conditional statement.

- **and:** indicates that both conditions must be true for the if-statement to succeed. For example, say a player wants to join a match that has requirements. To qualify, they must be level five or higher and have won at least two previous matches. For that scenario, you can use "if playerLevel >= 5 and victoryCount > 1."
- **or:** indicates that either one of the conditions must be true. For example, the price of a shop item is 10 gold or 100 silver. In that case, use "if gold = 10 or silver = 100."

Extra Practice

Practice creating conditions for the following scenarios. Write them on your own and then check the example for the answers. Write code to check if

1. a number is greater than 10.
2. a player's score is 200 or less.
3. a number has any value other than 10.

```
1    --answers for practice
2    local numValue = 0
3
4    --#1
5    ▾ if numValue > 10 then
6        --
7    end
8
9    --#2
10   ▾ if numValue <= 200 then
11       --
12   end
13
14   --#3
15   ▾ if numValue ~= 10 then
16       --
17   end
```

PRACTICAL EXERCISE USING TRAPS

Let's use conditionals to set a trap in your obby. Add a new object to act as the base of your trap and name it accordingly (mine is trapBase). Add another object onto it to act as the trap itself (trap-Part). Make sure the parts look different enough that the trap stands out. Play around with colors and textures to make it look dangerous. The point of the trap part will be to kill the player if they touch it.

Move the base and trap parts around so that a player would have to maneuver around the trap to get around it. Make it as hard or as easy as you want.

Attach a script to trapPart. In it, create a variable that will represent the trap. For convenience, I named the variable the same as
the part itself. Go ahead and create code for the .Touched event
and event handler, and add a line of print code to test if it works.
Try doing this yourself. You can look at previous examples if you
need to, but really give it a try before looking at the example
below.

```
1    local trapPart = script.Parent
2    --assign code object for trap
3
4    local function onTouch (otherPart)
5        print("trap was touched")
6    end
7
8    trapPart.Touched:Connect(onTouch)
9
```

If you run it as is, the event will fire immediately since the trapPart
is touching the base. For an easy fix, go into your Explorer, find
the base part, and look at its properties. Under Collision, you'll
find a property called CanTouch. As implied, this determines
whether or not the part can touch other objects. You can disable
this property to make sure it doesn't trigger the Touched event for
now, although the code we add in later will also fix this.

Now comes the tricky part. This trap is meant to react to player characters, but how do we distinguish players from other objects?

Let's take a moment to talk about how Roblox handles players. Roblox avatars aren't a single unified object. Instead, they're collections of individual parts. Each limb, clothing item, accessory, and feature is a unique object—each with its own properties and abilities.

Go back to your obby, run the game, and take a look at the Explorer. In Workspace, there will be a new object added for your character. If you open it, you'll see a whole list of child objects.

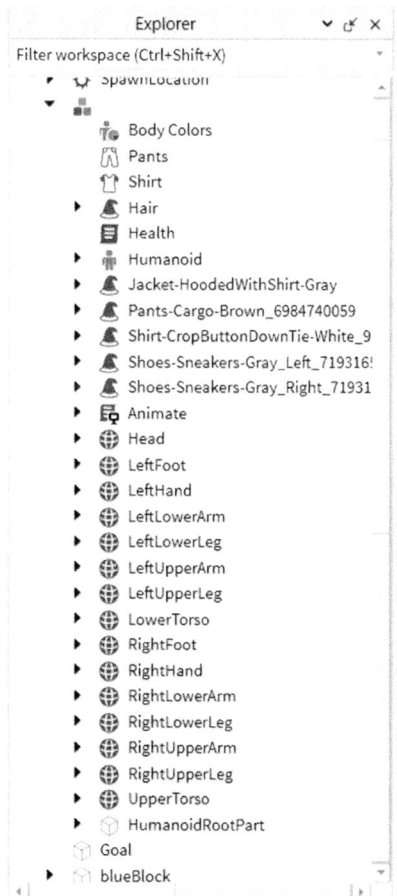

When a player comes into contact with other objects, each individual part of the avatar registers as a unique touch. In other words, each body part or clothing item touches the trap separately. This is why we get multiple outputs like this:

The onTouch function takes otherPart as its parameter. In our case, otherPart takes the value of the object that touched the trap, likely a limb or clothing item. If, say, my character's LeftFoot set off the event, otherPart will be LeftFoot, but that doesn't help us. We still need to test whether or not otherPart is a player character, and we can't do that with a foot or hand.

For that reason, we create a function-local variable called character and assign it the value otherPart.Parent. That means that character will be whatever object otherPart is attached to. In other words, character will reference the player object. This is important because player objects automatically have a child called "Humanoid."

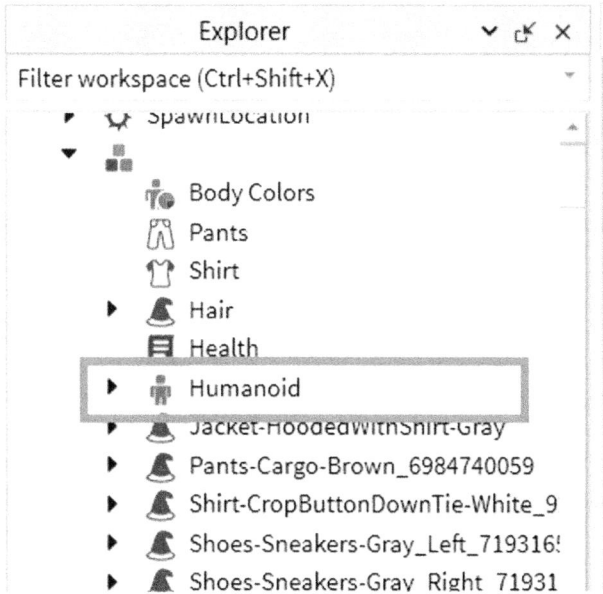

All avatars come with this child and it's highly unlikely that you'll see other objects with this feature. That means that we can use Humanoid to test whether or not the part that touched the trap was a player. To use this in a condition, we first need a way to locate the Humanoid part in our character.

Roblox has a predefined method called FindFirstChildWhichIsA that lets us search through an object's children to find a specific one. First, create a second local variable called humanoid in the function and add "character:FindFirstChildWhichIsA("Humanoid")" as its value. This will prompt the program to search for a Humanoid child in character. If it finds one, it will store the reference to that object in our humanoid variable. If it cannot find one, the variable will be nil.

```
3
4  ▾ local function onTouch (otherPart)
5        print("trap was touched")
6        local character = otherPart.Parent
7        local humanoid = character:FindFirstChildWhichIsA("Humanoid")
8    end
9
```

Now that we have humanoid, we can create the if-statement to test
for a player's touch.

```
1    local trapPart = script.Parent
2    --assign code object for trap
3
4  ▾ local function onTouch (otherPart)
5        print("trap was touched")
6        local character = otherPart.Parent
7        local humanoid = character:FindFirstChildWhichIsA("Humanoid")
8    ▾   if humanoid then
9            --conditional that checks if otherPart is a humanoid character
10           print ("trap was touched by a player")
11       end
12   end
13
14   trapPart.Touched:Connect(onTouch)
15
16 ▾ --[[code sourced from
17   https://create.roblox.com/docs/education/coding-3/traps-with-if-statements
18   retrieved in March 2023]]
```

The statement "if humanoid then" tests whether or not the variable humanoid contains a value. The condition "if humanoid then"
means the same as "if humanoid ~= nil then." Nils will fail this
condition since they are the absence of a value. Thus, if there was
no Humanoid child in character, it would not pass the if-statement
and the trap would not be sprung.

Run the game with this code and test whether or not you can see
the display message when you touch the part. If it does not work,
check that

- the touched event is connected to the right function.
- there is an end for both the function and if-statement.
- everything is capitalized and spelled correctly.
- all brackets that were opened were closed. If you have two
  "(" you should have two ")."

Changing Player Health

The same Humanoid object that lets us recognize player objects also lets us manipulate stats like their health. If you select the Humanoid object and look at its properties, you'll see all the characteristics of a player in a game. Things like health, walking speed, and movement properties can all be found here. It is thus through the Humanoid that we can make objects kill players or otherwise affect their abilities.

Player characters die when their health reaches zero. This is built into Studio. All we have to do is write code to set the player's health to zero when they touch the trap.

In your if-statement, add the following code: humanoid.Health = 0. Hit play and see what happens.

```lua
4   local function onTouch (otherPart)
5       print("trap was touched")
6       local character = otherPart.Parent
7       local humanoid = character:FindFirstChildWhichIsA("Humanoid")
8       if humanoid then
9           --conditional that checks if otherPart is a humanoid character
10          print ("trap was touched by a player")
11          humanoid.Health = 0
12          --kills the character
13      end
14  end
```

Once the Touched event is fired, onTouch will check whether the object that triggered it contains a Humanoid object. If it does, that part's Health property will be set to zero, which kills the player. If it does not, nothing will happen.

EXTRA PRACTICE

Use what you learned in the previous example and try to create a power-up feature. Add the following features:

- Once a certain object is touched, the player's speed increases temporarily.
- The power-up disappears once it's been touched.
- The power-up effect should go away after a few seconds.

MULTIPLE CONDITIONS WITH ELSEIF

An elseif is basically a collection of if-statements grouped together with which you can set out various alternative conditions that can be tested if the first one does not succeed.

```
1    --example elseif that tests a value against multiple options
2    numValue = 3
3
4  ▾ if numValue == 1 then --first condition
5        print("first")
6  ▾ elseif numValue == 2 then --second option
7        print("second")
8  ▾ elseif numValue == 3 then --third option
9        print("third")
10 ▾ elseif numValue == 4 then --fourth condition
11        print("fourth")
12 ▾ elseif numValue == 5 then --fifth condition
13        print("fifth")
14 ▾ else --if none of the conditions were true, do this
15        print("sorry, wrong number")
16   end
17
```

For example, the above code will first test if a number is equal to one. If it's not, it will move on through the list until it gets to the end or finds a match for numValue.

PRACTICAL EXERCISE WITH ELSEIF

To illustrate an elseif properly, let's add a race to the obby. You can create a whole new project if you want or add an additional section into your obby. Alternatively, you can just use the one you already have. I added a short racetrack onto my obby.

Tip: You can group different parts together into a folder by selecting them, right-clicking, and then choosing Group As A Folder. This makes managing and organizing big projects a lot easier.

At minimum, you need a racetrack and a finish line for the player to cross. I use a block with the texture ForceField for my part finishLine; I also disabled its CanCollide so players can run through it. If you aren't building something new, just use the last part in your obstacle course as the finish line.

In short, this racetrack is going to record how long it takes players to reach the finish line and then give them a reward based on that time. Try this on your own first before looking at the example for the answer. The only part of this exercise that involves new elements is the section on measuring time.

If you have no idea how to do this, that's fine. Here's a hint: For the game to time players, it needs a way of knowing when the race ends. The race ends when players cross the finish line. How will the game know when the player crosses the finish line?

Setting Up the Race

Before we begin, let's walk through the logic of what we'll attempt. While the race is active, the game will time the player. The race ends once they cross the finish line. Mine is an object players have to pass through. Alternatively, it might be an object they run across. Either way, the player will eventually touch the object that represents the finish line. That means that we can use a Touched event to judge when the race is over. However, since finishLine is part of a bigger environment, we need to test whether the event was triggered by a player object before ending the race.

Once the race has finished, we need to see how long it took them and then assign a reward based on the amount of time it took to finish the race. To do that, we'll need to find a way to track time while the race is active.

Since this is all dependent on the finishLine, attach a script to whatever object acts as yours. Begin by creating two variables, one to represent the part and one to track time. For now, assign the value zero to the latter.

```
1    local finishLine = script.Parent
2    local timePassed = 0
3    |
```

Code the necessary statements to handle a Touched event. The onTouch event handler will decide when the race will end. Only the touch of a player object should end the race. Use the previous example to construct code that will test if the object that touched the finishLine is a player. Add a suitable display message and test it to see if it works.

```
5   · local function onTouchFinish (otherPart)
6         local character = otherPart.Parent
7         local humanoid = character:FindFirstChildWhichIsA("Humanoid")
8   ·     if humanoid then
9             print("player crossed the finish line")
10        end
11    end
12
```

Create a second function called finish. We're adding a second function to split the workload; the onTouch will determine when the race ends, whereas the finish function will determine what happens once the race is over. For now, cut and paste the print code into the finish function. In its place in onTouchFinish, call finish.

```
5   - local function finish ()
6         print("player crossed the finish line")
7     end
8
9   - local function onTouchFinish (otherPart)
10        local character = otherPart.Parent
11        local humanoid = character:FindFirstChildWhichIsA("Humanoid")
12  -     if humanoid then
13            finish()
14        end
15    end
```

As it is now, once the part is touched, the event will trigger and call the onTouchFinish function. Here, the game will test whether a player has touched the finish line. If it is a player object, the finish function will be called. It, in turn, will print the display message.

If you run the code now, it will successfully recognize a player's touch, but the code will run multiple times as shown in the output.

To fix this, we need to add something extra to the conditional. Try to come up with a solution on your own.

Stopping Repetition

If your answer was debounce, congratulations! You're mostly correct. The solution is to create and use a boolean variable that will deactivate the race after the finish line was touched the first time. This uses the same logic as debounce.

First, create a local variable called raceActive and assign it the value true. Make sure that it isn't declared inside either of the functions. As implied, while the race is active, raceActive is true. Once the race has stopped, raceActive will become false. Add it to the conditional statement. This will make the game check if the race is still active before running finish. Next, add code to the finish function to turn raceActive false.

```
 5   · local function finish ()
 6         print("player crossed the finish line")
 7         raceActive = false
 8    end
 9
10   · local function onTouchFinish (otherPart)
11         local character = otherPart.Parent
12         local humanoid = character:FindFirstChildWhichIsA("Humanoid")
13    ·    if humanoid and raceActive == true then
14             finish()
15         end
16    end
17
```

Now, once the player crosses the finish line, the code will call onTouchFinish. It will check conditions and then call finish, who will then end the race.

Hit play and check to see that the game no longer spams the display message.

Measuring Time

To track the amount of time that's passed, we use a loop. We'll look at loops in the next chapter, so if you have a hard time following this next section, that's okay. The logic in it is pretty simple and works by waiting one second and then increasing a counter. Add the code in the example below to the bottom of your script. This code increases the value of timePassed by one (1) for each second that passes while the race is active. It will keep doing this until raceActive becomes false.

```
19    finishLine.Touched:Connect(onTouchFinish)
20
21  ▾ while raceActive == true do
22        wait (1)
23        --wait 1 second
24        timePassed = timePassed + 1
25        --increase timePassed by 1
26        print(timePassed)
27        --display the value of timePassed to test
28    end
```

The compiler reads and executes code the same way we do, from top to bottom. Our two functions are only executed when the Touched event fires. Touched only fires once the finishLine part has been touched. Until then, raceActive remains true. Neither function will be called until onTouch has been connected to the event. If the loop is above the Touched:Connect code, the computer will begin executing the loop before it makes the connection, meaning the functions can't be called. Since neither finish nor onTouch will get called in that scenario, raceActive will never turn false, meaning the code will keep repeating into infinity. To avoid this, make sure the loop is at the very bottom of the script so that the compiler reads everything else before it begins executing the loop.

Now that we have timePassed working, turn back to the finish function and clean up your code. Replace the test print with a new message. Instead of printing "player crossed the finish line," try crafting a message that tells the player their result. Use an appropriate statement like "player finished in" and add timePassed. To combine two values in print, separate them by a comma (i.e., "player finished in", timePassed), or use the concatenation operator (..). The latter is an operator that combines multiple values into one. Note, however, that it does not automatically add space between the two values like a comma does. In that case, your statement will be: "player finished in " .. timePassed.

Additionally, you can remove the print(timePassed) code from the while loop to make your output cleaner if you want to. An easy way to do this without losing the code is to just place that line in comments.

```
1    local finishLine = script.Parent
2    local timePassed = 0
3    local raceActive = true
4
5  ▾ local function finish ()
6        raceActive = false
7        print("player finished in ".. timePassed)
8    end
9
10 ▾ local function onTouchFinish (otherPart)
11        local character = otherPart.Parent
12        local humanoid = character:FindFirstChildWhichIsA("Humanoid")
13 ▾      if humanoid and raceActive == true then
14            finish()
15        end
16    end
17
18    finishLine.Touched:Connect(onTouchFinish)
19
20 ▾ while raceActive == true do
21        wait (1) --wait 1 second
22        timePassed = timePassed + 1 --increase timePassed by 1
23        print(timePassed) --display the value of timePassed to test
24    end
25
26 ▾ --[[code sourced from
27    https://create.roblox.com/docs/education/coding-3/multiple-conditions
28    retrieved in March 2023]]
29
```

Defining Rewards

Finally, we get to the elseif. The whole point of tracking time is to create a rewards system based on how long it takes players to finish the race. Run your game and see what result you get. For example, it took me 12 seconds to beat mine.

Use this value to determine the minimum requirement for a gold medal. Since you created the course and have, by now, run it a few times, you can safely qualify this as a fast run and measure other results against it. In other words, use it as a guideline for what deserves a gold medal. For example, it took me 12 seconds, so I can set the requirement for gold at 14 seconds. Therefore, my gold medal condition will be timePassed < 14.

This will be the first condition of my elseif. Use your result to create your own gold requirement and then create alternative conditions for silver and bronze. Finally, add a message for if they failed to get either gold, silver, or bronze.

```lua
 5   local function finish ()
 6       raceActive = false
 7       print("player finished in ".. timePassed)
 8
 9       if timePassed < 14 then
10           print("you got gold!")
11       elseif 14 <= timePassed and timePassed <= 18 then
12           print("you got silver!")
13       elseif timePassed > 18 and timePassed < 22 then
14           print("you got bronze!")
15       else print("Try again!")
16       end
17
18   end
19
20   --[[code adapted from
21   https://create.roblox.com/docs/education/coding-3/multiple-conditions
22   retrieved in March 2023]]
```

That's it! Run the game and test all the different rewards to make sure the game works.

LOOPS

WHAT ARE LOOPS?

A loop is a sequence of code that is repeated multiple times. Based on the way it is defined, loops can run a set number of times or until a condition is no longer true. Together with conditionals, loops are known as control structures, and we use them to manage the flow of execution in code. With conditionals, we determine when code should run, whereas loops let us determine how many times it runs.

Loops are a common technique used in most programming languages. You'll also find them in most online exercises and examples. Luckily, they're pretty easy to use once you understand how they work.

Lua has three main loops: for, while, and repeat. Most of what can be done with a repeat loop can also be done with a while loop. Because of this overlap, I will not cover repeat loops in this book and will instead focus on for and while loops.

WHILE LOOPS

While loops run on the basis of a condition. It works a lot like an if-statement, except that it runs more than once. With these loops, we tell the computer to keep repeating code as long as the condition remains true. The loop will only stop running once the condition becomes false.

We don't always know how many times a loop will need to run, and while loops let us base them on a condition. This means that the code will run as many times as it should without needing to know how many times it should happen. Based on the condition, it can run once, multiple times, or not at all.

While loops use the basic structure of "while [condition] do [code] end." Everything between "do" and "end" is considered part of the loop's code block and will be repeated with each iteration of the loop.

The conditions used in while loops are the same as those used in if-statements. For example, debounce == false, or number > 10. Regardless of what the condition is, it will return a true or false value. For the loop to run, the condition needs to be true. If it's false, the loop won't run, even if it returns false on the very first pass.

We can bypass the condition entirely to create a loop that will run independently of any condition. To do that, use "while true do."

```
1    while true do
2      --code
3    end
4
```

Using While to Create Color Loop

Pick any of the parts in your obby and add a script named ColorChange. In it, create a variable to store the reference to the part with script.Parent. This script will use a loop to let the part continually change color every two seconds.

Once you have the variable, type "while true do" and hit enter to autofill the "end." Now, add the code that will change the part's color. If you don't remember how to do this, turn back to Chapter 4, or take a peek at the image below:

```
1   local changePart = script.Parent
2
3 ▾ while true do
4       changePart.Color = Color3.fromRGB(255, 41, 34) --red
5   end
6
```

For the sake of functionality, add a wait between each color change. If there is no pause between the changes, the program will loop through colors faster than we can see. It's generally a good idea to include some kind of pause in loops to avoid overloading the game, especially when it comes to game-changing features like changing colors or disappearing platforms. Computers parse through code a lot faster than we as humans can. As such, it can run through an entire script in a second. Adding wait forces the program to take pauses in loops, which can greatly reduce strain on the system. You can put any value in the brackets, but for this example, it should be higher than one.

```
1   local changePart = script.Parent
2
3 ▾ while true do
4       changePart.Color = Color3.fromRGB(255, 41, 34) --red
5       wait(2)
6   end
7
```

Repeat this for however many colors you want. I want my part to cycle through the rainbow, so I'll have six color changes. Tip: Copy the two lines of code you already have and paste them for each color. You can then simply change the values in brackets.

```
1    local changePart = script.Parent
2
3  - while true do
4        changePart.Color = Color3.fromRGB(255, 41, 34) --red
5        wait(2)
6        changePart.Color = Color3.fromRGB(255, 152, 7) --orange
7        wait(2)
8        changePart.Color = Color3.fromRGB(255, 255, 3) --yellow
9        wait(2)
10       changePart.Color = Color3.fromRGB(6, 255, 0) --green
11       wait(2)
12       changePart.Color = Color3.fromRGB(0, 176, 255) --blue
13       wait(2)
14       changePart.Color = Color3.fromRGB(255, 3, 255) --purple
15       wait(2)
16   end
17
18 - --[[code adapted from
19       https://create.roblox.com/docs/education/coding-4/repeating-code-with-while-loops
20       retrieved in April 2023]]
```

Run the game to test if you can see all the colors you coded. If one gets skipped, check that you have a wait after each of them. If that doesn't fix it, check that the code is between the "do" and "end" of the loop.

FOR LOOPS

While loops work on the basis of a condition and use it to determine whether or not the code should be executed for each iteration. For loops, on the other hand, run a predefined number of times. It uses a control variable, or counter, with a defined starting and end point. The counter is increased with each iteration of the loop until it reaches the defined end point, which terminates the loop.

A for loop consists of three elements: namely, the control variable or counter, end point, and increment value. It is defined using the formula "for [control variable], [end point], [increment value] do." The counter acts as the determiner for the loop; it determines how many times the loop repeats. With each iteration, its value is increased or decreased with the increment value. Once it reaches the end point, the loop stops running. For example:

```
1    ▾ for count = 0, 5, 1 do
2          --count is the counter variable the loop uses to manage iterations
3          --5 is the end value
4          --1 determines how much count increases with each iteration
5          print(count)
6      end
7
8
```

Output

All Messages ⌄   All Contexts ⌄   Filter...

```
0    Server - For loops:5
1    Server - For loops:5
2    Server - For loops:5
3    Server - For loops:5
4    Server - For loops:5
5    Server - For loops:5
```

In this example, count starts with the value zero (0), which is printed in the output. Once the code has been executed, its value is increased with one, as per the increment value. On the next run of the loop, count has the value 1 and is printed as such. After this, it's increased to 2. This keeps repeating until count reaches the value 6. At this point, it has passed the end value (5), and the loop stops running.

In essence, this works the same as the conditions in if-statements and while loops. In this case, it tests whether count is less than the end point. If it is, the code is executed, and the increment value is added to the control variable (count). Each time the loop repeats, it tests count's new value against the end point.

For loops can also count backward if you use a negative value as an increment. For example:

```
1   ▾ for count = 10, 0, -1 do
2           print(count)
3     end
4
5
```

```
Output                                                    ⌄ ⧉ ✕
All Messages  ⌄    All Contexts  ⌄                        Filter...        ✍ ...

first Obby.rbxl auto-recovery file was created    Studio
10  ·  Server - For loops:2
9   ·  Server - For loops:2
8   ·  Server - For loops:2
7   ·  Server - For loops:2
6   ·  Server - For loops:2
5   ·  Server - For loops:2
4   ·  Server - For loops:2
3   ·  Server - For loops:2
2   ·  Server - For loops:2
1   ·  Server - For loops:2
0   ·  Server - For loops:2
```

In this example, the loop counts down from ten to zero. If we add "wait(1)" to this loop, we can turn this into an actual countdown by making it loop once per second.

For loops automatically use an increment of 1 if no other value is defined. As such, you can omit it and use "for count = 0, 10 do" and it will still add one at the end of each iteration.

For Loop Exercises

Code loops for the following exercises:

- Count up from 0 to 20.
- Count in even numbers from 0 to 20.

Do this on your own before looking at the answer below.

```
1     --for loop answers
2
3     --#1
4   ▾ for count = 0, 20, 1 do
5        --code
6     end
7
8     --#2
9   ▾ for count = 0, 20, 2 do
10       --code
11    end
12
13  ▾ --[[examples found on
14       https://create.roblox.com/docs/education/coding-4/intro-to-for-loops
15       retrieved in April 2023]]
```

Troubleshooting

If a for loop doesn't run the way you expect, check the following things. Check that

- the definition values are separated by commas.
- there is an appropriate wait time if the loop runs too fast.
- the starting value is less than the end point if you have a positive increment (e.g., for count = 0, 10, 1), or greater than the end point if you have a negative increment (e.g., for count = 10, 0, -1).

NESTED LOOPS

Loops can be nested, i.e., placed within each other. Each individual loop runs a certain number of times before the computer moves on to the next line of code. If one loop is contained within another, it will run in its entirety with each iteration of the parent loop.

To illustrate, look at the following example:

```
1    --nested loops
2   ▾ for counter = 0, 3, 1 do --loop A
3   ▾     for count = 3, 0, -1 do --loop B
4             print(count)
5         end
6         print("counter =", counter)
7     end
8
```

Output

All Messages ∨   All Contexts ∨   Filter...

```
first Obby.rbxl auto-recovery file was created    Studio
3    Server - Script:4
2    Server - Script:4
1    Server - Script:4
0    Server - Script:4
counter = 0    Server - Script:6
3    Server - Script:4
2    Server - Script:4
1    Server - Script:4
0    Server - Script:4
counter = 1    Server - Script:6
3    Server - Script:4
2    Server - Script:4
1    Server - Script:4
0    Server - Script:4
counter = 2    Server - Script:6
3    Server - Script:4
2    Server - Script:4
1    Server - Script:4
0    Server - Script:4
counter = 3    Server - Script:6
```

As you can see from the output, for each single iteration of loop A, loop B is run fully. Once loop B is finished with all its iterations, the print code in loop A is run, and then it repeats. The entirety of loop B is run for each single iteration of loop A.

Nested loops may seem abstract, but they have many applications. They can be used to repeat functional loops (like countdowns or color changes), create multiple game objects, or control the execution of other loops. Below is an example of a nested loop.

PRACTICAL EXERCISE – GLOWING LIGHTS

In this exercise, we'll create a light source that brightens and dims continually. Try the coding sections on your own before looking at the examples.

To see the light better, let's switch the project to a nighttime environment. In Explorer, find Lighting.

With it selected, turn to Properties, and find ClockTime. Set this to zero to darken the environment.

Properties - Lighting "Lighting"	⌄ ⌐ ×

Filter Properties (Ctrl+Shift+P)

▼ **Appearance**

Ambient	■ [70, 70, 70]
Brightness	3
ColorShift_Bottom	■ [0, 0, 0]
ColorShift_Top	■ [0, 0, 0]
EnvironmentDiffuseS...	1
EnvironmentSpecular...	1
GlobalShadows	☑
OutdoorAmbient	■ [70, 70, 70]
ShadowSoftness	0.2
Technology	ShadowMap

▼ **Data**

Archivable	☑
ClassName	Lighting
ClockTime	0
ClockTime cLatitude	0
Name	Lighting
Parent	first Obby.rbxl
TimeOfDay	00:00:00

▼ **Exposure**

ExposureCompensation	0

▼ **Attributes**

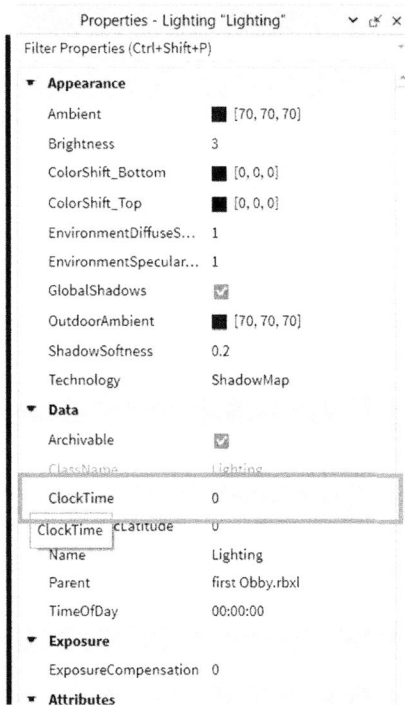

In your obby, add an object that will act as the light source and rename it Lamp. You can choose an ordinary object or find one from the Toolbox. I added a cylinder to the racetrack we made earlier. Once you have the object in a position you like, add a light part to it the same way you would add a script. You can use either PointLight or SpotLight. If you use a Toolbox model, it will likely already have one attached, but double-check.

The PointLight part has a default brightness of 1. To get the effect we want, we're going to cycle this property through different values. The value assigned to its Brightness property will act as the counter of a for loop. It will start at 0 and end at 5.

Attach a script to the Lamp part. In it, create two variables to store references to Lamp and the PointLight.

```
1    local lamp = script.Parent
2    --variable for lamp object
3    local light = lamp.PointLight
4    --variable for PointLight
5
```

Create two more variables. The first, brightnessChange, will store the value with which the lamp's brightness will increase. In this case, its value will be 1. The second variable, timeChange, will indicate how much time passes between each change in brightness. In other words, it will contain the value we'll use in wait statements. The reason we use a variable is to make it easier if we later want to change how much time passes.

```
1    local lamp = script.Parent
2    local light = lamp.PointLight
3    local brightnessChange = 1
4    --variable for how much the brightness changes
5    local timeChange = 1
6    --variable to indicate how much time passes
7
```

Glowing Loop

First, we need to create a loop that will increase the light's brightness. It will start at a brightness of 0 and end with a brightness of 5. To slowly increase it, we use a control variable called currentBrightness.

```
1    local lamp = script.Parent
2    local light = lamp.PointLight
3    local brightnessChange = 1
4    local timeChange = 1
5
6  ▾ for currentBrightness = 0, 5, brightnessChange do
7
8    end
9
```

In it, we set the PointLight's Brightness to currentBrightness's value and add a wait time. The time the program has to wait is the value of timeChange.

```
1    local lamp = script.Parent
2    local light = lamp.PointLight
3    local brightnessChange = 1
4    local timeChange = 1
5
6  ▾ for currentBrightness = 0, 5, brightnessChange do
7        light.Brightness = currentBrightness
8        wait(timeChange)
9    end
10
```

Run your game to see if the light increases in brightness.

Fading Loop

Next, we code the loop that will decrease the lamp's brightness back to 0. This loop works exactly the same as the glowing loop, only in reverse. Since we are using variables as values, you can simply copy the code for the previous loop, paste it, and change the defining values. This loop counts backward from 5 to 0, which means the control value and end value need to be adjusted. We can change the positive value of brightnessChange by putting a dash (-) in front of it to make it a negative number.

```
6     --to increase brightness
7   ▾ for currentBrightness = 0, 5, brightnessChange do
8         light.Brightness = currentBrightness
9         wait(timeChange)
10    end
11
12    --to decrease brightness
13  ▾ for currentBrightness = 5, 0, -brightnessChange do
14        light.Brightness = currentBrightness
15        wait(timeChange)
16    end
17
```

Simple as that. Run it to check that the light increases and then decreases.

Making the Loops Repeat

Finally, we need to write code to repeat these two loops continuously. Take a moment to try and find the solution on your own. Ask yourself how you can make a loop repeat itself. When you think you have the answer, look at the example below.

```
1     local lamp = script.Parent
2     local light = lamp.PointLight
3     local brightnessChange = 1
4     local timeChange = 1
5
6   ▾ while true do
7         --to increase brightness
8     ▾     for currentBrightness = 0, 5, brightnessChange do
9             light.Brightness = currentBrightness
10            wait(timeChange)
11        end --of first for
12
13        --to decrease brightness
14    ▾     for currentBrightness = 5, 0, -brightnessChange do
15            light.Brightness = currentBrightness
16            wait(timeChange)
17        end --of second for
18
19    end --of while
20
21  ▾ --[[code sourced from
22        https://create.roblox.com/docs/education/coding-4/glow-lights-with-for-loops
23        retrieved in April 2023]]
```

The answer is to place both loops in a while loop. On their own, each loop will run once. The first one will run until the brightness reaches 5 and then the second one will run until it's back to 0. By placing them in a while loop, we can make the program cycle through both loops repeatedly.

Run the game to test it. If it doesn't work as expected, check that both for loops are contained between the while loop's "do" and "end." You can also check that the code for each for loop is contained within their respective blocks. It sometimes helps to add a comment after each end to indicate which block it belongs to—like I did above.

This script is duplicable, so you can attach it to any object with a light source. This means you can run multiple lights on the same cycle. The code will also work for other light-giving objects like glowing crystals or celestial bodies. Because we're using variables for brightnessChange and timeChange, you can easily adjust the script to suit any circumstances by simply changing their values.

PRACTICAL EXERCISE – TIMED BRIDGE

For this exercise, we're going to use the script we already have for the button-activated bridge we made in Chapter 5. We are going to add the humanoid test to it and then set it on a timer. Once the button is pressed, it will activate a countdown. While the countdown is active, the bridge will be solid, and players can run across it. After the time has run out, the bridge should return to being transparent and impassable.

Before we get to that, add a new object to the obby to act as a display for the timer. Move and scale it into a position where players can see it as they approach and cross the bridge. Once you have it, add a SurfaceGui, and then attach a TextLabel to it.

These two items will let us display text on the block. Players can't access the output window and, as such, can't see any messages displayed there. Thus, we need to display things we want players to see in some other way.

If you can't immediately see the TextLabel on the block, don't panic. They start out pretty small and don't always attach where you expect them to. Select the SurfaceGui and find its Face property.

Properties - Surf...eGui "SurfaceGui" ∨ ⌖ ×

Filter Properties (Ctrl+Shift+P)

- ▼ **Appearance**
  - ZOffset   0
- ▼ **Data**
  - Archivable ☑
  - ▶ AbsolutePosition   0, 0
  - AbsoluteRotation   0
  - ▶ AbsoluteSize   500, 400
  - Active ☑
  - Adornee
  - AlwaysOnTop ☐
  - ClassName   SurfaceGui
  - Enabled ☑
  - Face   Top
  - LightInfluence   1
  - Name   SurfaceGui
  - Parent   timeDisplay
  - ResetOnSpawn ☑
  - ToolPunchThro...   0
  - ZIndexBehavior   Sibling
- ▼ **Behavior**
  - ClipsDescendants ☑
- ▼ **Localization**
  - AutoLocalize ☑

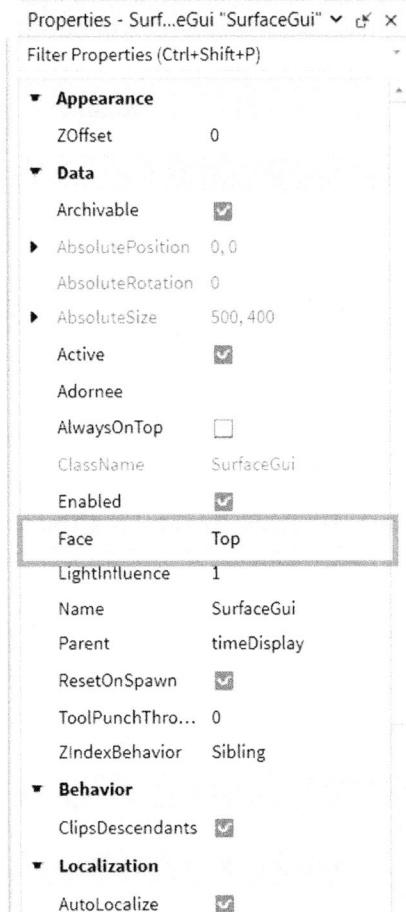

Changing this affects where the TextLabel is placed on the block. I had to move it to Top, but yours might be different depending on how it's been moved. Once you have it on the right face, it'll look like this:

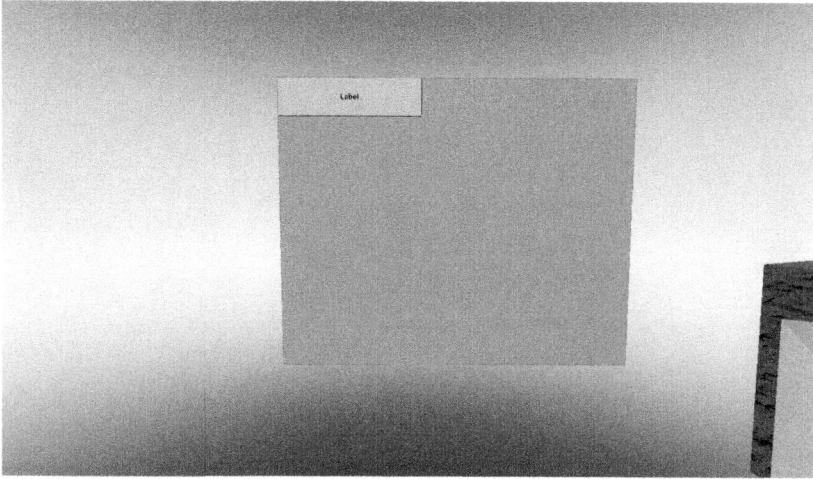

Now we have to resize it. Select TextLabel in Explorer and go to its Size property. Under it, there are two subproperties, X and Y. For both, set their Scale to 1 and Offset to 0. This centers the text on the block. Next, scroll down to TextScaled. Enable this to automatically scale the text to the size of the block. Finally, find Text and delete what's in it.

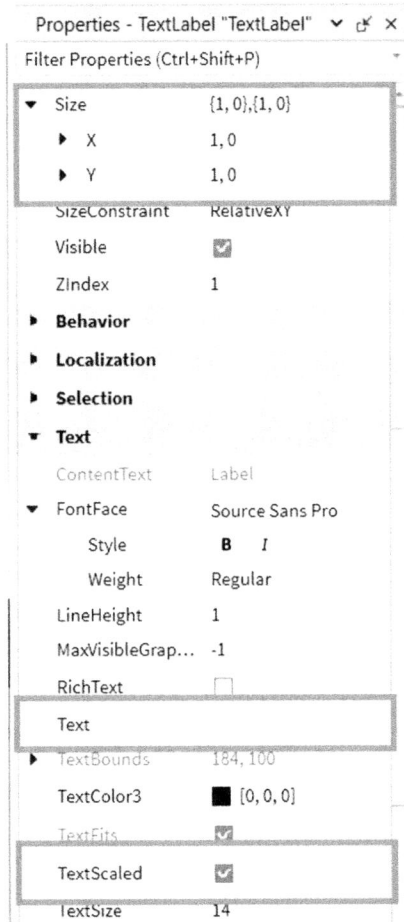

Changing the Script

Since we already have code managing the button's Touched event, we'll simply add onto it. You can, of course, start over from scratch if you want to. This is where we left off in this script:

```lua
1    local button = script.Parent
2    local bridge = game.Workspace.Bridge.bridge
3    local debounce = false
4
5  - local function onButtonPress ()
6  ▾     if debounce == false then
7            debounce = true
8            button.Color = Color3.fromRGB(0, 255, 0)
9            bridge.Transparency = 0
10           bridge.CanCollide = true
11           print("button pressed, bridge available")
12        end
13    end
14
15    button.Touched:Connect(onButtonPress)
16
```

What we need to do is

1. create variables to reference the block's textlabel and the maximum timer value (this will determine how long the bridge stays up).
2. include a humanoid condition to test for players touching the button.
3. create a new function called startTimer and move the code from the onButtonPress if-statement to it. In the if-statement, call startTimer.
4. use a loop to create a timer that counts down from the maximum timer value to 0.
5. create code that reverts the bridge to impassable once the time runs out.

These are all things you've done before. Try doing them yourself before looking at the answer. Below, I'll walk you through the code and the steps involved.

First, create a variable for the display text, called timerText. To display the countdown, we need to change the Text property of the TextLabel. To access this property, we'll have to use the TextLabel's whole path. While we're up here, let's also create the variable to store how long the bridge will stay traversable. My bridge is pretty

short, so 5 seconds will be enough time to cross it. Thus, timerDuration = 5.

```
1    local button = script.Parent
2    local bridge = game.Workspace.Bridge.bridge
3    local timerText = game.Workspace.Bridge.timeDisplay.SurfaceGui.TextLabel
4    local timerDuration = 5
5    local debounce = false
6
```

Second, we need to add code to make the button test whether a
player touched it. Simply add the variables for character and
humanoid to the existing function and add the condition to the if-
statement. I also added otherPart as a parameter since we reference it for the character variable's initialization.

```
6
7    local function onButtonPress (otherPart)
8        local character = otherPart.Parent
9        local humanoid = character:FindFirstChildWhichIsA("Humanoid")
10
11       if humanoid and debounce == false then
12           debounce = true
13           button.Color = Color3.fromRGB(0, 255, 0)
14           bridge.Transparency = 0
15           bridge.CanCollide = true
16           print("button pressed, bridge available")
17       end
18   end
19
```

Third, create a new function called startTimer. Cut the code from
the if-statement in onButtonPress and paste it into startTimer.
Call this new function in the if-statement.

```
6
7   ▾ local function startTimer ()
8         debounce = true
9         button.Color = Color3.fromRGB(0, 255, 0)
10        bridge.Transparency = 0
11        bridge.CanCollide = true
12        print("button pressed, bridge available")
13    end
14
15  ▾ local function onButtonPress (otherPart)
16        local character = otherPart.Parent
17        local humanoid = character:FindFirstChildWhichIsA("Humanoid")
18
19  ▾     if humanoid and debounce == false then
20            startTimer()
21        end
22    end
23
24    button.Touched:Connect(onButtonPress)
25
```

Play the game to test that the bridge button still works.

Create a Timer

This timer will manage how long the bridge is open. While the timer is active, the player can walk across the bridge. Once the time runs out, the bridge becomes impassable again. To do this, we need a for loop that will count down from timerDuration to zero. If you haven't yet created the loop on your own, try. In the loop block, change the TextLabel's Text property to reflect the value of the counter used in the loop. Add a wait(1) to make the loop run once per second.

```
7   ▾ local function startTimer ()
8         debounce = true
9         button.Color = Color3.fromRGB(0, 255, 0)
10        bridge.Transparency = 0
11        bridge.CanCollide = true
12        print("button pressed, bridge available")
13
14  ▾     for count = timerDuration, 0, -1 do
15            timerText.Text = count
16            wait(1)
17        end
18    end
```

Run your game to check that the bridge is only solid while the timer is running. If it isn't, check that all the code is where it should be, that everything is spelled correctly, and that the parts are assigned to the correct variables.

ARRAYS AND DICTIONARIES

W e've covered tables a little in a previous chapter. Tables are collections of related data gathered in one object. Unlike regular variables, they do not just store a single value. Instead, they contain multiple values, each with its own unique identifier.

In Lua, there are two types of tables: namely, arrays and dictionaries.

ARRAYS

Arrays are a common feature of most programming languages. They also have tons of applications; people use them in data management, game development, general-purpose programming, system engineering, and more. They're a very common programming technique and being able to work with them is a useful skill.

An array is declared with a name like any other code object. It can also be given local scope or left as global. Its values are listed in curly brackets (i.e., {...}) and separated by commas. For example:

```
local testArray = {"one", "two", "three", "four", "five"}
```

Arrays are tables that store ordered lists. Values are listed in a specific order and given a corresponding numerical index number based on the order in which they are listed. The first entry is stored at index 1, the second at index 2, and so on. Above, value "one" is linked to 1, "two" to 2, "three" to 3, and so on. Unlike many other languages, indexes in Lua start at 1 and not 0 (zero).

Lua arrays don't have a fixed length. Length refers to the number of elements contained in an array, elements meaning the items contained within it. In Lua, length is determined automatically by the number of elements. If you add or remove items, the length is adjusted. This means that arrays can grow and shrink as needed. If an array has no items, it is given the value nil.

To access specific values in an array, you need to reference the name of the array, and then the index number of the value you're looking for. The index is always placed in square brackets (i.e., [...]). For example, testArray[2].

To access elements of the array, we use a for loop to cycle through all the available indexes. The control variable represents the value of the index. For example, if I wanted to print all elements of test-Array, I'd use the following code:

```
1    local testArray = {"one", "two", "three", "four", "five"}
2
3  ▾ for k = 1, 5, 1 do
4        print(testArray[k])
5    end
6
7
```

```
Output                                          ⌄ ⊡ ×
All Messages ⌄    5 Contexts ⌄              Filter...         ⚲ ...
one   -  Server - Arrays:5
two   -  Server - Arrays:5
three    Server - Arrays:5
four  -  Server - Arrays:5
five  -  Server - Arrays:5
```

You'll notice that I use the variable k as a control. This is mostly for the sake of habit and convenience. It's common to use variable names like k or i for counters since they're unspecific and unlikely to be used in any other circumstances. Since I always use k for array loops, I won't ever name any other variable k and can thus immediately tell what this loop is for.

In this example, I use 5 as the end value. Since you won't always know the length of the array, it's better to use #arrayName instead. Coding "for k = 1, #testArray, 1 do" will have the same result but makes provision for if the array grows or shrinks.

```
1    local testArray = {"one", "two", "three", "four", "five"}
2
3  · for k = 1, #testArray, 1 do
4        print(testArray[k])
5    end
6
```

Output

All Messages ⌄   All Contexts ⌄   Filter...

first Obby.rbxl auto-recovery file was created - Studio
one   - Server - Arrays:4
two   - Server - Arrays:4
three - Server - Arrays:4
four - Server - Arrays:4
five - Server - Arrays:4

PRACTICAL EXERCISE USING ARRAYS

In your obby, create a segmented path consisting of multiple blocks. Use at least three parts and line them up to create a path. These parts will disappear separately one after the other and then reappear. First, create a folder called disappearingPath. In it, create a script and then another folder named Parts. The subfolder will contain the various parts that form the path.

Next, create the individual parts. I'd recommend making one, transforming it into what you want, and then duplicating it for the others. Rename them something like pathPart1, pathPart2, and pathPart3. Make sure that they are in the Parts folder.

Now create variables in the script to reference these folders.

```
1    local path = script.Parent
2    local partsFolder = path.Parts
3
```

Define an array and reference each of the path parts in it. Place each item on a separate line to make it easier to read and remember to separate them with commas. Your path can include as many parts as you want, just make sure to reference each part in the array. If, for example, you have five path parts, you need five array elements.

```
3
4  • local partsArray = {
5        partsFolder.pathPart1,
6        partsFolder.pathPart2,
7        partsFolder.pathPart3
8    }
9
```

To run through the different parts and make them disappear, we use a loop. This will let us make them disappear one at a time with a pause in between. First, set up the loop to run from 1 to #parts-Array. Next, declare a variable outside the loop to represent how long the game should pause between each disappearance. For testing purposes, make this time short, one or two seconds. You can change this later to give players enough time to cross the path.

In the loop, add code to make the game wait. This should be the first line of the loop since we want to delay the disappearance of the first block.

```
 9
10    local disappearTime = 2
11
12  ▾ for k = 1, #partsArray, 1 do
13        wait(disappearTime)
14    end
15
16
```

Next, we want a variable to contain a reference to the part we're managing. Create a local variable called whichPart in the loop and assign it the value partsArray[k]. In this case, k represents the index value of each array element.

```
 9
10    local disappearTime = 2
11
12  ▾ for k = 1, #partsArray, 1 do
13        wait(disappearTime)
14        local whichPart = partsArray[k]
15    end
16
```

We'll use whichPart to access each part's properties. Do you remember how we made the button-activated bridge vanish? Use that example to write the code to make whichPart disappear. If you can't remember, turn back to the bridge examples from Chapter 5 or Chapter 7. Finally, add a suitable display message to test the loop.

```
11
12  ▾ for k = 1, #partsArray, 1 do
13        wait(disappearTime)
14        local whichPart = partsArray[k]
15        whichPart.CanCollide = false
16        whichPart.Transparency = 1
17        print("Part #", k, "has disappeared")
18    end
19
```

Run the game and check that the parts vanish one after the other. It takes time to load into the game, and by the time you spawn in, the path could already be gone. If this happens, increase the value of disappearTime.

If it doesn't work, check that you reference the correct parts in the array, that values in it are separated by commas, and that you have the correct values in the for loop declaration.

As is, the parts only disappear once at the start of the game and then they remain gone, meaning players can't get across at all. To fix this, let's add another loop to make them reappear. To do this, copy the existing loop and paste it below the first. Leave the loop declaration as is and change the whichPart properties to make the objects visible again. You can choose to leave the wait period to make them reappear in sequence or remove it to make them reappear all at once. If you remove the wait from the second loop, add a wait between the loops to create a delay between the last disappearance and the path's reappearance.

```
21    wait(disappearTime)
22
23  ▾ for k = 1, #partsArray, 1 do
24        local whichPart = partsArray[k]
25        whichPart.CanCollide = true
26        whichPart.Transparency = 0
27        print("Part #", k, "has reappeared")
28    end
29
```

Finally, place both loops in a while loop. Without the while loop, the parts will disappear and then reappear permanently. For it to be a continuous cycle, the loops should repeat. Run the game and test that it works. Once it does, you can remove the print code since we only use it to test that the loops work as intended.

```
1    local path = script.Parent
2    local partsFolder = path.Parts
3
4  - local partsArray = {
5        partsFolder.pathPart1,
6        partsFolder.pathPart2,
7        partsFolder.pathPart3
8    }
9
10   local disappearTime = 2
11
12 - while true do
13 •     for k = 1, #partsArray, 1 do --disappear loop
14            wait(disappearTime)
15            local whichPart = partsArray[k]
16            whichPart.CanCollide = false
17            whichPart.Transparency = 1
18        end
19
20        wait(disappearTime)
21
22 •     for k = 1, #partsArray, 1 do --reappear loop
23            local whichPart = partsArray[k]
24            whichPart.CanCollide = true
25            whichPart.Transparency = 0
26        end
27    end
28    --[[code adapted from https://create.roblox.com/docs/education/coding-5/loops-and-arrays
29       retrieved in April 2023]]
```

MODIFYING ARRAYS

Arrays aren't static; their values can still change after they've been declared. You can change the values assigned to elements, add new entries, and remove existing items. These are useful tricks to know since we often use arrays for inventory systems and when managing player data.

Adding Elements

The simplest way to add new entries is to add another line in the array declaration. Since this isn't always possible, you can also use code outside the definition. To do this, use "table.insert(...)." This function takes two parameters, the name of the array and then the value you want to assign to it. This will assign that value to the next available index number.

```
1     local modifyArray = { }
2
3     table.insert(modifyArray, "one")
4     table.insert(modifyArray, "two")
5     table.insert(modifyArray, "three")
6
7   ▾ for k = 1, #modifyArray,1 do
8         print(modifyArray[k])
9     end
10
```

Output

All Messages ▾   5 Contexts ▾   Filter...

one	Server • Arrays 2:8
two	Server • Arrays 2:8
three	Server • Arrays 2:8

Above, I declared an empty array and then used table.insert to add three new elements. As you can see, this array displays exactly the same as the other example despite it being initialized differently. You can also use this to add onto arrays with preexisting values.

```
1     local modifyArray = {"one", "two", "three"}
2
3     table.insert(modifyArray, "four")
4     table.insert(modifyArray, "five")
5     table.insert(modifyArray, "six")
6
7   ▾ for k = 1, #modifyArray,1 do
8         print(modifyArray[k])
9     end
10
```

Output

All Messages ▾   5 Contexts ▾   Filter...

one	Server • Arrays 2:8
two	Server • Arrays 2:8
three	Server • Arrays 2:8
four	Server • Arrays 2:8
five	Server • Arrays 2:8
six	Server • Arrays 2:8

Remove Elements

There's also a function to remove items. For this, use table.remove to delete the last entry in an array. Unlike its counterpart, it only takes the array name as a parameter, i.e., table.remove(modify-Array). Let's add this to modifyArray.

```lua
1    local modifyArray = {"one", "two", "three"}
2
3    table.insert(modifyArray, "four")
4    table.insert(modifyArray, "five")
5    table.insert(modifyArray, "six")
6
7    table.remove(modifyArray)
8
9  ▾ for k = 1, #modifyArray, 1 do
10       print(modifyArray[k])
11   end
12
```

Output

All Messages ∨   5 Contexts ∨   Filter...

```
one      Server - Arrays 2:10
two      Server - Arrays 2:10
three    Server - Arrays 2:10
four     Server - Arrays 2:10
five     Server - Arrays 2:10
```

As you can see, the last element we inserted was removed and is thus missing from the output.

You can also remove items per their index by adding them as a second parameter. If I wanted to remove the third element from modifyArray, I would use table.remove(modifyArray, 3).

```lua
1    local modifyArray = {"one", "two", "three"}
2
3    table.insert(modifyArray, "four")
4    table.insert(modifyArray, "five")
5    table.insert(modifyArray, "six")
6
7    table.remove(modifyArray, 3)
8
9  ▾ for k = 1, #modifyArray, 1 do
10       print(modifyArray[k])
11   end
12
```

Output

All Messages ∨   5 Contexts ∨   Filter...

```
one      Server - Arrays 2:10
two      Server - Arrays 2:10
four     Server - Arrays 2:10
five     Server - Arrays 2:10
six      Server - Arrays 2:10
```

Note that this affects the index numbers of the rest of the array. Arrays are ordered lists, and indexes follow an ordinal pattern. If I display the array with its indexes, you'll see that modifyArray[3] now has the value "four" instead of "three" as it was defined.

```
1    local modifyArray = {"one", "two", "three"}
2
3    table.insert(modifyArray, "four")
4    table.insert(modifyArray, "five")
5    table.insert(modifyArray, "six")
6
7    table.remove(modifyArray, 3)
8
9  ▾ for k = 1, #modifyArray, 1 do
10       print(k, modifyArray[k])
11   end
12
```

Output

All Messages ⌄   5 Contexts ⌄   Filter...

```
1 one    Server - Arrays 2:10
2 two    Server - Arrays 2:10
3 four   Server - Arrays 2:10
4 five   Server - Arrays 2:10
5 six    Server - Arrays 2:10
```

Searching for a Value

You can also search through the elements of an array to find a specific element. We can use a for loop to cycle through the indexes and a conditional to test each value against what we're looking for. Create a function with the name of the array and value you're searching for as parameters. In it, create the for loop.

```
1    local searchArray = {"one", "two", "three", "four", "five", "six"}
2
3  ▾ local function findValue(arrayName, searchValue)
4  ▾     for k = 1, #arrayName, 1 do
5
6          end
7    end
8
```

Here, searchValue contains the value we're looking for, and each array value should be compared to it via a conditional. In this case, the condition will be "if searchArray[k] == searchValue." If the condition succeeds (i.e., the values match), the function returns the index number of the element.

```
1    local searchArray = {"one", "two", "three", "four", "five", "six"}
2
3  ▾ local function findValue(arrayName, searchValue)
4  ▾     for k = 1, #arrayName, 1 do
5  ▾         if arrayName[k] == searchValue then
6              return k
7          end --of if
8      end --of for
9    end --of function
10
```

To test the function, create a variable called valueFound. For its initialization, call the function and give it the necessary arguments. Then, print valueFound with an appropriate message.

```
1   local searchArray = {"one", "two", "three", "four", "five", "six"}
2
3 ▾ local function findValue(arrayName, searchValue)
4 ▾     for k = 1, #arrayName, 1 do
5 ▾         if arrayName[k] == searchValue then
6               return k
7           end --of if
8       end --of for
9   end --of function
10
11  local valueFound = findValue(searchArray, "two")
12
13  print("value found at index", valueFound)
14
```

Output   ∨ ⅆ ×
All Messages ∨   5 Contexts ∨   Filter...   ⋀
▌ value found at index 2   · Server · Arrays 2:13

The reason why we might search an array is to find specific elements so that we can use, display, or remove them. For example, let's remove the value we found. Above, the function searched for "two" and found it at index 2. To remove it, use the valueFound variable as a parameter in table.remove.

```
1   local searchArray = {"one", "two", "three", "four", "five", "six"}
2
3 ▾ local function findValue(arrayName, searchValue)
4 ▾     for k = 1, #arrayName, 1 do
5 ▾         if arrayName[k] == searchValue then
6               return k
7           end --of if
8       end --of for
9   end --of function
10
11  local valueFound = findValue(searchArray, "two")
12
13  print("value found at index", valueFound)
14
15  table.remove(searchArray, valueFound)
16
17 ▾ for k = 1, #searchArray, 1 do
18      print(searchArray[k])
19  end
20
```

Output   ∨ ⅆ ×
All Messages ∨   5 Contexts ∨   Filter...   ⋀
▌ value found at index 2   · Server · Arrays 2:13
▌ one   · Server · Arrays 2:18
▌ three · Server · Arrays 2:18
▌ four   · Server · Arrays 2:18
▌ five   · Server · Arrays 2:18
▌ six   · Server · Arrays 2:18

Simplify the code by moving the remove statement inside the loop and deleting valueFound. This makes code more effective since it will remove all elements with that value and not just the first one it finds.

```
1    local searchArray = {"one", "two", "three", "four", "five", "two", "six"}
2
3  ▾ for k = 1, #searchArray, 1 do
4  ▾     if searchArray[k] == "two" then
5            print("value found at index", k)
6            table.remove(searchArray, k)
7        end --of if
8    end --of for
9
10 ▾ for k = 1, #searchArray, 1 do
11        print(searchArray[k])
12    end
13
14 ▾ --[[code adapted from
15        https://create.roblox.com/docs/education/coding-5/making-changes-to-arrays
16        retrieved in April 2023]]
```

Output

All Messages ∨   5 Contexts ∨   Filter...

```
value found at index 2    Server · Arrays 2:5
value found at index 5    Server · Arrays 2:5
one      Server · Arrays 2:11
three    Server · Arrays 2:11
four     Server · Arrays 2:11
five     Server · Arrays 2:11
six      Server · Arrays 2:11
```

Above, I added an additional element with the value "two" into the array, and the function removed both instances.

Arrays aren't always as simple as this in practice. These examples use simplified objects to illustrate the basics. However, the logic remains the same regardless of how complex the array or project is. Keep this in mind for when your projects start growing in complexity.

EXTRA PRACTICE

For some extra practice, create an NPC and post them somewhere in your obby. When you make them (or choose them from the Toolbox) make sure they have a ClickDetector child.

This NPC will react to player clicks with dialogue. The dialogue it responds with will be stored in an array called dialogueArray. To make the NPC speak, use the Chat method stored in the Chat service. If you call this method, it will ask you for two parameters. The first will refer to the object that speaks, and the second will refer to what it says. Use a combination of functions, variables, and array management to set up an array that contains a few different sentences the NPC can cycle through.

The answer is below but try this on your own first.

```
1    local Chat = game:GetService("Chat")
2
3    local npc = script.Parent
4    local characterParts = npc.CharacterParts
5    local head = characterParts.Head
6    local clickDetector = npc.ClickDetector
7
8    --Add table below
9    local dialogueArray= {"Hi!", "Do I know you?", "How are you?"}
10   local arrayIndex = 2 --value of index number
11
12  ▾ local function speak()
13       local dialogue = dialogueArray[arrayIndex]
14       Chat:Chat(head, dialogue)
15       arrayIndex = arrayIndex + 1
16   end
17
18   clickDetector.MouseClick:Connect(speak)
19
20   --[[code sourced form https://create.roblox.com/docs/education/coding-5/intro-to-
     arrays#creating-the-talking-character
21      retrieved in April 2023]]
```

DICTIONARIES

The second type of table you'll encounter is a dictionary. Dictionaries are similar to arrays in that they store multiple values within one object. However, here, values are stored in relation to a key instead of a sequential index number. Where arrays act as ordered lists, dictionaries label values.

Each entry has a key and assigned value. The key acts similar to indexes in that it differentiate values from other entries. The difference is that keys aren't limited to sequential numbers. While you can add keys of various data types, it's better to stick to one. This makes dictionaries easier to manage and manipulate. Each key needs to be unique so it can act as an identifier. In other words, you cannot have two keys with the same name in the same dictionary.

Where arrays can be used to store and manipulate ordered lists, dictionaries are better suited to more complex structures like inventory systems or item stats.

Dictionaries are defined the same way arrays are, with a name, "=" and curly brackets. Each entry is placed on a new line with the formula key = value. Each item is separated by a comma. For example:

```
1    ▾ local cutlass = {
2         name = "Cutlass",
3         description = "A pirate's weapon",
4         atk = 17,
5         def = 3,
6         spd = 2,
7         critDamage = 0.1
8      }
9
```

In this example, the dictionary contains data related to a weapon. To use any of these values, we need to call the item by the name of the dictionary and the key; e.g., cutlass["atk"].

```
1    ▾ local cutlass = {
2         name = "Cutlass",
3         description = "A pirate's weapon",
4         atk = 17,
5         def = 3,
6         spd = 2,
7         critDamage = 0.1
8      }
9
10     print(cutlass["atk"])
11
```

Output

All Messages ⌄   5 Contexts ⌄   Filter...

▌ 17   ⌄   Server ▸ Dictionaries:10

Modifying Dictionaries

You can modify a dictionary by referencing the table and key and then assigning a new value to it. This overrides the previous value. For example:

```
1   - local cutlass = {
2         name = "Cutlass",
3         description = "A pirate's weapon",
4         atk = 17,
5         def = 3,
6         spd = 2,
7         critDamage = 0.1
8   }
9
10   cutlass["atk"] = 25
11
12   print(cutlass["atk"])
13
```

Output ⌄ ⟲ ×

All Messages ⌄   5 Contexts ⌄   Filter...

▌ 25   Server - Dictionaries:12

To create a new entry, simply reference a new key, and then assign it a value. For example:

```
1   - local cutlass = {
2         name = "Cutlass",
3         description = "A pirate's weapon",
4         atk = 17,
5         def = 3,
6         spd = 2,
7         critDamage = 0.1
8   }
9
10   cutlass["critRate"] = 0.5
11
12   - for key, value in pairs(cutlass) do
13         print (key, "=", value)
14   end
```

Output ⌄ ⟲ ×

All Messages ⌄   5 Contexts ⌄   description = A pirate's weapon   Filter...

▌ description = A pirate's weapon   Server - Dictionaries:13
  name = Cutlass   Server - Dictionaries:13
  def = 3   Server - Dictionaries:13
  critRate = 0.5   Server - Dictionaries:13
  spd = 2   Server - Dictionaries:13
  atk = 17   Server - Dictionaries:13
  critDamage = 0.1   Server - Dictionaries:13

Here you can see that I added a new item called critRate. When the dictionary is displayed, you can see that the new item is included. If you're wondering about the loop I used to display it, we generally use a function called pairs to manipulate dictionaries. Unlike arrays, dictionaries don't have sequential keys we can use as a counter. Instead, we use pairs to loop through each key-value pair contained in the table.

Removing items from a dictionary is as simple as adding them. Simply change the value of the item you want to remove to nil. For example, if I change cutlass["description"] to have the value nil, it will be removed from the dictionary.

```
1  - local cutlass = {
2        name = "Cutlass",
3        description = "A pirate's weapon",
4        atk = 17,
5        def = 3,
6        spd = 2,
7        critDamage = 0.1
8  }
9
10    cutlass["description"] = nil
11
12 - for key, value in pairs(cutlass) do
13        print (key, "=", value)
14    end
```

Output

All Messages   5 Contexts

```
name = Cutlass      Server - Dictionaries:13
def = 3             Server - Dictionaries:13
spd = 2             Server - Dictionaries:13
atk = 17            Server - Dictionaries:13
critDamage = 0.1    Server - Dictionaries:13
```

Dictionaries and Other Variables

You can use preexisting variables to supply data to a table. Say you want to use the value of a predefined variable as the key in a dictionary. Think, for example, of scenarios where you want to use the name of a player or value that will be calculated in a function. In that case, you can use the variable as the key. Instead of the key being the name of the variable, it will instead be its value. For example:

```
1  - local cutlass = {
2        name = "Cutlass",
3        description = "A pirate's weapon",
4        atk = 17,
5        def = 3,
6        spd = 2,
7        critDamage = 0.1,
8  }
9
10    local newKey = "critRate" --variable containing the new key
11    cutlass[newKey] = 0.5 --new entry using the variable
12
13 - for key, value in pairs(cutlass) do
14        print (key, "=", value)
15    end
```

Output

All Messages   5 Contexts

```
description = A pirate's weapon   Server - Dictionaries:14
name = Cutlass      Server - Dictionaries:14
def = 3             Server - Dictionaries:14
critRate = 0.5      Server - Dictionaries:14
spd = 2             Server - Dictionaries:14
atk = 17            Server - Dictionaries:14
critDamage = 0.1    Server - Dictionaries:14
```

In this example, you can see that I use newKey to create a key called "critRate." When the table is displayed, it displays "critRate" and not newKey.

This example is somewhat abstract since this isn't really a situation in which you would use a variable. However, you can use the same logic to reference things like players' names retrieved from events or objects instanced through code.

PAIRS AND IPAIRS

Pairs and ipairs are built-in functions you can use to work with dictionaries and arrays when you want to manipulate their data. Both are used with a for loop. In this case, the for loop does not use a control, end value, or increment. Instead, it uses the key or index and their corresponding values along with the table name.

Pairs and Dictionaries

When working with dictionaries, we use the function pairs. This lets us access table keys and their corresponding values without needing to specify which entry we're working with. It basically lets us work with each entry as a pair. Pairs is used with the following code: for key, value in pairs(dictionaryName) do. For example, in "atk = 17," atk is the key, and 17 is the value. This is then stored in the key and value variables to be used however needed.

To illustrate, let's create a quick script that organizes players into a dictionary based on assigned colors. Use any colors or names to create a few entries. Then use a for loop and pairs to display both the name and color.

```lua
1  - local players = {
2       blue = "Tommy",
3       red = "Mark",
4       green = "John",
5       purple = "June",
6       yellow = "Mary"
7  }
8
9  - for key, value in pairs(players) do
10      print(value, "is", key)
11  end
12
```

```
                                            Output                                    ∨ ⊘ ×
   All Messages  ∨    All Contexts  ∨                              Filter...              ⚲  ⋯

   first Obby.rbxl auto-recovery file was created      Studio
 | Tommy is blue    ·   Server · pairs:10
 | John is green    ·   Server · pairs:10
 | Mary is yellow   ·   Server · pairs:10
 | June is purple   ·   Server · pairs:10
 | Mark is red      ·   Server · pairs:10
```

Note that you don't have to use "key" and "value" with this loop.
You can give them any name you want, like assignedColor and
playerName. These are just temporary variables that store the keys
and values of each item in the dictionary. The code "for color,
name in pairs(players) do" will work just as well as the above
example.

Ipairs and Arrays

When working with arrays, there are two ways you can go about
it. You can use a control variable that represents the index number,
or you can use ipairs. Ipairs lets us link the value to the index
number and work with them as a pair. You use it with a for loop
and declare it with the code "for index, value in ipairs(arrayName)
do."

This is a great alternative to normal for loops for cases where the
item value should be tied to the index. If, for example, your array
represents a leaderboard, the index values have meaning beyond
just indicating the location of the value. In that case, the value of
the index number has a meaning.

For example, let's assume the following array contains the names
of players sorted by their highest score. Index 1 represents the
player with the highest score while index 5 contains the name of

the one with the lowest score. Placed in an ipairs loop, we can individually reference both values independently to create a display message.

```
1   - local leaderboard = {
2         "Ali",
3         "May",
4         "Cammy",
5         "Ben",
6         "Alex"
7     }
8
9   - for rank, name in ipairs(leaderboard) do
10        print("#"..rank.." is ".. name)
11    end
12
13  - --[[code adpated from
14       https://create.roblox.com/docs/education/coding-5/pairs-and-ipairs
15       retrieved in April 2023]]
```

```
Output                                                    v d x
All Messages  v   5 Contexts  v                Filter...
#1 is Ali   - Server - ipairs:10
#2 is May   - Server - ipairs:10
#3 is Cammy   Server - ipairs:10
#4 is Ben   - Server - ipairs:10
#5 is Alex   Server - ipairs:10
```

Like above, the names you use to represent the index and value don't matter. You can use specific descriptors like above or general words like index and value.

PRACTICAL EXERCISE

Let's combine arrays and dictionaries into one exercise. Here, we are going to create a simplified soup simulator. The game will have a dictionary that stores potential ingredients. The player will select a few, and those will be added into a soup. The soup will be represented by an array that will store the chosen ingredients. Finally, we will display the soup to the player using the array.

For now, we are only going to make the code for this simulator without creating the game itself. As always, try this on your own first before looking at the walkthrough of the answer below. Here is a list of the things you'll need to do:

- Create an ingredients dictionary. The key for each item is the name of the ingredient, and the value represents whether it is added to the soup. All items should start off as false. They become true once they've been chosen by a player.
- Make a loop to search through the items to find any with the value true. The ones that are true should be added into an array.
- Find a way to test whether the array has any elements. If it does, display those elements as the chosen ingredients; if it doesn't, display an appropriate message.

First, create a dictionary of ingredients. This dictionary acts as a menu from which players can choose. Add as many items as you want but try to add at least five. The name of the ingredient is the key, and all the values are false. You can also create an empty array called inSoup.

```
1   - local ingredients = {
2         potato = false,
3         tomato = false,
4         kale = false,
5         chicken = false,
6         rice = false,
7         beef = false,
8         beans = false,
9         peas = false,
10    }
11
12    local inSoup = {}
13
```

Second, code a loop that will cycle through all these items. I use the variables menuChoice and value to contain the key and value of each item. In this loop, set up a conditional that will test whether any of the values are true. You can use the condition "if value then" to do this. Any item with the value false will fail this condition. Create code to sort the items that succeed into the inSoup array using table.insert.

```
 1   local ingredients = {
 2       potato = false,
 3       tomato = false,
 4       kale = false,
 5       chicken = false,
 6       rice = false,
 7       beef = false,
 8       beans = false,
 9       peas = false,
10   }
11
12   local inSoup = {}
13
14   for menuChoice, value in pairs(ingredients) do
15       if value then
16           table.insert(inSoup, menuChoice)
17       end
18   end
```

This code will test the value of each item and then store the key to the array. For example, if tomato was chosen and thus true, it would pass the conditional. Only "tomato" will be inserted into the array.

Thirdly, we need to code appropriate responses. If this was an actual game, it would need to know if any ingredients were chosen to determine how to react. If something is chosen, the game has to respond by making soup with the chosen ingredients. If nothing was chosen, there shouldn't be any soup.

In our case, if items were selected, they will be displayed in the output. If nothing was chosen, an alternative message should be displayed instead. To test if ingredients were selected, we have to see whether the array has any entries. Remember, items will only be added to the array if they are true. If none are, the array will be empty. So how do we test this? With an if-statement to test whether the array's length is more than zero with "if #array > 0 then."

```
14    for menuChoice, value in pairs(ingredients) do
15        if value then
16            table.insert(inSoup, menuChoice)
17        end
18    end
19
20
21    if #inSoup > 0 then
22        print("Your soup contains:")
23        for itemNumber, chosen in ipairs(inSoup) do
24            print(chosen)
25        end
26    else print("Nothing was chosen, aren't you hungry?")
27    end
28
29    --[[code adapted from
30        https://create.roblox.com/docs/education/coding-5/pairs-and-ipairs
31        retrieved in April 2023]]
32
```

To test whether the code works, make one or two of the ingredients true and hit play. If it works, those ingredients will be displayed.

For example, here's what happens when I run it with all ingredients false:

```
1    local ingredients = {
2        potato = false,
3        tomato = false,
4        kale = false,
5        chicken = false,
6        rice = false,
7        beef = false,
8        beans = false,
9        peas = false
10   }
11
```

Output

All Messages   5 Contexts   Filter...

Nothing was chosen, aren't you hungry?   Server - Soup simulator:26

Here's what happens if some are true:

```
1   · local ingredients = {
2        potato = false,
3        tomato = true,
4        kale = false,
5        chicken = true,
6        rice = false,
7        beef = true,
8        beans = true,
9        peas = false
10   }
11
```

```
                                            Output                                              ⌄  ⌐  ×
All Messages  ⌄    All Contexts  ⌄                               Filter...                        ⌷  ···
   first Obby.rbxl auto-recovery file was created     Studio
 │ Your soup contains:       Server · Soup simulator:22
 │ chicken      Server · Soup simulator:24
 │ beef      Server · Soup simulator:24
 │ beans      Server · Soup simulator:24
 │ tomato      Server · Soup simulator:24
```

Don't worry if the items don't print in the same order they're listed in the table. While arrays are handled sequentially, dictionaries aren't. This means that items aren't handled in the order you might expect.

If your code doesn't work, check that all the names were typed correctly in the loop and conditional, that lines of code are where they should be, and that the final if-statement comes after the for loop.

Additional Challenges

If you want to get more out of this exercise, try making this into an actual game by adding the following features:

- Create visual items for each ingredient and use their Touched to turn the values true.
- Add an NPC or display object that will show the output message to a player.
- Turn the game around entirely and add dictionaries that store specific recipes. Use the code logic to make the

player the chef who has to choose ingredients based on those recipes.

NEXT UP

Now that we've covered the basics of coding, we're going to put it into practice. In the next two chapters, you're going to build two different experiences: an adventure game and a battle royale. These two games will reinforce different coding concepts as well as teach you different techniques to build game environments.

BUILD AN ADVENTURE GAME

PROJECT PLANNING

P lanning is the first and most important step of any project. This is called pre-production and involves creating a game design document where you explore your ideas in more detail. This document doesn't have to be long and complicated, and you can do it in a Word editor or on a piece of paper.

This document should contain the following:

- the concept of the game
- what players will do when playing
- the game loop
- basic mechanics
- description of the setting (the world the game takes place in)
- a rough sketch of the map and environment
- any items or tools added to the game
- possible upgrades for equipment.

This game is an adventure game. Its objective is to make players explore a world to find specific objects. It features a fairly simple game loop or premise: Players explore, harvest items, sell them, and upgrade their gear. Then, they can return to exploring.

In this project, we'll

- make a map.
- code a leaderboard.
- create items to harvest and a tool to use.
- provide a selling feature.
- create an upgrade system.

CREATE A MAP

Make a rough sketch of the map. Plan where players will spawn, where items can be harvested and sold, and an upgrade station. You can also map out environment details like trees, water, mountains, and paths. Once you have that, create a new Roblox project with the Flat Terrain template.

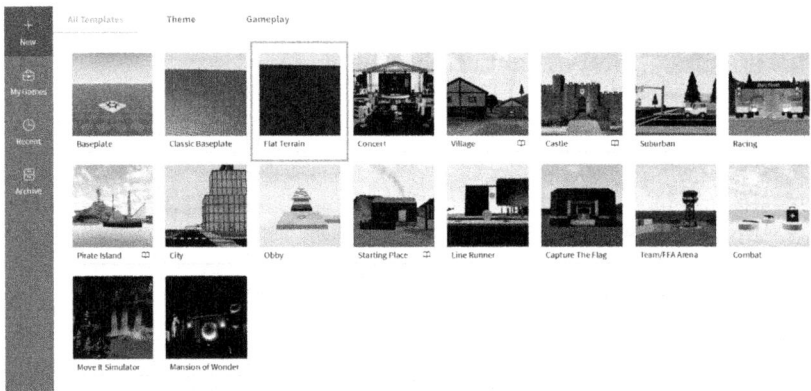

For this project, we are going to create the world from scratch using the Terrain Editor. Once you have the project ready, open the Terrain Editor and click on Edit. There you'll see these tools:

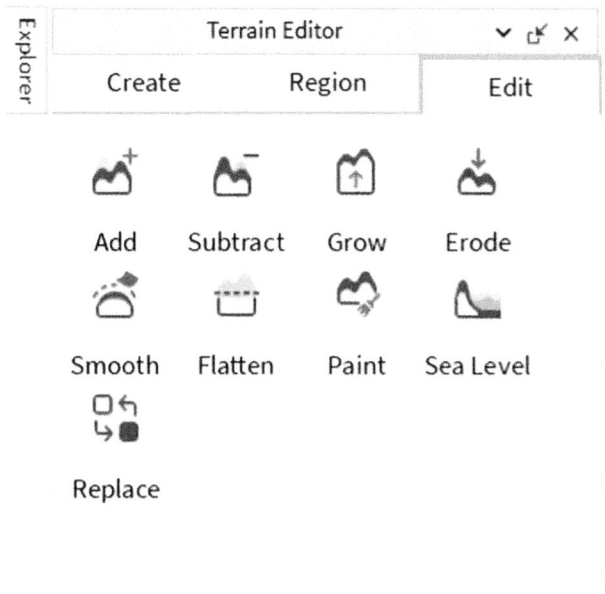

First, use Paint to create the basic layout of your map. Keep your planning sketch nearby for reference. Experiment with different areas, materials, and brushes. Remember to save regularly and view your project from different angles.

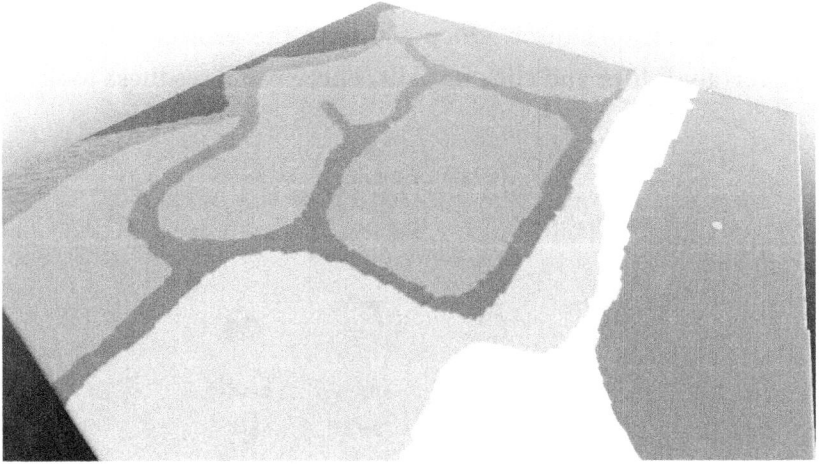

Next, use the other tools to add variety to the environment. Add lets you build onto the terrain to create mountains and hills. Subtract lets you cut out sections of the terrain to create valleys and dips. Other tools like Smooth and Flatten can help you refine these shapes while Grow and Erode can help you add more dimension. Take this opportunity to play around with the Terrain Editor. See what you can accomplish and build. Add mountains, dig trenches for rivers, erode areas to create bumpier terrain, etc.

To illustrate, I added some mountains and a river to the project.

You can go ahead and add a SpawnLocation. Don't worry about adding any other decorations or items just yet.

CODE A LEADERBOARD

Roblox automatically creates a leaderboard in every experience. At default, it only displays the names of the players who join. Since this is an automatic feature, we can use it to also display player stats. We do this first to make playtesting other game mechanics easier.

Create a script in ServerScriptService and name it PlayerSetup. Here, we'll instance a folder that will be attached to each player and then store three variables in that folder to represent three stats. We'll use the PlayerAdded event to do this.

In the script, create a function to connect to the event. It will take the parameter player. In it, create a variable called leaderstats. Its value is an instance of the type "Folder." Use the properties .Name and .Parent to give it the name "leaderstats" and set its parent as player. It's important that its name be "leaderstats" since this will let us use it for the leaderboard.

```
1  ‣ local function onPlayerJoin(player)
2        local leaderstats = Instance.new("Folder")
3        leaderstats.Name = "leaderstats"
4        leaderstats.Parent = player
5    end
6
```

Our leaderboard will track three stats:

- Gold: represents how much money the player has available
- Items: how many items are in their possession
- Spaces: the amount of inventory space they have

Each of these variables will be instances of the type "IntValue." IntValues are just number variables, but this method lets us attach them to each player as an object.

Declare a new variable called "gold" in the function and initialize it with Instance.new("IntValue"). Change its .Name to "Gold." To give it a value, use its .Value property and set it to 0. Finally, make it a child of the leaderstats folder.

```
6
7        local gold = Instance.new("IntValue")
8        gold.Name = "Gold"
9        gold.Value = 0
10       gold.Parent = leaderstats
11       --adding a Gold section to the leaderboard
12   end
13
```

Do the same thing for the other two variables (items and spaces). Copy and paste this code, and change the values as needed. For spaces, assign the value 2.

```lua
1   - local function onPlayerJoin(player)
2        local leaderstats = Instance.new("Folder")
3        leaderstats.Name = "leaderstats"
4        leaderstats.Parent = player
5        --adding the player to the leaderboard
6
7        --adding sections into the leaderboard to display Gold, Items, and Spaces
8        local gold = Instance.new("IntValue")
9        gold.Name = "Gold"
10       gold.Value = 0
11       gold.Parent = leaderstats
12
13       local items = Instance.new("IntValue")
14       items.Name = "Items"
15       items.Value = 0
16       items.Parent = leaderstats
17
18       local spaces = Instance.new("IntValue")
19       spaces.Name = "Spaces"
20       spaces.Value = 2
21       spaces.Parent = leaderstats
22   end
```

Run the game to check that you can see these stats on the leaderboard.

While the game is running, take a look at the Explorer. If you open Players, you'll see that the leaderstats folder and variables have been attached to your character.

▶ 🌐 Workspace
▼ 👥 Players
  ▼ 👤
    ▼ 🗂 leaderstats
        # Gold
        # Items
        # Spaces
    ▶ 🎒 Backpack
      ◇ StarterGear
    ▶ ◇ PlayerGui
    ▶ ◇ PlayerScripts
▶ 💡 Lighting
  🛠 MaterialService
▶ 📡 NetworkClient

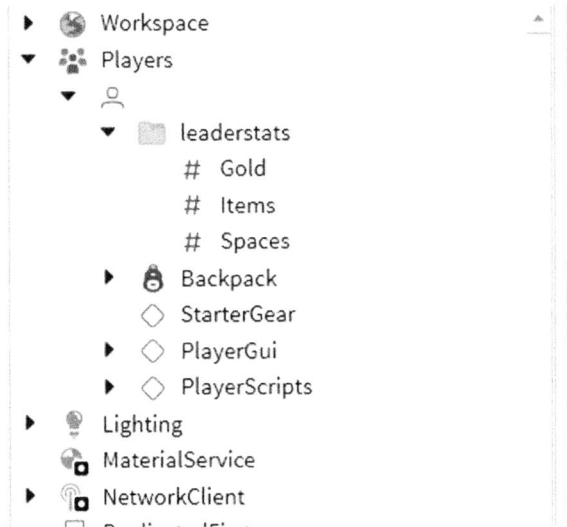

MAKING ITEMS TO HARVEST

Harvesting items is the first part of the game loop and will be one of the first things players do. Thus, they need something to harvest.

You can build something from scratch by using parts and then grouping them together as a model. Alternatively, use the Toolbox to find something instead. I chose @ropeccool's Pink Crystal. You can add this directly from the Toolbox or go to create.roblox.com and click on Marketplace. Search for the item you want and Click Get Model.

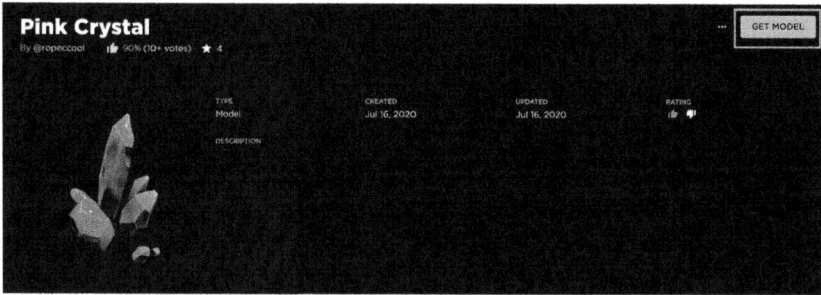

Items added through the Marketplace will be added to your Toolbox inventory.

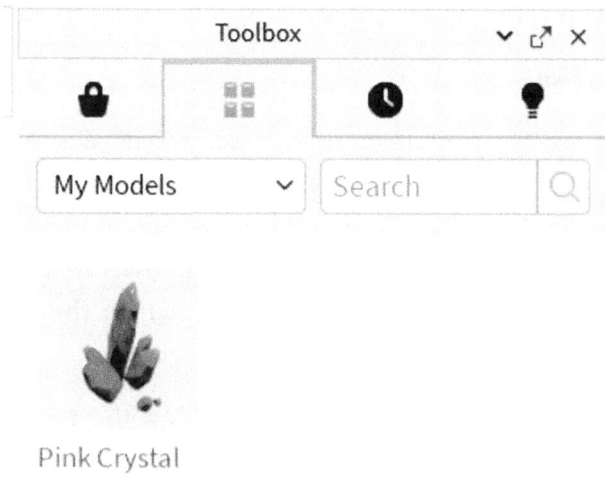

Add one to your experience and place it close to your spawn. Attach a BoolValue object and rename it canHarvest. Don't add multiple items just yet. It's easier to work with one until it's functional and then add more from there.

Select canHarvest and find its Value property. Make sure it's enabled. This is the equivalent of giving it the value true in code.

Creating a Tool

Now that we have an item to harvest, we need something to harvest it with. Go over to the Toolbox or Marketplace and look for a tool that matches your item. Look for models that have animations. I chose @gorosae's StarterTool. Insert it and drag it to the StarterPack. This will automatically include the tool into a player's backpack when they join the experience.

To test, run the game and see if you spawn in with a tool item.

CODING HARVEST MECHANICS

The logic is simple; to harvest an item, players need to touch it with the tool. Once the tool makes contact, the code should

- check whether the item is harvestable, and that the player has space.
- increase the Items stat.
- temporarily make the item disappear from the environment.

Tip: Most models have a Handle child or some other basepart to which a mesh is attached. For our code to work, your script needs to be attached to this part. We need a Touched event to harvest the item, but models don't have Collision properties and thus no Touched events. To remedy this, we need a basepart object like Handle through which to access Touched.

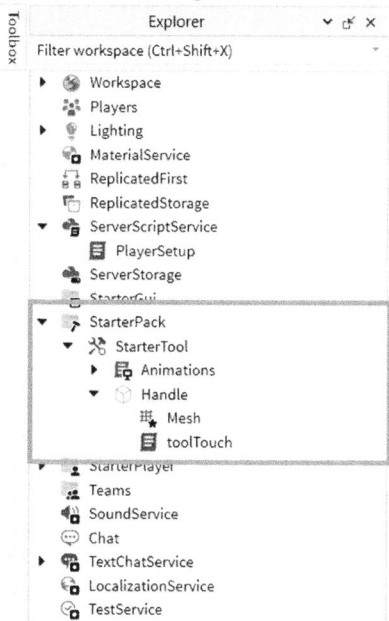

Try to code the mechanics I listed above on your own before looking at the example.

Touched Event

First, create a script and attach it to the Handle object. Then, create a variable to reference that handle as the tool. Code an onTouch function and connect it to the tool's Touched event.

```
1    local tool = script.Parent
2
3  ▾ local function onTouch(otherPart)
4
5    end
6
7    tool.Touched:Connect(onTouch)
8
```

To determine whether otherPart is a harvestable item, we test if it has a child called "canHarvest." In this case, we use FindFirstChild instead of FindFirstChildWhichIsA. The difference between these two functions lies in what they search for. The first searches for something with the name supplied as an argument. The latter searches by type. If we wanted to use FindFirstChildWhichIsA in this context, we would need to search for "BoolValue" instead of "canHarvest."

```
1    local tool = script.Parent
2
3  ▾ local function onTouch(otherPart)
4        local canHarvest = otherPart:FindFirstChild("canHarvest")
5  ▾     if canHarvest then
6            print("part was touched")
7        end
8    end
9
```

Run the game and try to harvest your item. Check that you see the print message.

Note: The if-statement will check whether canHarvest is present in otherPart; it does not test its value.

Next, we need to test whether the player has enough space for the item. Before we can do that, we need to access the player's stats. Create variables to reference the tool model, backpack (in which the tool is stored during gameplay), and finally the player themself.

```
1    local tool = script.Parent --the tool part handle
2    local toolitem = tool.Parent --the tool model
3    local backpack = toolitem.Parent --the backpack
4    local player = backpack.Parent --the player character
5
```

This might seem excessive, but it's necessary. The leaderstats folder is only created when a player joins the game, and to get to it, we need to first get to the player character.

Create three variables to reference the leaderstats folder and the items and spaces stats. Use FindFirstChild for all three.

```
5
6    local playerStats = player:FindFirstChild("leaderstats")
7    local items = playerStats:FindFirstChild("Items")
8    local spaces = playerStats:FindFirstChild("Spaces")
9
```

We want code that will check whether the player has enough space for a new item. One way of doing that is to check whether items' value is less than spaces' value with the condition items.Value < spaces.Value. We also need to check whether canHarvest is true by testing its .Value. Both these comparisons need to occur simultaneously in an if-statement.

In the if-statement, add code that will increase items by one.

```
9
10   local function onTouch(otherPart)
11       local canHarvest = otherPart:FindFirstChild("canHarvest")
12       if canHarvest then
13           if canHarvest.Value == true and items.Value < spaces.Value then
14               print("part was touched")
15               items.Value = items.Value + 1
16           end
17       end
18   end
19
```

Run the game. Check to see that you can successfully touch the item and that your Items stat increases. If the code doesn't work, check that you reference all the names correctly and that you have .Value added for canHarvest, items, and spaces.

Making the Item Disappear

Once an item has been harvested, it should vanish temporarily. For this, its Transparency, CanCollide, and canHarvest should change to make it invisible and unharvestable. Add a wait time, and then reverse the changes to make it harvestable again.

```
9
10    local function onTouch(otherPart)
11        local canHarvest = otherPart:FindFirstChild("canHarvest")
12        if canHarvest then
13            if canHarvest.Value == true and items.Value < spaces.Value then
14                print("part was touched")
15                items.Value = items.Value + 1
16
17                --making the item disappear
18                canHarvest.Value = false
19                otherPart.Transparency = 1
20                otherPart.CanCollide = false
21                wait(5)
22
23                --making it reappear
24                canHarvest.Value = true
25                otherPart.Transparency = 0
26                otherPart.CanCollide = true
27            end
28        end
29    end
30
31    tool.Touched:Connect(onTouch)
32
33    --[[code adapted from
34        https://create.roblox.com/docs/education/adventure-game-series/collect-items
35        retrieved in April 2023]]
36
```

Run the game and test that the item disappears after being touched and then reappears after some time.

SELLING ITEMS

The second part of the game loop is selling the items that have been harvested. Create a space where your player can sell their items. Make something that fits your environment. For convenience, place it close to the SpawnLocation and item you created. I use a basic block with a SurfaceLight and TextLabel to act as a selling platform.

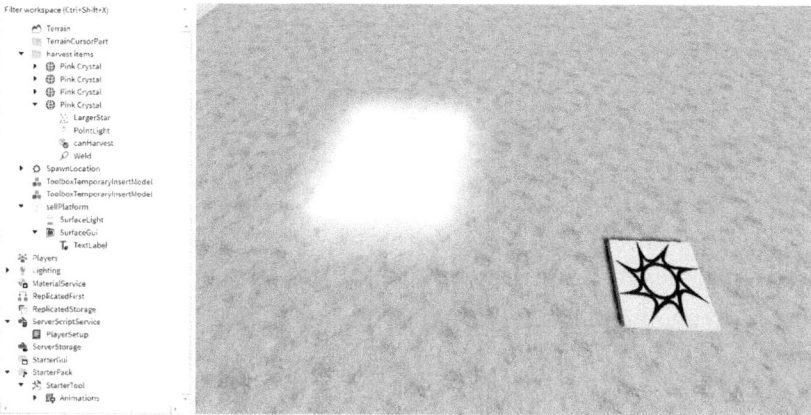

Attach a script to it and rename it accordingly. The platform should decrease Items to zero and increase Gold once the player steps on it. Go ahead and set up the Touched event and event handler and code a humanoid test and conditional.

```
1    local platform = script.Parent
2
3    local function onTouch(otherPart)
4        local character = otherPart.Parent
5        local humanoid = character:FindFirstChildWhichIsA("Humanoid")
6        if humanoid then
7
8        end
9    end
10
11   platform.Touched:Connect(onTouch)
12
```

Once again, to access the player stats, we need to get the player character. This time, we'll use game.Players:GetPlayerFromCharacter(humanoid.Parent). The Humanoid object is added into the player character found in Workspace. The leaderstats folder, on the other hand, is added to the character object in Players. This function lets us access the Players object that corresponds to the one Humanoid is attached to.

```
1    local platform = script.Parent
2
3  • local function onTouch(otherPart)
4        local character = otherPart.Parent
5        local humanoid = character:FindFirstChildWhichIsA("Humanoid")
6  •     if humanoid then
7            local player = game.Players:GetPlayerFromCharacter(humanoid.Parent)
8        end
9    end
10
```

Add variables for the leaderstats folder, Items, and Gold, and include a print code to test the function.

```
1    local platform = script.Parent
2
3  • local function onTouch(otherPart)
4        local character = otherPart.Parent
5        local humanoid = character:FindFirstChildWhichIsA("Humanoid")
6  •     if humanoid then
7            local player = game.Players:GetPlayerFromCharacter(humanoid.Parent)
8            -- get player stats
9            local playerStats = player:FindFirstChild("leaderstats")
10           local items = playerStats:FindFirstChild("Items")
11           local gold = playerStats:FindFirstChild("Gold")
12           print("player touched platform")
13       end
14   end
```

Selling Mechanics

Create a second function that will process the sale. It should take gold and items as parameters.

Decide what your items should sell for. For example, one crystal is worth 100 gold. In your function, create a variable called totalSum. This variable will contain the number of items multiplied by the selling price.

```
2
3  • local function sellItems(items, gold)
4        local totalSum = items.Value * 100
5    end
```

To check that the math works, add a print to display the value of totalSum. Next, add this sum to the player's gold and decrease the value of items to zero. Once that's done, call the sellItems function from the onTouch.

```lua
1    local platform = script.Parent
2
3    local function sellItems(items, gold)
4        local totalSum = items.Value * 100
5        print(totalSum)
6        gold.Value = gold.Value + totalSum
7        items.Value = 0
8    end
9
10   local function onTouch(otherPart)
11       local character = otherPart.Parent
12       local humanoid = character:FindFirstChildWhichIsA("Humanoid")
13       if humanoid then
14           local player = game.Players:GetPlayerFromCharacter(humanoid.Parent)
15           --get player stats
16           local playerStats = player:FindFirstChild("leaderstats")
17           local items = playerStats:FindFirstChild("Items")
18           local gold = playerStats:FindFirstChild("Gold")
19           print("player touched platform")
20           sellItems(items, gold)
21       end
22   end
23
24   platform.Touched:Connect(onTouch)
25
26   --[[code sourced from
27       https://create.roblox.com/docs/education/adventure-game-series/selling-items
28       retrieved in April 2023]]
```

Run the game. Check that once you touch the platform, the items and gold stats change correctly.

BUYING UPGRADES

Use the same steps to create an option to upgrade the number of spaces a player has. First, create the part through which the player will access an upgrade. In this case, I use a block with a display label. Then, add a clickDetector. With it, we'll use a different event; instead of using part.Touched, we can use clickDetector.Mouse-Click. This event works the exact same way as Touched, except that we don't need to test for humanoid with it.

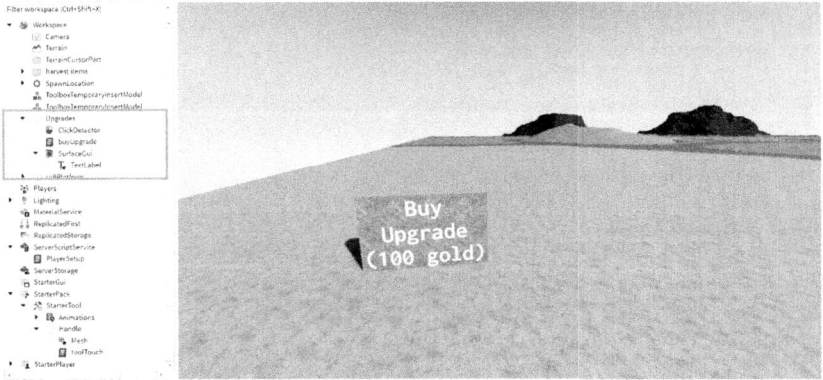

I want you to code this section on your own. The process is the same as above, with some minor changes. Once the player clicks the upgrade, their gold will decrease, and their spaces will increase. Try on your own before looking at the answer.

```
1   local button = script.Parent
2   local clickDeterctor = button.ClickDetector
3   local newSpaces = 5
4   local upgradeCost = 100
5
6   local function onClick (player)
7       print("someone clicked the button")
8
9       --get player stats
10      local playerStats = player:FindFirstChild("leaderstats")
11      local gold = playerStats:FindFirstChild("Gold")
12      local spaces = playerStats:FindFirstChild("Spaces")
13
14      if gold.Value >= upgradeCost then
15          gold.Value = gold.Value - upgradeCost
16          spaces.Value = newSpaces
17      end
18  end
19
20  clickDeterctor.MouseClick:Connect(onClick)
21
22  --[[code sourced from
23      https://create.roblox.com/docs/education/adventure-game-series/buying-upgrades
24      retrieved in April 2023]]
```

FINAL TOUCHES

Once the game mechanics are up and running, you can add some final touches. When coding, we used relatively small values for things like wait times, upgrade costs, and inventory space. This made it easier to test the game but isn't suitable for actual gameplay. Go through the code and adjust these values to something more appropriate. Keep testing the game as you adjust these values to make sure they still work and that changes don't affect functionality.

Move the sell and upgrade objects to their proper positions and begin adding more harvestables. Duplicate the item you already have and move them into position. Then, take the time to flesh out your terrain more and turn it into a world players want to explore. Make sure that your items are accessible to players and that they won't struggle too much to reach them.

While you do this, consider what would be enjoyable for a player. Remember to test the game periodically. It's difficult to judge scale and distance when designing the environment, and sometimes you just need to play it and see things for yourself. Once you think the game is ready, ask someone else to play it as a final test before publishing it if you want to.

CREATE A BATTLE ROYALE

A battle royale is a multiplayer game where different players face off against each other to see who remains as the last one standing. They're typically fighting games but can also be any game where the goal is to eliminate other players.

PROJECT PLANNING

Before we start the project, we need to plan it out. This game has a lot of features and is more complex than the adventure game from the previous chapter. In it, we'll

- manage players.
- set up timers and events.
- create a user interface.
- define the start and end of matches.
- handle the aftermath of each round.

For it, you'll need to create two areas: one for the lobby and one for the arena. Take the time to sketch out a plan for both.

The lobby is going to be pretty simple. All you need is a walled-off space with a spawn location and whatever decorations you want to add.

For the arena, your plan should include multiple spawn points, obstacles, and walls to create enclosed spaces, and varying levels of playable space. Use basic shapes to get an idea of the layout you want. Think about where and how your players would move during a match. If you're stuck, try to imagine a fun place to hold a fight and then go from there.

The way this game will work is that players spawn into the lobby when they first join. Once there are enough players, they will be transported to an arena and a timer will start. Once a player dies, they will be transported to the lobby. The match will end when only one player remains, or the time runs out. Finally, the game resets and runs cleanup, which usually involves transporting any remaining players to the lobby, finding winners, and resetting the arena for the next match. A GUI will keep players informed of the time on the clock, the number of players remaining, and the status of the game.

CREATE THE MAP

Once you have planning sketches ready, create a new Baseplate project in Roblox Studio. Our two areas will essentially be two separate, floating rooms. We don't need a baseplate, so go ahead and remove it from the Workspace if you want to. Of course, you can also leave it in while building and then remove it later if you want to.

For the lobby, use base parts to create a walled-off space with a floor. Tip: To make the process easier, go to the Model tab and find the Snap to Grid sections. There, you'll be able to specify how the parts move when you transform them. Objects move according to studs, and you can change exactly how many studs they should move along. You can also change the angle of rotation here for more precise orientations.

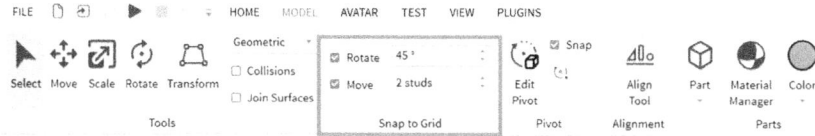

You can also go to View and enable the Show Grid option. These will help you align your objects more easily to each other.

When you add parts, group them together using models and folders. At the end of the day, all parts that are used in the lobby should be in a separate folder from the rest of the Workspace.

Here is my lobby:

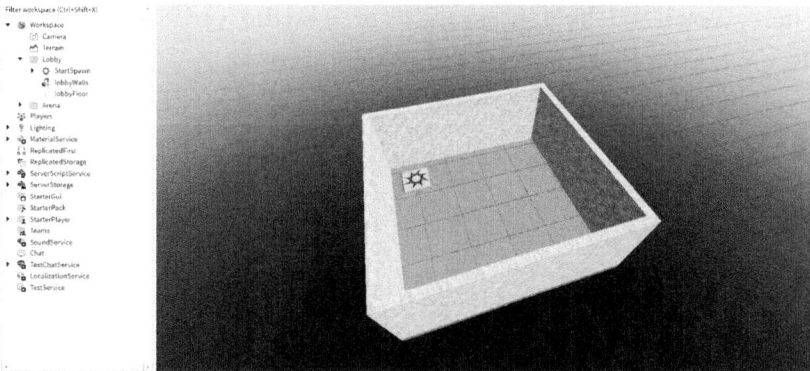

Building the arena won't be as simple. Create a new folder in your workspace. As you did for the lobby, create a room that will contain the match. We're going to use a technique called gradoxing where we use simple shapes to create the basic structure of the room you envisioned. Go to the Toolbox and click on the filter options.

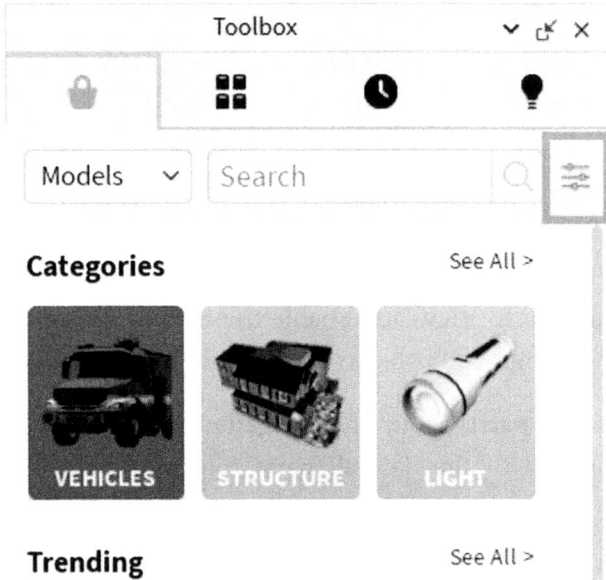

There, you'll be able to search for specific creators. Type in "Roblox_Educators" and select this one:

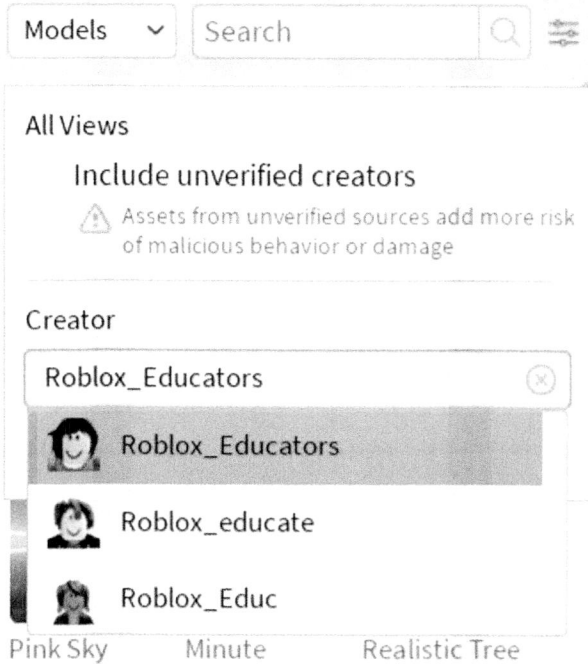

Hit apply. If you don't see their models show up, redo the search but select the "Include unverified creators" option. Roblox_Educators has a basic graybox assets kit that's freely available for your use.

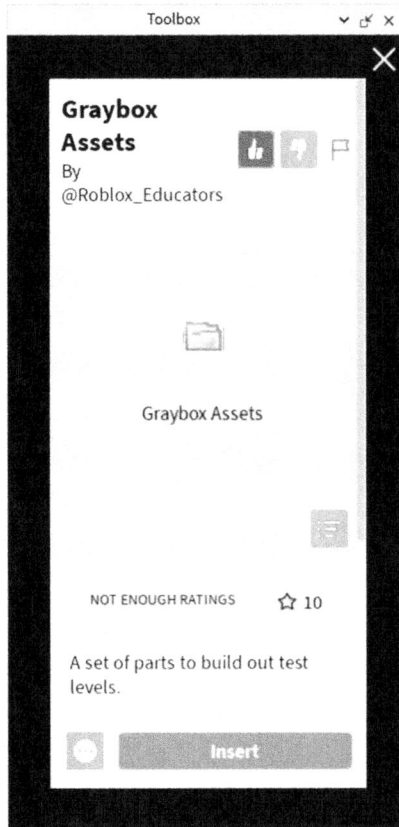

Click Insert and the entire kit will be added into your workspace. Use the shapes as you want and delete the ones you don't want to use. If you want multiple copies of one, simply duplicate it. Remember to move the assets into your arena folder. You can also use regular base parts if you want to.

Take the time to flesh out your arena. Use different shapes, sizes, and heights to add variety to the space. Include things like ramps, stairs, ladders, and various platforms to create a dimensional environment. Find places for multiple spawn locations. Matches will consist of multiple players, so consider how many participants you want in each round. If you want eight players, add eight spawn locations.

Try to keep your Workspace organized. Keep the spawn locations in one folder, related parts in another, and so on. If you have multiple parts that make up a single unit, group them together as a model. This will also help you scale and position them more accurately.

It's difficult to judge scale without playing in the environment, so make sure to regularly run the game and test the features you're adding. Make sure you can get around objects, reach the ones you want to jump on, and fit onto ramps. Once you're satisfied with the layout of the arena, run it a final time, and run through it like you would if you were a player in a match.

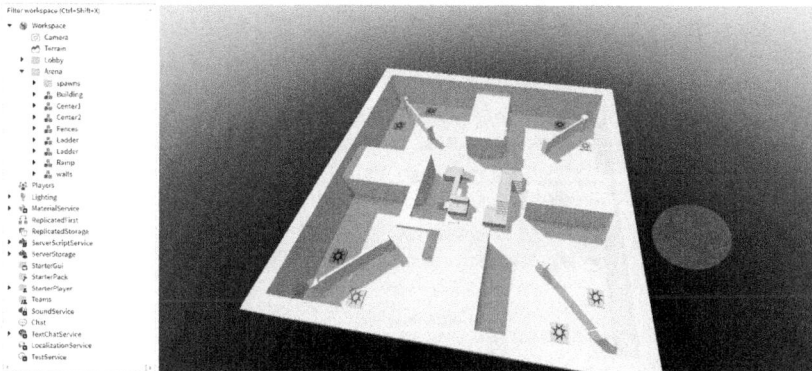

Don't start adjusting the look of the arena beyond this yet. Focus only on creating the layout of it. It's easier to make sure you have a working game before you spend time making it look nice.

CODING THE GAME LOOP

To begin, create a folder in ServerStorage called "ModuleScripts." In this folder, create two ModuleScripts, called GameSettings and

MatchManager. GameSettings will store common values and variables that determine certain functional features. MatchManager will store functions and events related to the arena matches.

Next, go to ServerScriptService and create an ordinary script called GameManager. This script will call and manage code from other scripts. Since ModuleScripts cannot run code themselves, we need a regular script that will be able to call the code from these modules at the right times.

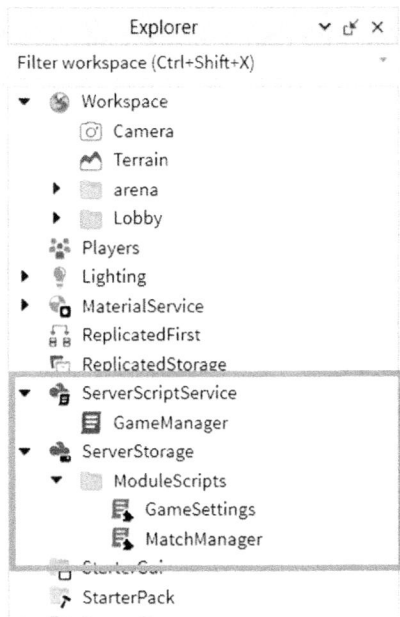

GameSettings

Let's quickly recap ModuleScripts. These scripts store different variables and functions as members of a module. This allows us to keep related code separate from other nonrelated code and helps us keep scripts better organized. The variables and functions contained in ModuleScripts exist as members of that module. To access them from other scripts, we import the module using "require()" and then access its members using moduleName.memberName.

In GameSettings, you'll find the autofilled module declaration and return module. Replace "module" with gameSettings. Do so for both the declaration and the return code at the bottom.

Next, create the following variables:

- intermissionTime: how long players will wait between matches
- matchDuration: how long each round or match will last
- minimumPlayers: the lowest number of players necessary for a match
- transitionTime: a brief pause between the changes from intermission to match and vice versa

For now, assign small values to each to make testing easier.

```
1    local gameSettings = {}
2
3    -- game variables added to the module
4    gameSettings.intermissionDuration = 5
5    gameSettings.matchDuration = 10
6    gameSettings.minimumPlayers = 2
7    gameSettings.transitionTime = 5
8
9    return gameSettings
10
11   --[[code sourced from https://create.roblox.com/docs/education/battle-royale-series/
     coding-the-game-loop#gamesettings-script
12       retrieved in April 2023]]
13
```

MatchManager

This script will contain various functions related to the arena rounds. Replace "module" with matchManager. We aren't going to add too much to this script just yet. For now, create a module function called prepareGame and code a basic print statement in it.

```
1    local matchManager = {}
2
3  · function matchManager.prepareGame()
4        print("Game starting!")
5    end
6
7    return matchManager
8
9    --[[code sourced from https://create.roblox.com/docs/education/battle-royale-series/
     coding-the-game-loop#gamesettings-script
10        retrieved in April 2023]]
11
```

When working in module scripts, there are two kinds of functions: namely, local functions and module functions. Local functions are declared with local scope and a name as usual. Module functions, on the other hand, are direct members of the module itself. It is not declared with local scope, and its name always includes the module name. For example, function matchManager.prepareGame().

GameManager

For this script to access the modules, create variables to store references to the ServerStorage, ModuleScripts folder, and the ModuleScripts. You'll also need a variable to reference the Players service. When importing a ModuleScript, we use the function require().

```
1    local ServerStorage = game:GetService("ServerStorage")
2    local Players = game:GetService("Players")
3
4    local moduleScripts = ServerStorage:WaitForChild("ModuleScripts")
5    local matchManager = require(moduleScripts:WaitForChild("MatchManager"))
6    local gameSettings = require(moduleScripts:WaitForChild("GameSettings"))
```

In the above example, I use the method WaitForChild. When we run the game, it's first run through the compiler and then built. This can sometimes take a few moments and means that objects like parts and scripts don't come online at the same time. If the code executes before they are built, it will try to find an object that doesn't exist, and an error will occur. WaitForChild tells the code to wait until the object comes into existence before moving on. If, for example, the GameManager code runs before the ModuleScripts folder is accessible, the game will wait for the folder and then store it as a reference. We'll use this method in most of the variable references moving forward. The only times we don't use it are when referencing services like Players or ServerStorage.

Since this game runs on a repetitive cycle of matches and intermissions, most of its code will need to be placed inside a while loop. Insert a basic while true do loop into this script.

```lua
1    local ServerStorage = game:GetService("ServerStorage")
2    local Players = game:GetService("Players")
3
4    local moduleScripts = ServerStorage:WaitForChild("ModuleScripts")
5    local matchManager = require(moduleScripts:WaitForChild("MatchManager"))
6    local gameSettings = require(moduleScripts:WaitForChild("GameSettings"))
7
8    while true do
9
10   end
```

CODING THE INTERMISSION

Starting Intermission

The intermission starts at the beginning of the game while it waits for enough players to run a match. For this, we need two main variables: the number of players in the experience (as stored under players in GameManager) and minimumPlayers (as per GameSettings).

Our code will compare the value of players to the value of minimumPlayers in GameManager to test if there are enough players. Once the player count is equal to or greater than minimumPlayers, the game can move from an intermission state to a match state. Currently, my minimumPlayers is set to 2, meaning there need to be at least two players in the lobby for the intermission to end.

How would you code this? Take a moment to consider the problem and try to think of a solution. If your answer is to use an if-statement to check a condition, you're halfway right. We do need to test a condition, but we can't do this with a simple conditional. Since we don't know when the minimum number of players will be reached, we cannot define when the condition needs to run. For this reason, we need code that will run multiple times to test it. The answer is to use a loop that tests a condition.

You have two options, a while loop, or a repeat loop. Both of them will test the condition for each iteration of the code. Since we've covered while loops, I'm going to use a repeat loop in this example. Know, however, that you can use a while loop to get exactly the same effect.

Repeat loops work on the same logic as while loops. They repeat code based on a condition. While loops use the structure "while condition do [code]." Repeat loops approach it from the other direction, and they use the structure "repeat [code] until condition." They essentially execute code repeatedly until the condition becomes true.

Try to construct a condition that will work for our purpose. Do this on your own first before reading further.

In the case of a while loop, we want code to loop while the number of players is less than minimumPlayers, thus players < minimumPlayers. In the case of a repeat loop, we want code to keep repeating until the number of players is equal to or greater than minimumPlayers, thus players >= minimumPlayers.

With all that in mind, construct the intermission loop in GameManager; it needs to go into the while loop that's already there. Inside the loop, code a basic print statement for testing purposes, and add a wait with the intermissionDuration value.

```
 7
 8   ▾ while true do
 9   ▾     repeat --intermission loop
10             print("Starting intermission")
11             wait(gameSettings.intermissionDuration)
12         until Players.NumPlayers >= gameSettings.minimumPlayers
13     end
14
```

Run the game and check that you see the "Starting intermission" display in the output. Check that the message repeats within the time you defined in intermissionDuration.

Ending Intermission

Once there are enough players, the game should end the intermission and start the match. After the intermission loop, add a print statement to display "Intermission over" and add a wait code with the transitionTime variable as parameter. Then, call the prepare-Game function from MatchManager.

```
 8   ▾ while true do
 9   ▾     repeat --intermission loop
10             print("Starting intermission")
11             wait(gameSettings.intermissionDuration)
12         until Players.NumPlayers >= gameSettings.minimumPlayers
13
14         --moving out of intermission
15         print("Intermission over")
16         wait(gameSettings.transitionTime)
17         matchManager.prepareGame()
18     end
19
```

To test this code, we need multiple players. As is, there need to be at least two players in the game for it to end the intermission. Regular testing won't cover this since you're only one character. For this, we need a local server to simulate multiple players. Go to the Test tab and find the Clients and Servers section. This gives you the option of hosting a test server with multiple characters. Select the option that matches your minimumPlayers value.

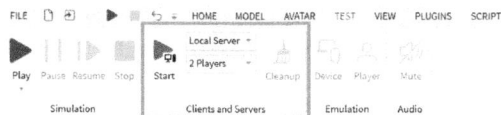

Once you hit start, Studio will open several new windows, a server, and then a client for each player in the experience. This can take some time, especially the first time you do it. It might also prompt you to give it security access. Click Allow Access if prompted and wait for all the windows to load in. Find the one marked as the Server; you'll be able to see the print statements in its Output. Check that you see the "Starting intermission" and "Intermission over" messages. They'll keep repeating since we haven't provided any other code yet. Once you're satisfied, click the Cleanup button to close all the server-related windows.

If the game doesn't work as expected, make sure that you have all the names referenced correctly. If your objects are named differently than mine, your code will use different names. Use your Explorer to double-check the identifiers. Identify the statement that isn't printing and use it to pinpoint where the problem is. Check that the code there is in the right blocks. Finally, if the intermission isn't ending, check that the number of players you added to the local server is equal to or greater than minimumPlayers. If your minimum is four, you'll need four players.

MANAGING PLAYERS

All players are automatically spawned into the lobby at the start of the game. Once the match begins, they will be transported to the arena. Players will be returned to the lobby once they are defeated or if the match ends. For this, we need a way to manage different players.

Create a new ModuleScripts in the ServerStorage folder. Rename it PlayerManager and replace the "module" with playerManager. In the script, create variables to reference Players and ServerStorage.

```
1    local playerManager = {}
2        --service variables
3        local Players = game:GetService("Players")
4        local ServerStorage = game:GetService("ServerStorage")
5
6    return playerManager
7
```

Next, create three variables called lobbySpawn, arenaSpawns, and the arena folder. These will store location references we need to transport players. Finally, create an empty table that will track active players.

```
1    local playerManager = {}
2
3    --service variables
4    local Players = game:GetService("Players")
5    local ServerStorage = game:GetService("ServerStorage")
6
7    --map variables
8    local lobbySpawn = workspace.Lobby.StartSpawn
9    local arenaMap = workspace.Arena
10   local spawnLocations = arenaMap.SpawnLocations
11
12   --player table
13   local activePlayers = {}
14
15   return playerManager
16
```

Make sure that you name them correctly. If your parts and folders are stored under different names, your code will need to reflect that. You don't need to reference each individual arena spawn location, just the folder in which they're kept. Make sure there's nothing else in that folder besides SpawnLocations.

Next, create a module function called sendPlayersToMatch. For now, it has no parameters and no code other than a print display.

```
15       --module functions
16   ▾ function playerManager.sendPlayersToMatch ()
17       print("sending players to match")
18   end
19
```

Then, create a local function called onPlayerAdded with player as a parameter. We'll use this function to ensure that players spawn into the lobby and not one of the other spawns. As is, a player can spawn into any of the possible locations, and we want to make it so they can only spawn into the lobby. Where someone spawns are determined by their RespawnLocation property. This is attached to the player themselves, and to access it, we need access to that player.

Using PlayerAdded will let us create a reference for each player as they're added. We can also set their RespawnLocation at the same time. In the function, write the code "player.RespawnLocation = lobbySpawn." Then, connect the function to the PlayerAdded event.

```
19    --local functions
20    local function onPlayerAdded (player)
21        player.RespawnLocation = lobbySpawn
22    end
23
24    Players.PlayerAdded:Connect(onPlayerAdded)
25
26    return playerManager
27
28    --[[code sourced from https://create.roblox.com/docs/education/battle-royale-series/
      managing-players
29        retrieved in April 2023]]
```

To use these functions, we need to link them to the MatchManager module. Go to Matchmanager and create variables for ServerStorage, the ModuleScripts folder, and the PlayerManager script. Call the sendPlayersToMatch function from prepareGame.

```
1     local matchManager = {}
2
3     --PlayerManager variables
4     local serverStorage = game:GetService("ServerStorage")
5     local moduleScripts = serverStorage:WaitForChild("ModuleScripts")
6     local playerManager = require(moduleScripts:WaitForChild("PlayerManager"))
7
8     function matchManager.prepareGame()
9         print("game is starting!")
10        playerManager.sendPlayersToMatch()
11    end
12
13    return matchManager
14
15    --[[code sourced from https://create.roblox.com/docs/education/battle-royale-series/
      managing-players
16        retrieved in April 2023]]
17
```

Run the game with a local server. Make sure that all player characters join into the lobby and that you see the print message from sendPlayersToMatch. If you don't, go back and double-check that you used the right name for the lobbySpawn object when assigning the variable. You can also check other names and references for mistakes. Finally, double-check that you connected the onPlayerAdded function with the PlayerAdded event.

Transporting Players to the Arena

In PlayerManager, create a new local function called preparePlayer. It will take two parameters—player and whichSpawn. In its code block, set the player's RespawnLocation to whichSpawn. This variable (whichSpawn) will contain a reference to one of the arena spawnLocations.

Then, use the built-in function LoadCharacter() to reload the player's position and transport them to the new spawn point. LoadCharacter essentially resets the player object with each reload. This is important for later features of the game.

```
26    ▾local function preparePlayer (player, whichSpawn)
27         player.RespawnLocation = whichSpawn
28         player:LoadCharacter()
29    end
30
31    return playerManager
```

To determine where players load in, we have to identify each of the various arena spawns that are available. Create a variable called arenaSpawns and initialize it with spawnLocations:GetChildren(). This will essentially create an array of possible values that we can assign to whichSpawn.

Remember that empty table we created earlier called activePlayers? We're going to add players to it as they join the experience.

This will help us track the players as well as assign their respawn locations.

First, create a for loop in the sendPlayersToMatch function. This loop will run through players:GetPlayers using pairs as though it were a dictionary. It uses playerKey for the key value, and which-Player to contain the name of the player. For each iteration, it will store the name of the player as a new entry of activePlayers.

```
14    --module functions
15  • function playerManager.sendPlayersToMatch ()
16        print("sending players to match")
17        local arenaSpawns = spawnLocations:GetChildren()
18  •     for playerKey, whichPlayer in pairs(Players:GetPlayers()) do
19            table.insert(activePlayers,whichPlayer)
20        end
21    end
22
```

In this same loop, create a local variable called spawnLocation that will take the value of the first entry of our arenaSpawns array (local spawnLocation = arenaSpawns[1]). Then, call preparePlayers, and pass whichPlayer and spawnLocation as arguments.

If you're confused, slow down a moment to think about it. This game's code can and will get complex, so take your time to work through the logic step by step. The variable whichPlayer contains the name of a specific player while spawnLocation contains a reference to a specific spawn. When their values are passed to preparePlayer, it will transport the player in question to the SpawnLocation identified by the variables. Then, the code will move on to the next player and spawnLocation.

```
26    --module functions
27  • function playerManager.sendPlayersToMatch ()
28        print("sending players to match")
29        local arenaSpawns = spawnLocations:GetChildren()
30  •     for playerKey, whichPlayer in pairs(Players:GetPlayers()) do
31            table.insert(activePlayers,whichPlayer)
32            local spawnLocation = arenaSpawns[1]
33            preparePlayer(whichPlayer, spawnLocation)
34            table.remove(arenaSpawns, 1)
35        end
36    end
37
```

Run the game to test that your character respawns to the arena. Tip: If you don't want to boot up a local server each time to test these features, change your minimumPlayers in GameSettings to one. This will let you test the game normally. However, keep in mind that this game is intended for multiple players. While this code works for single and multiple players, make sure to increase the minimum every once in a while and test it with more than one player.

ADDING A TOOL

Find a weapon model that you would like your players to use. It can be any weapon or tool that fits the concept of the game you have in mind. I'm using @Roblox_Educators' *Battle Royale Weapon*.

In the previous chapter, we added the tool directly to the StarterPack so that players would have the tool immediately after joining. For this game, however, we won't be doing that. LoadCharacter resets a character regardless of what they had in their inventory, and it would still spawn them with the weapon if it was in the StarterPack. However, it would be a neat feature if players don't have a tool while they're in the lobby but then get one when they enter the arena, don't you think?

For this, add the tool model to ServerStorage. Make sure it's not in the ModuleScripts folder. Then, return to PlayerManager and create a variable to reference that model. If you added it into its own folder, you'll need to include a variable for the folder as well.

```
3    --service variables
4    local Players = game:GetService("Players")
5    local ServerStorage = game:GetService("ServerStorage")
6    --map variables
7    local lobbySpawn = workspace.Lobby.StartSpawn
8    local arenaMap = workspace.Arena
9    local spawnLocations = arenaMap.spawns
10
11   --player variable
12   local activePlayers = {}
13   local playerWeapon = ServerStorage.Weapon
```

Turn to the preparePlayer function and add two variables there to represent the character and sword. While the above playerWeapon variable represents the model itself, the sword variable will represent a copy of that object that is attached to a specific player.

For character, initialize it using "player.Character or player.Character:Wait()." Using or in this case lets us add an alternative option for the game to ensure that it runs well. Like with WaitForChild, using Character:Wait gives the game the option to wait for the object to become available before trying to reference it. This will stop the game from throwing errors if it cannot immediately find a character object.

For sword, we will use the function Clone. This is a built-in function that lets us duplicate the playerWeapon model and attach it to the player character once the game moves into a match state.

```
22   local function preparePlayer (player, whichSpawn)
23       player.RespawnLocation = whichSpawn
24       player:LoadCharacter()
25
26       local character = player.Character or player.CharacterAdded:Wait()
27       local sword = playerWeapon:Clone()
28       sword.Parent = character
29   end
```

Run the game and test that you receive a tool once you spawn into the arena. Check also that this tool isn't available to you while in the lobby during the intermission.

MATCH EVENTS

The code we have created thus far provides for starting and ending the intermission and teleporting players. Once they have been transported, however, the intermission will start again. To enable players to actually play a match, we need events to trigger the start of a new round (to pause the game loop) and signal the end of the match (to resume the game loop).

In ServerStorage, create a new folder called Events, and then attach two BindableEvent objects to it. Rename them matchStart and matchEnd, respectively.

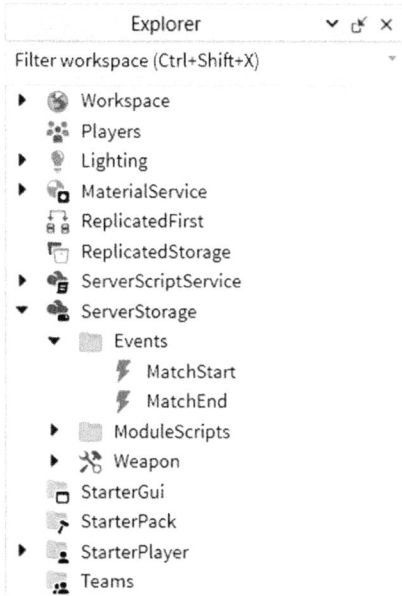

In GameManager, create two new variables to reference the Events folder and matchEnd event.

```
 8    --event variables
 9    local events = ServerStorage.Events
10    local matchEnd = events.MatchEnd
11
```

If you'll remember, when we want to access built-in functions of the BindableEvents class, we need to use .Event. One of these functions, called Wait, will let the script pause until matchEnd is triggered. In other words, we can use matchEnd.Event:Wait() to pause the game loop and stop the intermission from restarting until the match is over.

```
18        --moving out of intermission
19        print("Intermission over")
20        wait(gameSettings.transitionTime)
21        matchManager.prepareGame()
22
23        --matchEnd
24        matchEnd.Event:Wait()
25    end
```

TIMER

To set up a customizable timer, we are going to use a prebuilt timer module. Go to create.roblox.com and search for their Battle Royale tutorial. Under the Timers and Events section, there will be a subsection called "Setting Up The Timer." Here you will find a comprehensive timer module that you can copy and paste into your project. Look for this:

```
1     local Timer = {}
2     Timer.__index = Timer
3
4   ▾ function Timer.new()
5         local self = setmetatable({}, Timer)
6
7         self._finishedEvent = Instance.new("BindableEvent")
8         self.finished = self._finishedEvent.Event
9
10        self._running = false
11        self._startTime = nil
12        self._duration = nil
```

Once you have the code, create a new ModuleScript called Timer and paste the code you copied into it. Then, require this module and GameSettings into MatchManager. From MatchManager, create a new instance of the timer module.

```
8     local gameSettings = require(moduleScripts:WaitForChild("GameSettings"))
9     local timer = require(moduleScripts:WaitForChild("Timer"))
10
11    local myTimer = timer.new()
12
```

This timer has access to all the functions set out in the module it was created from. This includes functions like start and stop that we can use to trigger matchStart and matchEnd.

Create two new functions in MatchManager called timeUp and startTimer. Add an appropriate print message to each. In start-Timer, call the timer's start function and use gameSettings and matchDuration as the parameters. Then connect its .finished to our timeUp function.

```
 8    local gameSettings = require(moduleScripts:WaitForChild("GameSettings"))
 9    local timer = require(moduleScripts:WaitForChild("Timer"))
10
11    local myTimer = timer.new()
12
13  ▾ local function timeUp()
14        print("time's up!")
15    end
16
17  ▾ local function startTimer()
18        print("timer started")
19        myTimer:start(gameSettings.matchDuration)
20        myTimer.finished:Connect(timeUp)
21    end
22
```

Starting the Timer

In MatchManager, create three new variables for the events folder, matchStart, and matchEnd.

```
 6    local playerManager = require(moduleScripts:WaitForChild("PlayerManager"))
 7    local gameSettings = require(moduleScripts:WaitForChild("GameSettings"))
 8    local timer = require(moduleScripts:WaitForChild("Timer"))
 9
10    --event variables
11    local events = serverStorage:WaitForChild("Events")
12    local matchStart = events:WaitForChild("MatchStart")
13    local matchEnd = events:WaitForChild("MatchEnd")
14
15    local myTimer = timer.new()
```

Then, just above return, connect matchStart to startTimer. Finally, fire startMatch from the prepareGame function.

```
27   ▾ function matchManager.prepareGame()
28        print("game is starting!")
29        playerManager.sendPlayersToMatch()
30        matchStart:Fire()
31   end
32
33   matchStart.Event:Connect(startTimer)
34
35   return matchManager
36
37   --[[code sourced from https://create.roblox.com/docs/education/battle-royale-
        series/timers-and-events#setting-up-the-timer
38        retrieved in April 2023]]
39
```

Run the game to make sure you can see the message that indicates the timer is starting.

CREATING A USER INTERFACE

Thus far, we've been using print and the Output window to communicate changes in the program. However, players don't have access to the output and thus can't see the status of the game. So let's add an interface to display the status of the game to players.

GUI elements are generally added to the StarterGui to ensure that players can all see the same thing. The GUI communicates with clients, and each player is a unique client that needs to receive that information individually. As such, we need a way to guarantee consistent communication across all clients, and StarterGui does that.

In StarterGui, add a ScreenGui object and then a TextLabel. Rename the label ScreenDisplay.

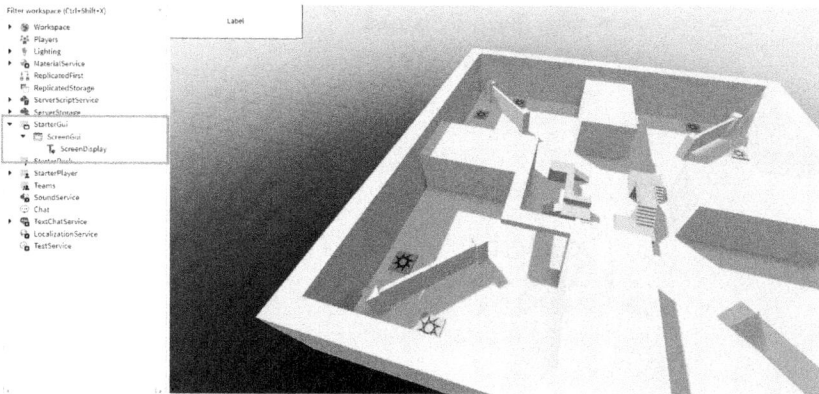

The label acts as a display board for players. If you want to change its location, click on it, and then drag it into position. You can also change its size.

Since GUIs communicate across the client-server boundary, the values it needs to access can't be in the ServerStorage. Go to ReplicatedStorage and create a new folder called Values. In it, add a StringValue and name it Status. Go to its properties and change its Value to "Welcome to the game!"

Then, attach a LocalScript to the TextLabel. Rename it DisplayStatus.

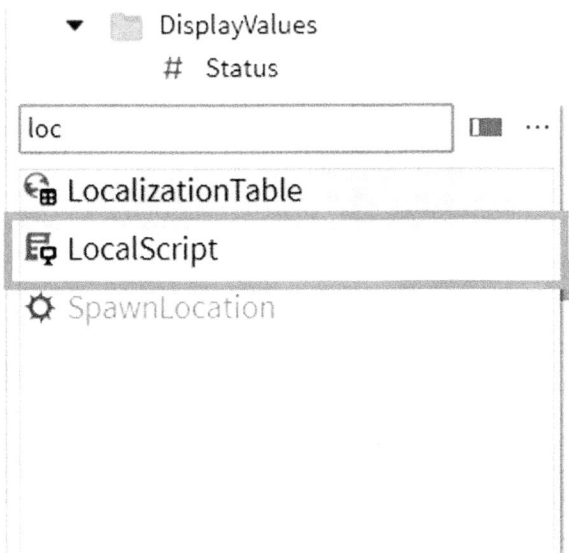

Open the script and create variables to reference ReplicatedStorage, the DisplayValues folder, and the Status string value. Finally, create a variable to store the text label the script is attached to.

The value currently in ReplicatedStorage contains the message we want to display. Its value will change depending on the status of the game. For example, while the game is in an intermission, Status will have a value of "waiting for players" or "in intermission." Once the game switches to a match, Status will also change.

To reflect this on the TextLabel, assign the TextLabel's Text property to the value contained in Status. Do this in a new function called updateText.

```
1    --display variables
2    local ReplicatedStorage = game:GetService("ReplicatedStorage")
3    local displayValues = ReplicatedStorage:WaitForChild("DisplayValues")
4    local status = displayValues:WaitForChild("Status")
5    local screenDisplay = script.Parent
6
7    local function updateText ()
8        screenDisplay.Text = status.Value
9    end
```

Since Status's value will fluctuate with the game flow, we can use its Changed event to call the updateText function to change the GUI. Connect updateText to the Changed event and then, beneath it, call the updateText function. This will ensure more frequent updates.

```
1    --display variables
2    local ReplicatedStorage = game:GetService("ReplicatedStorage")
3    local displayValues = ReplicatedStorage:WaitForChild("DisplayValues")
4    local status = displayValues:WaitForChild("Status")
5    local screenDisplay = script.Parent
6
7    local function updateText ()
8        screenDisplay.Text = status.Value
9    end
10
11   status.Changed:Connect(updateText)
12   updateText()
13
14   --[[code sourced from https://create.roblox.com/docs/education/battle-royale-
     series/creating-a-gui
15       retrieved in April 2023]]
```

Run the game. Check that the display changes to the value you assigned to status. If it doesn't, make sure you use the TextLabel's .Text property and status's .Value.

DisplayManager

Take a moment to think about how the game works. We want a GUI that will inform the player of the various statuses the game goes through during its game loop. How would you go about making that happen?

To let the GUI change along with the rest of the game, we need to manage it the way we've managed everything else. Create a new ModuleScript called DisplayManager in the same folder as the other ModuleScripts. In it, create variables for ReplicatedStorage, displayStatus, and status.

```
1   local displayManager = {}
2
3   local ReplicatedStorage = game:GetService("ReplicatedStorage")
4   local displayValues = ReplicatedStorage:WaitForChild("DisplayValues")
5   local status = displayValues:WaitForChild("Status")
6
```

This module will contain code that manages the status updates. Then, call it from GameManager to run alongside the other modules. Next, create a module function called updateStatus. Here, code will manage the value of status. In the previous section, we made it so that the TextLabel displays status each time it changes, and in updateStatus, we can assign a new value to be displayed.

```
1    local displayManager = {}
2
3    local ReplicatedStorage = game:GetService("ReplicatedStorage")
4    local displayValues = ReplicatedStorage:WaitForChild("DisplayValues")
5    local status = displayValues:WaitForChild("Status")
6
7    --local functions
8
9    --module functions
10   function displayManager.updateStatus(newStatus)
11       status.Value = newStatus
12   end
13
14   return displayManager
15
16   --[[code sourced from https://create.roblox.com/docs/education/battle-royale-
     series/creating-a-gui
17       retrieved in April 2023]]
```

This function takes the parameter newStatus, which will contain the replacement value.

Updating Status

Now that we have that, let's go over to gameManager to code the change in status to feed to this function. Add variables for ReplicatedStorage and the displayManager module.

```lua
1    --services
2    local ServerStorage = game:GetService("ServerStorage")
3    local Players = game:GetService("Players")
4    local ReplicatedStorage = game:GetService("ReplicatedStorage")
5
6    --module scripts
7    local moduleScripts = ServerStorage:WaitForChild("ModuleScripts")
8    local matchManager = require(moduleScripts:WaitForChild("MatchManager"))
9    local gameSettings = require(moduleScripts:WaitForChild("GameSettings"))
10   local displayManager = require(moduleScripts:WaitForChild("DisplayManager"))
11
```

The very first thing the game should do is update the status to "Waiting for players" while the intermission is active. In the very first line after the while loop declaration, add the code to call the updateStatus function and pass it the message you want to display. You can remove the print statement from the repeat loop since the message will be displayed on the GUI.

```lua
16   ▾ while true do
17        displayManager.updateStatus("Waiting for players")
18
19   ▾    repeat --intermission loop
20            wait(gameSettings.intermissionDuration)
21        until Players.NumPlayers >= gameSettings.minimumPlayers
22
```

Next, replace the print "intermission is over" message with one that changes the status to "Match is starting." Again, this replaces the output display since the label itself acts as a means to test the code.

```lua
23        --moving out of intermission
24        displayManager.updateStatus("Match is starting")
25        wait(gameSettings.transitionTime)
26        matchManager.prepareGame()
27
28        --matchEnd
29        matchEnd.Event:Wait()
30   end
```

Run the game and check if the text label changes as the game does. If it doesn't, check that you're referencing the correct names when assigning variables and that you call updateStatus in the correct places.

Match Displays

Aside from displaying the current state of the game, we also want the GUI to display certain match statistics, like the amount of time left and the number of players still remaining. To do that, create two IntValue objects in DisplayValues; rename them playersLeft and TimeLeft. Create two variables to reference them in display-Manager.

```
1    local displayManager = {}
2
3    local ReplicatedStorage = game:GetService("ReplicatedStorage")
4    local displayValues = ReplicatedStorage:WaitForChild("DisplayValues")
5    local status = displayValues:WaitForChild("Status")
6    local timeLeft = displayValues:WaitForChild("TimeLeft")
7    local playersLeft = displayValues:WaitForChild("PlayersLeft")
8
9    --local functions
```

Create a new module function called updateMatchStatus that will change the value of status to include playersLeft and timeLeft. Then, connect both values to a Changed event and the function.

```
9     --local functions
10    local function updateMatchStatus()
11        status.Value = "Time left: "..timeLeft.Value.." / Players left: "..playersLeft.Value
12    end
13
14    --module functions
15    function displayManager.updateStatus(newStatus)
16        status.Value = newStatus
17    end
18
19    timeLeft.Changed:Connect(updateMatchStatus)
20    playersLeft.Changed:Connect(updateMatchStatus)
21
22    return displayManager
```

The value you see assigned to status uses a technique called string building. This is when we combine different values into one string value, often for display purposes. It lets us craft values like time-Left and playersLeft into a meaningful message. We use the concatenate operator here to mash different data types together. In this example, we combine strings with numbers. In print, we can use commas, but not when creating a value to assign to a variable.

The next step is to get the values that will be displayed in those variables. For playersLeft, turn to the PlayerManager script and create variables to store ReplicatedStorage, DisplayValues, and playersLeft.

```
3    --service variables
4    local Players = game:GetService("Players")
5    local ServerStorage = game:GetService("ServerStorage")
6    local ReplicatedStorage = game:GetService("ReplicatedStorage")
7
8    local lobbySpawn = workspace.Lobby.StartSpawn
9    local arenaMap = workspace.Arena
10   local spawnLocations = arenaMap.spawns
11   local displayValues = ReplicatedStorage:WaitForChild("DisplayValues")
12   local playersLeft = displayValues:WaitForChild("PlayersLeft")
```

The value of playersLeft should be the length of the activePlayers array. Its length represents the number of players that each match starts out with. This will later change as we begin coding when players are removed from the match.

```
34   --module functions
35   function playerManager.sendPlayersToMatch ()
36       print("sending players to match")
37       local arenaSpawns = spawnLocations:GetChildren()
38       for playerKey, whichPlayer in pairs(Players:GetPlayers()) do
39           table.insert(activePlayers,whichPlayer)
40           local spawnLocation = arenaSpawns[1]
41           preparePlayer(whichPlayer, spawnLocation)
42           table.remove(arenaSpawns, 1)
43       end
44       playersLeft.Value = #activePlayers
45   end
46
```

Tip: Our code is becoming complex, and it's getting more and more difficult to manage the various variables, functions, and modules. We're also jumping around between scripts a lot. Now more than ever, use comments to create sections in your code and use white space to your advantage. This project is a good example of how proper organization can help make sense of code.

Find the startTimer function we created earlier. Underneath the finished event connection but before the function's end, create a while loop with the condition myTimer:isRunning(). Then, add the code "timeLeft.Value = (math.floor(myTimer:getTimeLeft() + 1))." Add "wait()" but do not pass a value into this wait. This will allow the game to manage its own time for better accuracy.

```
28   ▾ local function startTimer()
29        print("timer started")
30        myTimer:start(gameSettings.matchDuration)
31        myTimer.finished:Connect(timeUp)
32
33   ▾    while myTimer:isRunning() do
34            timeLeft.Value = (math.floor(myTimer:getTimeLeft() + 1))
35            wait()
36        end
37   end
```

Lua has a math library with functions (like floor) that let us perform more complex math like conversions and trigonometry. The function math.floor rounds the number passed as argument to the nearest integer value (i.e., whole number). This particular line of code takes the value left in myTimer, adds 1 to it, and then rounds it out to the nearest whole number. For example, if there are 5.4 seconds left, it will increase it to 6.4, and then round it out to 6. This accounts for the milliseconds that pass between each second without overburdening the game by displaying each of those minuscule changes.

ENDING MATCHES

Respawn Defeated Players

Players are eliminated when their health is decreased to zero. The actual elimination is managed by the weapon's scripts. If you used a model from the Toolbox, it likely comes with a script that determines what happens when it hits another player. If it doesn't, find another tool that does, or refer to the trap exercise from Chapter 6 to create one that reduces the other player's health on contact. As extra practice, try to code a script for this on your own, even if your weapon already has one. I'll include a very basic example of what it would look like without any animations or special moves.

```
1    local players = game:GetService("Players")
2    local tool = script.Parent
3    local damage = 5
4
5    local function attack (opponent)
6        local character = opponent.Parent
7        local humanoid = character:FindFirstChildWhichIsA("Humanoid")
8        if humanoid then
9            humanoid.Health = humanoid.Health - damage
10       end
11   end
12
13   local function onTouch (otherPlayer)
14       attack(otherPlayer)
15   end
16
17   tool.Touched:Connect(onTouch)
```

As is, when a player is defeated, they'll be respawned into the arena when they should be removed from the match and be taken to the lobby instead.

In PlayerManager, create a new function called respawnToLobby. Make sure that it's somewhere before the preparePlayer function. Use it to set the player's new spawn point as the lobbySpawn, and then use the LoadCharacter function to reset them.

```
24
25   local function respawnToLobby(player)
26       player.RespawnLocation = lobbySpawn
27       player:LoadCharacter()
28   end
29
30   local function preparePlayer (player, whichSpawn)
```

Roblox has a built-in event that automatically references when a character dies. This event is named Died and is attached to the Humanoid object. We can use this event to determine when players should be removed from the arena and taken back to the lobby.

Find the preparePlayer function. At the end, declare a new variable to store a reference to humanoid.

Use "character:WaitForChild("Humanoid")." Then, connect humanoid. Died to an anonymous function.

If you'll remember, anonymous functions are functions that aren't named. In this case, using an anonymous function will let us define it in the brackets of Died:Connect so that we can also reference who died specifically. Remember, we are using an array to track active players, and when one dies, we want to remove them from that array. This will also let us decrease the value of our players-Left value in the GUI.

Code the connect event like you normally would. In this case, it's humanoid.Died:Connect(). In the brackets of Connect, type function () and then press enter to autofill the "end." Make sure it is still within the brackets of the Connect. You should see this:

```
31   ▾ local function preparePlayer (player, whichSpawn)
32         player.RespawnLocation = whichSpawn
33         player:LoadCharacter()
34
35         local character = player.Character or player.CharacterAdded:Wait()
36         local sword = playerWeapon:Clone()
37         sword.Parent = character
38
39         --respawn after death
40         local humanoid = character:WaitForChild("Humanoid")
41
42   ▾     humanoid.Died:Connect(function ()
43
44         end)
45   end
```

In the anonymous function's block, call respawnToLobby and pass player as a parameter to it.

```
38         --respawn after death
39         local humanoid = character:WaitForChild("Humanoid")
40
41   ▾     humanoid.Died:Connect(function ()
42             respawnToLobby(player)
43         end)
44   end
```

END STATES

A match can end in two ways: when the time runs out or there's only one player left standing. Since they're two very different outcomes, we'll need to manage them separately.

Timer Ending

In GameSettings, create a new table called endStates. In it, declare two members called foundWinner and timerUp. Give them string values.

```lua
 7    gameSettings.transitionTime = 5
 8
 9  ▾ gameSettings.endStates = {
10        foundWinner = "foundWinner",
11        timerUp = "timerUp"
12    }
13
14    return gameSettings
```

Once that's done, return to GameManager and find "match-End.Event:Wait()." Assign it to a variable by adding "local endState =" in front of it:

```lua
28        --matchEnd
29        local endState = matchEnd.Event:Wait()
30        print("match ended with", endState)
31    end
```

For the sake of testing, add a print statement to display its value. It won't work just yet.

In MatchManager, find the timeUp function. Replace its print statement with code that will fire the matchEnd event and pass it gameSettings.endStates.timerUp as a parameter.

```lua
22    local myTimer = timer.new()
23
24  ▾ local function timeUp()
25        matchEnd:Fire(gameSettings.endStates.timerUp)
26    end
27
```

Run the game; test that you see timerUp displayed in the output once the time runs out.

Finding a Winner

In PlayerManager, declare variables for the ModuleScripts folder, GameSettings, the events folder, and matchEnd event.

```
 3    - service variables
 4    local Players = game:GetService("Players")
 5    local ServerStorage - game:GetService("ServerStorage")
 6    local ReplicatedStorage = game:GetService("ReplicatedStorage")
 7
 8    --module scripts
 9    local moduleScripts = ServerStorage:WaitForChild("ModuleScripts")
10    local gameSettings = moduleScripts:WaitForChild("GameSettings")
11
12    - event variables
13    local events = ServerStorage:WaitForChild("Events")
14    local matchEnd = events:WaitForChild("MatchEnd")
```

Then, add a new function above respawnToLobby and call it checkPlayerCount. Add code to it that will check if the length of activePlayers is 1, and then add code to fire the matchEnd event. Reference the foundWinner object in its parameters.

```
33
34  - local function checkPlayerCount()
35  -     if #activePlayers == 1 then
36            matchEnd:Fire(gameSettings.endStates.FoundWinner)
37        end
38    end
39
```

This function will test how many players are left in activePlayers each time it is called. Once there is only one person left in the array, the function will end the match with the FoundWinner end state.

Removing Players from activePlayers

When a player dies, they are removed from the arena, but not from this array. To fix that, we need code that will remove defeated players. This will also let us use the array to identify the winner.

Create a function called removeActivePlayer (still in PlayerManager). It should be placed directly under checkPlayer-Count in the script. Give it player as an argument.

```
40   local function removeActivePlayer(player)
41
42   end
```

It will loop through activePlayers to find a match for the player it receives as argument.

```
40   local function removeActivePlayer(player)
41       for playerKey, whichPlayer in pairs(activePlayers) do
42           if whichPlayer == player then
43
44           end
45       end
46   end
```

If it finds a match, that entry should be removed from activePlayers, and the value of playersLeft should be adjusted. Then, the checkPlayerCount function should be called to check how many entries are left in the array.

```
40   local function removeActivePlayer(player)
41       for playerKey, whichPlayer in pairs(activePlayers) do
42           if whichPlayer == player then
43               table.remove(activePlayers, playerKey)
44               playersLeft.Value = #activePlayers
45               checkPlayerCount()
46           end
47       end
48   end
49
```

Scroll down until you find preparePlayer. Find the .Died connect code where we defined the anonymous function. In it, call removeActivePlayer the same way you called respawnToLobby.

```
69       humanoid.Died:Connect(function ()
70           respawnToLobby(player)
71           removeActivePlayer(player)
72       end)
73   end
```

Stopping the Timer

When a winner is found before the time runs out, the timer will keep going. To fix this, we need to stop the timer once a winner has been identified. To do this is pretty simple. Go to MatchManager and add a new function called stopTimer. I'd recommend putting it above timeUp, but anywhere above the event connection is fine. To stop the timer, use the code "myTimer:stop()."

```
24   • local function stopTimer ()
25        myTimer:stop()
26     end
27
```

Once you've done that, scroll to the bottom of the script where you connected matchStart to startTimer. There, connect matchEnd to stopTimer.

```
49     matchStart.Event:Connect(startTimer)
50     matchEnd.Event:Connect(stopTimer)
51
52     return matchManager
```

UPDATING THE GUI

Now that the code works, let's update the GUI to match. We'll need two more functions in PlayerManager. The first will be a module function called getWinnerName that will retrieve the winner's name.

```
84
85   • function playerManager.getWinnerName ()
86
87     end
88
```

In it, write code to access the remaining player in activePlayers. I do this with an if-statement to avoid any errors if, for some reason, it tries to run with an empty array. Next, add code that creates a new variable, winningPlayer, that stores the value of activePlayers[1]. Then, return winningPlayer.Name.

```
85   · function playerManager.getWinnerName ()
86   ·     if activePlayers[1] then
87             local winningPlayer = activePlayers[1]
88             return winningPlayer.Name
89         end
90   end
```

Now we can use this in the second function called getEndStatus. This is a module function in MatchManager that takes endState as a parameter. In it, create an empty variable that will hold the result.

```
48
49   · function matchManager.getEndStatus(endState)
50         local statusToReturn
51   end
52
```

Use an if-elseif statement to test whether the game ended with foundWinner or timerUp by testing endState.

```
49   · function matchManager.getEndStatus(endState)
50         local statusToReturn
51
52   ·     if endState == gameSettings.endStates.foundWinner then
53
54   ·     elseif endState == gameSettings.endStates.timerUp then
55
56         end
57
58   end
```

The variable statusToReturn will eventually store the value we want to display to the GUI. Its final value will depend on the outcome of these conditions. If a winner was found, we want to include the name of that player. We'll thus have to use the getWinnerName function, and then use its return as a string for display.

```
49   function matchManager.getEndStatus(endState)
50         local statusToReturn
51
52   ·     if endState == gameSettings.endStates.foundWinner then
53             local winnerName = playerManager.getWinnerName()
54             statusToReturn = "Winner is : " .. winnerName
55
56   ·     elseif endState == gameSettings.endStates.timerUp then
57
58   end
```

If the time runs out, the value of statusToReturn will simply be something like "time ran out!" Finally, add an else condition, and then return statusToReturn outside the conditional. Make sure you have an end for both the if-statement and the function.

```
49   ▾ function matchManager.getEndStatus(endState)
50        local statusToReturn
51
52   ▾    if endState == gameSettings.endStates.foundWinner then
53            local winnerName = playerManager.getWinnerName()
54            statusToReturn = "Winner is : " .. winnerName
55   ▾    elseif endState == gameSettings.endStates.timerUp then
56            statusToReturn = "Time ran out!"
57        else statusToReturn = "Error occurred"
58        end
59
60        return statusToReturn
61    end
```

To display this, go to GameManager and scroll down to the bottom. Find the print statement that displayed the value endState. Replace it with a new local variable called endStatus and call the getEndStatus function from it. The variable endStatus will thus reflect the value of statusToReturn. Then, use endStatus and the display function updateStatus to update the GUI. Finally, add a wait time with timerDuration as a parameter.

```
28        --matchEnd
29        local endState = matchEnd.Event:wait()
30        local endStatus = matchManager.getEndStatus(endState)
31        displayManager.updateStatus(endStatus)
32
33        wait(gameSettings.transitionTime)
34
35    end
```

CLEANUP

That does it for functional gameplay code. All that's left to do now is tidy up the remaining loose ends. As is, some players leave the arena with their weapons. To fix this, go to PlayerManager and create a new local function removePlayerWeapons with the parameter whichPlayer. In this function, create a conditional to test whether whichPlayer still exists (players have a tendency to quit the game when they die, which can cause an error). Store their

Character part in a variable, and then use it to find the weapon object. If the weapon is there, the function should destroy it.

```
72    local function removePlayerWeapon(whichPlayer)
73        if whichPlayer then
74            local character = whichPlayer.Character
75
76            if character:FindFirstChild("Weapon") then
77                character.Weapon:Destroy()
78            end
79        end
80    end
```

Next, create a module function called removeAllWeapons. This one will loop through activePlayers and remove the weapons of all players still in it.

```
102    function playerManager.removeAllWeapons()
103        for playerKey, whichPlayer in pairs(activePlayers) do
104            removePlayerWeapon(whichPlayer)
105        end
106    end
```

Switch to MatchManager to create a separate CleanUp function. For now, this will only call removeAllWeapons, but if you end up expanding the game and adding more features, you can use this function as a collection point for all other cleanup functions. Lastly, go to GameSettings, and call cleanUp before the final wait.

```
63    function matchManager.cleanUp()
64        playerManager.removeAllWeapons()
65    end
66
```

The only thing left now is to transport remaining players to the lobby and clear the activePlayers array. Go to playerManager and create a module function resetMatch. In it, set up a loop to run through the activePlayers array. Whichever players are still left in the game will be in here. They need to go back to the lobby, so call respawnToLobby. After the loop's end, clear the array.

```
108   ▾ function playerManager.resetPlayers ()
109   ▾     for playerKey, whichPlayer in ipairs(activePlayers) do
110           respawnToLobby(whichPlayer)
111       end
112       activePlayers = {}
113   end
114
```

Go to MatchManager and create a resetMatch function that will call resetPlayers.

```
67   ▾ function matchManager.resetMatch()
68       playerManager.resetPlayers()
69   end
70
```

Then, from GameSettings, call it after the final wait statement. I place it after the wait to give victors an extra moment in the arena before taking them to the lobby. If you don't want to do this, you can just call resetMatch from cleanUp to execute it at the same time as removeAllWeapons.

```
33       matchManager.cleanUp()
34
35       wait(gameSettings.transitionTime)
36
37       matchManager.resetMatch()
38   end
39
40   --[[code sourced from https://create.roblox.com/docs/education/battle-royale-series/cleanup-and-reset
41       retrieved in April 2023]]
```

FINAL TOUCHES

That was a pretty big project, and it isn't quite finished yet. The values we assigned in GameSettings were kept small for testing purposes. If you want to make this a proper game, those values need to be adjusted for proper gameplay. Remember to play your game periodically to test the values.

There's also the matter of making the project look like a game. As of yet, the maps are still very unfinished, but now that the game is working, you can take the time to make it look nice. Spend some time with this one, you've worked hard on it. Play around with visual styles and really flesh out the maps you have. Add decorations, textures, and extra features as you see fit. Once you're happy with it, you can publish it to Roblox if you want to.

CODING CHALLENGES

In this chapter, you'll find extra coding challenges. These are a bit harder than the projects we did previously, so take your time with them. I'm not going to give you answers to these challenges, but I will give you some insight into them. I want you to think about the problems and find your own solutions. A good developer knows how to solve problems and find answers to issues they haven't encountered before—so use this chapter to develop those skills.

These challenges were created by user starmaq on devforum.roblox.com, and they do a fantastic job of explaining their work and providing solutions. They also have a few extra challenges I didn't include if you want more. You can find these challenges and their answers at https://devforum.roblox.com/t/list-of-coding-challenges/485248.

#1 – NUMBERS TO FRENCH

French has a notoriously complex numerical system with several odd rules, which makes it the perfect language to test your problem-solving skills. Create an algorithm that will take a number and translate it into written French. If you don't know any French, take the time to look up its language rules for numbering. If French is too hard, use another language.

Method:

1. Identify unique values that are translated the same regardless of context and assign them to a table. In French, this means the numbers 0–16. Notice the correlation between value and index. For example, 0 is at [1], 1 at [2], and 2 at [3].
2. Assign multiples of 10 to a second table. Again, notice the relationship between value and index number. For example, 10 is at [1], 20 at [2], and 30 at [3].
3. Create a third table for the powers of 10, i.e., 10, 100, 1,000, etc.
4. Break numbers up into sections. For example, the number 1,359,876 can be broken up into millions (1), thousands (359), and tens and hundreds (876). Each of these chunks can then be further broken down. In 876, the first number (8) represents hundreds, the second (7) tens, and the third (6) is ones. With 359, the first (3) is hundred thousands, the second (5) is ten thousands, and the third (9) is thousands.
5. With that in mind, code the conversion. Make code that will test if the number can be translated directly from the tables. If not, the code should break the number up as we did above, convert it into a manageable format, and then

start finding matches from the tables you created. Make sure to provide for any special translations (like the numbers 90–99 in French, which are translated differently from other numbers).

6. Combine your various functions together to craft a single string.

#2 – SORT A TABLE

Arrays, as you know, are ordered lists. The order of values is determined by the index number. But what if you wanted to change that order based on the values and not the indexes? Sorting algorithms are code that tests and compares the values of array elements and then changes their location based on specific criteria. Think of alphabetizing names, or sorting based on scores.

Try to create an algorithm of your own that will sort an array of numbers in descending order (i.e., from largest to smallest). Again, consider how you would do it. Break that process down into simple steps. For example, I would identify two specific entries, compare their values to see which one was larger, and then swap them based on the answer. Find a way to translate that into code.

Explore different methods of sorting. One method is quick sorting, where you define a pivot point to create a partition in the array. Then use two pointers to move through the different sides to find values that are lesser than or greater than the pivot. Once both pointers find values that match, they swap them. Another way is to use bubble sort to compare two adjacent elements, e.g., [1] and [2]. If [2] is greater than [1], swap them. Then compare [2] and [3] and repeat the process until the array is sorted; this can take several passes.

There's no right or wrong way to do this, so play around with a few different ideas.

#3 – NON-REPEATING CHARACTERS

For this challenge, create code that will run through a string to find and display the first character that isn't repeated anywhere else.

```
--strings

"aabgafdd"  --b, g, and f are non-repeating

"rgggtffkrr"  --t is non-repeating

"vvssfgfg"  --no non-repeating characters
```

If there are no non-repeating characters, display an underscore.

The simplest solution is to sort through the string, identify each character, and test it against the others. If there are no matches, it is non-repeating. Alternatively, you can split the string wherever it finds a specified character and then test how many sections you end up with. If a string is split by a non-repeating character, there will be two sections while there would be more if the character repeats itself.

Here are three string manipulation functions that might help:

- match(string, pattern, initial): finds matches in a source string. String is the source, pattern the character you're looking for, and initial a numerical value that indicates where to start searching.

- split(string, separator): splits the string wherever it finds the separator value.
- sub(string, i, j): returns a substring from string position i to j.

#4 – FINDING THE FIRST DUPLICATE

Following the previous example, create an algorithm that will search through an array of numbers to find the first duplicate value. Use the same logic as above but apply it to a table with numbers. In this case, use loops to store a value and then compare it to other elements of the array. Return and display the value of the first duplicate you find.

#5 – ROTATING A MATRIX

Take a 2D table and rotate it 90 degrees clockwise.

```
--go from this
   {{1,2,3},
    {4,5,6},
    {7,8,9}}

--to this
   {{7,4,1},
    {8,5,2},
    {9,6,3}}
```

This challenge uses a 2D table or matrix (an array that contains other arrays). Data in these tables are organized into rows and columns. Each subarray forms a row and is stored under an index value. For example, the row {1,2,3} is stored at [1]. Corresponding indexes of different rows form a column. For example row1[1], row2[1], and row3[1] create the first column that reads {1,4,7}. Thus, {1,2,3} is the first row while {1,4,7} is the first column.

To rotate the table, you would need to adjust the values so that the first column becomes the top row, the top row becomes the third column, and so on.

#6 – PAIRS DIVISIBLE BY FIVE

For your next challenge, code an algorithm that will take two numbers (x and y) and find all possible pairs where m + n divided by 5 equals a whole number. M will be all numbers between 1 and x ($1 <= m <= x$), while n is all numbers between 1 and y ($1 <= n <= y$). In other words, x and y are the upper limits, and m and n include all numbers between 1 and them.

For example, if I give you the numbers 6 (x) and 12 (y), m will be 2–6, while n will be 2–12. In this example, there are 14 pairs that can work.

Tip: Use the operator "%" instead of "/" since it will test the residual and not the result. Finally, your code should return a number value to show how many pairs were successful. If you're still a little lost, consider this: A pair must satisfy the condition "(m+n)%5==0" to qualify as a divisible pair. Your function should take two integers and find how many pairs succeed that condition.

#7 – SNAKE_CASE TO CAMELCASE

This challenge is a bit easier. Write code that will convert a string from snake_case to camelCase. As you can guess, snake_case separates lowercase words with an underscore between each word; camelCase has no underscores but capitalizes the first letter of every new word in a compound string.

```
--for example

"hello_world" --snake_case

"helloWorld" --camelCase
```

Find a way for your code to find an underscore in the string and use it to determine where to capitalize. Refer to the string management functions from #3 if you're stuck.

#8 – RECAMÁN'S SEQUENCE

Recamán's sequence is a famous mathematical sequence that's made by subtracting the next index from the previous value. If the subtraction results in a value that is negative or already in the pattern, the index is added to the previous value instead. To illustrate how it works:

```
--Recaman's sequence
R = {0, 1, 3, 6, 2, 7, 13, 20, 12, 21, 11, 22, 10, 23, 9}
--[[ [0] = 0
     [1] = 1 (0 - 1 fails, therefore 0 + 1)
     [2] = 3 (1 - 2 fails, therefore 1 + 2)
     [3] = 6 (3 - 3 fails, therefore 3 + 3)
     [4] = 2 (6 - 2 succeeds)
     [5] = 7 (2 - 5 fails, therefore 2 + 5)
]]
```

For more on the sequence itself, try looking it up on YouTube.

Your challenge is to create an algorithm that will calculate these values without you supplying the numbers. Write code that will subtract the index from the previous value. If that results in a negative value or an existing value, it should add the index to the previous value. Use loops and conditionals to cycle through terms and use variables to represent the indexes. Display each new term and store it into an array.

#9 – NON-DECREASING ARRAYS

A non-decreasing array is any array where all elements are lesser than or equal to the element that follows them. In other words, they follow the rule array[k] <= array [k+1]. For example:

```
array1 = {2, 3, 6, 9}   non-decreasing array since each value is greater than the one before it
array2 =  {6, 5, 8, 9}   not a non-decreasing array since 6 is not lesser than 5
```

Write code that will test whether an array is non-decreasing. Use the rule above to test each element of an array with a for loop. Tip: Instead of testing it exactly as is, test whether [k] is greater than [k + 1], and any arrays that succeed this condition fail the non-decreasing test. If you want to add more to this challenge, try to figure out a way to test whether arrays that fail can become non-decreasing with change to a single element.

#10 – DRAW MULTIPLICATION

For this challenge, write code that will print a multiplication problem as you would if you wrote it out. To illustrate:

--go from this

(5,4)

--to this

$$
\begin{array}{r}
5 \\
\times \quad 4 \\
\hline
20
\end{array}
$$

This uses a combination of string manipulation and arithmetic. If you want to make this even more challenging, code your function to calculate and display the equation like you would for long multiplication. For example:

--go from this

(452, 21)

--to this

```
        452
  x      21
  ----------
        452
  +    9040
  ----------
       9492
```

If you're unsure how to approach this, look up the steps to long multiplication and consider how you would tell a program to do them.

Help Spread the Gaming Passion!

Your problem-solving skills are improving. And as you develop your coding and gaming skills, you begin to see just how much potential you have. Whether your goal is to create a solid profile or some extra income, it's happening. And now it's time to let others see just what they are capable of.

JUST ONE CLICK!

You know how much of a difference a single click can make! I would be super grateful if you could add one more click for the day and share your opinion with others. One click and one minute can make a huge impact – but who am I telling? Happy gaming!

▶▶▶**Click here to leave your review on Amazon.**

CONCLUSION

If you made it this far, well done! Really, you did a lot to get to this point, and it's something to be proud of. How does it feel to not only have new skills but also to have made two different, functional experiences? From one self-taught developer to another, this is only the beginning. You stand on the threshold of an incredible opportunity. We all start somewhere, and you've just started your journey.

Many people want to become a game developer or to make the next big game, but not many people actually take the steps to see it through. You did, and now you're ready for the next step. This isn't the end of your journey—not by far. There are still more things to learn, techniques to master, and experiences to explore. You have the tools to meet life as a Roblox developer head-on. Use what you've learned and grow beyond it. Experiment, be creative, and never stop developing your skills and interests.

If you enjoyed this book or found it at all helpful, please consider leaving a review. I'd love to hear your thoughts.

GLOSSARY

Anonymous function: a function with no defined name; often used as parameters or linked to other functions and methods.

Arguments/Parameters: variables through which information is passed from one area of code to another.

Array: a table of data values listed in a specific order as indicated by a numerical index.

Compiled: a process in which code is translated into machine language for execution.

Compiled language: a programming language that requires code to be compiled before execution.

Condition: a comparison of different values to return a value of true or false.

Data types: each value or object is classed into a data type depending on what information it is or what it can be used for.

- **Boolean:** a value that is either true or false.
- **Function:** a code object that groups different code statements aimed at executing a goal.
- **Nil:** the absence of any other value.
- **Number:** any numerical value, both decimal and whole.
- **String:** a collection of characters contained in quotation marks.
- **Table:** a collection of related values, objects, functions, and variables.
- **Thread:** references to threads of execution.
- **Userdata:** data that refers to individual users.

Debounce: a boolean value used to stop events from repeatedly firing.

Dictionary: a table that groups multiple values together, where each is identified by a unique key.

Element: an entry in an array.

Elseif: code that can be added onto an if-statement to provide an alternative condition.

Experience: a game hosted on the Roblox platform.

Event: something that occurs in response to a user interaction or when something happens in the game.

Event handler: a function that is dedicated to managing an event.

Function: a collection of code statements unified under a single name.

Humanoid: a child object that is added to a player's character once they join an experience.

If-statement: a statement in which a condition is tested to determine whether code should execute.

Instance: the process by which an object is created from a preexisting class or module.

Interpreted language: a programming language that's not compiled before execution but instead interpreted at run-time.

Ipairs: a function that is used in for loops with arrays.

Key: an identifying value used to distinguish members of a dictionary.

Loop: a coding technique that lets code be repeated on the basis of a condition or controller.

Method: a function that requires itself or parent object as parameter.

ModuleScript: a script in which members are grouped inside a module object.

Obby: a Roblox obstacle course.

Pairs: a function that is used in for loops with dictionaries.

Parent-child: a relationship that illustrates the connection between objects and structure in which they exist.

Part: a visual object that can be added into an experience.

ReplicatedStorage: a project service that contains objects meant to be involved in client-server communication.

Robux: the virtual currency used in Roblox.

Script: a container for code.

ServerScriptService: a project service that contains objects that communicate exclusively on the server side of the client-server barrier.

ServerStorage: a project service that stores objects used in accordance with server management.

Variable: a container for unspecified values.

Variadic function: a function that can take a varying number of arguments.

REFERENCES

AlvinBlox. (2018, April 9). *Roblox debounce tutorial.* [Video]. YouTube. https://www.youtube.com/watch?v=HoZkuvd6RPA.

Ben. (2021, September 13). *What's the difference between an array and a table?* https://devforum.roblox.com/t/whats-the-difference-between-an-array-and-a-table/1466701.

Bibard, F. (2021, August 23). *The easy guide to French numbers.* Talkinfrench.com. https://www.talkinfrench.com/french-numbers/.

Bindable events and functions. (n.d.). Create.roblox.com. https://create.roblox.com/docs/scripting/events/bindable-events-and-functions.

BindableFunction. (n.d.). Create.roblox.com. https://create.roblox.com/docs/reference/engine/classes/BindableFunction.

Boylls, T. (2023, January 24). *How to use Roblox Studio (with pictures).* WikiHow. https://www.wikihow.com/Use-Roblox-Studio.

Brumbaugh, Z. (2021). *Introducing Roblox development.* In Coding Roblox Games Made Easy. Packt. https://subscription.packtpub.com/book/game-development/9781800561991/2/ch02lvl1sec05/discovering-developer-types.

Buying upgrades. (n.d.). Create.roblox.com. https://create.roblox.com/docs/education/adventure-game-series/buying-upgrades.

CharlieJ. (2021, March 20). *The beginners guide to all things game development.* DevForum. https://devforum.roblox.com/t/the-beginners-guide-to-all-things-game-development/1121665.

Cleanup and reset. (n.d.). Create.roblox.com. https://create.roblox.com/docs/education/battle-royale-series/cleanup-and-reset.

Coding the game loop. (n.d.). Create.roblox.com. https://create.roblox.com/docs/education/battle-royale-series/coding-the-game-loop#gamesettings-script.

Coding the leaderboard. (n.d.). Create.roblox.com. https://create.roblox.com/docs/education/adventure-game-series/code-the-leaderboard.

Codotaku. (2018, November 10). *Variadic functions in Roblox Studio (Lua).* [Video]. https://youtu.be/KyX3HkEzZHI.

Collecting items. (n.d.). Create.roblox.com. https://create.roblox.com/docs/education/adventure-game-series/collect-items#troubleshooting-tips-1.

Color3. (n.d.). Create.roblox.com. https://create.roblox.com/docs/reference/engine/datatypes/Color3#fromRGB.

Create & Learn Team. (2022a, September 1). *How to make an obby in Roblox.* Kids'

Coding Corner | Create & Learn. https://www.create-learn.us/blog/how-to-make-an-obby-in-roblox/.

Create & Learn Team. (2022b, September 26). *How to use conditional statements (if, then) in Roblox Studio*. Kids' Coding Corner | Create & Learn. https://www.create-learn.us/blog/conditional-statements-roblox-studio/.

Create on Roblox. (n.d.-a). Create.roblox.com. https://create.roblox.com/docs/tutorials/scripting/basic-scripting/intro-to-scripting.

Create on Roblox. (n.d.-b). Create.roblox.com. https://create.roblox.com/docs/education/adventure-game-series/landing.

Create the map. (n.d.). Create.roblox.com. https://create.roblox.com/docs/education/adventure-game-series/create-the-map.

Creating a battle royale. (n.d.). Create.roblox.com. https://create.roblox.com/docs/education/battle-royale-series/landing.

Creating a GUI. (n.d.). Create.roblox.com. https://create.roblox.com/docs/education/battle-royale-series/creating-a-gui.

Creating a Script. (n.d.). Create.roblox.com. https://create.roblox.com/docs/education/coding-1/creating-a-script.

Curry, D. (2023, February 28). *Roblox revenue and usage statistics* (2021). Business of Apps. https://www.businessofapps.com/data/roblox-statistics/.

Danmaigoro, A. S. (2021, September 3). *What are conditional statements in programming?* Educative: Interactive Courses for Software Developers. https://www.educative.io/answers/what-are-conditional-statements-in-programming.

DeepAI. (2020, June 25). *Pattern Matching*. DeepAI. https://deepai.org/machine-learning-glossary-and-terms/pattern-matching.

Developer economics | Roblox creator documentation. (n.d.). Create.roblox.com. https://create.roblox.com/docs/production/monetization/economics.

Dodge, D. (2022, May 12). *The ultimate guide to making your first game on roblox studio*. CodaKid. https://codakid.com/ultimate-guide-making-your-first-game-on-roblox-studio/.

Ending matches. (n.d.). Create.roblox.com. https://create.roblox.com/docs/education/battle-royale-series/ending-matches.

Events. (n.d.). Create.roblox.com. https://create.roblox.com/docs/scripting/events.

Finishing the project. (n.d.-a). Create.roblox.com. https://create.roblox.com/docs/education/adventure-game-series/finishing-the-project.

Finishing the project. (n.d.-b). Create.roblox.com. https://create.roblox.com/docs/education/battle-royale-series/finishing-the-project.

Functions. (n.d.). Create.roblox.com. https://create.roblox.com/docs/scripting/luau/functions.

Gorosae. (2022). *StarterTool*. https://create.roblox.com/marketplace/asset/10837098513/StarterTool.

Grubb, J. (2013, January 22). *Roblox in 2012: Users played for over 176 million hours.* VentureBeat. https://venturebeat.com/games/roblox-in-2012-users-played-for-over-176-million-hours/.

Guiding your up-and-coming Roblox developer. (2023, February 17). Roblox Support. https://en.help.roblox.com/hc/en-us/articles/4438648708756-Guiding-Your-Up-and-Coming-Roblox-Developer.

How to make an obby on Roblox. (2023, February 24). WikiHow. https://www.wiki how.com/Make-an-Obby-on-Roblox.

Ierusalimschy, R. (2003). *Programming in Lua (1st ed.).* Lua.org, Cop. https://www.lua.org/pil/contents.html#P1.

Ierusalimschy, R., De Figueiredo, L. H., & Celes, W. (2022). *Lua 5.4 Reference Manual.* Lua.org. https://www.lua.org/manual/5.4/contents.html#index.

Ierusalimschy, R. (n.d.). *Programming in Lua: 1.3.* Www.lua.org. https://www.lua.org/pil/1.3.html.

If/then practice with powerups. (n.d.). Create.roblox.com. https://create.roblox.com/docs/education/coding-3/powerups-with-if-statements.

If/then practice with traps. (n.d.). Create.roblox.com. https://create.roblox.com/docs/education/coding-3/traps-with-if-statements.

Instance. (n.d.). Create.roblox.com. https://create.roblox.com/docs/reference/engine/classes/Instance.

Intro to arrays. (n.d.). Create.roblox.com. https://create.roblox.com/docs/education/coding-5/intro-to-arrays.

Intro to dictionaries. (n.d.). Create.roblox.com. https://create.roblox.com/docs/education/coding-5/intro-to-dictionaries.

Intro to for loops. (n.d.). Create.roblox.com. https://create.roblox.com/docs/education/coding-4/intro-to-for-loops.

Intro to if statements. (n.d.). Create.roblox.com. https://create.roblox.com/docs/education/coding-3/intro-to-if-statements.

Intro to Module Scripts. (n.d.). Create.roblox.com. https://create.roblox.com/docs/education/coding-6/intro-to-module-scripts.

Isaac. (2016, July 7). *Roblox studio tour - episode 1: home section.* [Video]. Youtube. https://www.youtube.com/watch?v=VpTFBSNFynk.

Kenlon, S. (2022, November 30). *Get to know Lua for loops in 4 minutes.* Opensource.com. https://opensource.com/article/22/11/lua-for-loops.

Landsberg, N. (2022, September 14). *56 amazing Roblox statistics: Revenue, usage & growth stats.* Influencer Marketing Hub. https://influencermarketinghub.com/roblox-stats/.

Layn333, & MrNicNacWIKI. (2010, June 18). *Loops.* Roblox Lua Wiki. https://arebeexlua.fandom.com/wiki/Loops.

Litt, S. (n.d.). *Callback functions in Lua.* Www.troubleshooters.com. http://www.

Loops. (n.d.). Create.roblox.com. https://create.roblox.com/docs/education/
coding-4/landing.

Loops practice - creating a timed bridge. (n.d.). Create.roblox.com. https://create.
roblox.com/docs/education/coding-4/creating-a-timed-bridge.

Loops practice - glowing lights with for loops. (n.d.). Create.roblox.com. https://create.
roblox.com/docs/education/coding-4/glow-lights-with-for-loops.

Lua array length | quick glance on Lua array length. (2021, May 19). Educba. https://
www.educba.com/lua-array-length/.

Lua - arrays. (n.d.). Www.tutorialspoint.com. https://www.tutorialspoint.com/lua/
lua_arrays.htm.

Lua - data types. (n.d.). Www.tutorialspoint.com. https://www.tutorialspoint.com/
lua/lua_data_types.htm.

Lua - math library. (n.d.). Www.tutorialspoint.com. https://www.tutorialspoint.
com/lua/lua_math_library.htm.

Lua - variables. (n.d.). Www.tutorialspoint.com. https://www.tutorialspoint.com/
lua/lua_variables.htm.

Making changes to arrays. (n.d.). Create.roblox.com. https://create.roblox.com/
docs/education/coding-5/making-changes-to-arrays.

Managing players. (n.d.). Create.roblox.com. https://create.roblox.com/docs/educa
tion/battle-royale-series/managing-players.

ModuleScripts. (n.d.). Create.roblox.com. https://create.roblox.com/docs/scripting/
scripts/modulescripts.

Monetization | Roblox creator documentation. (n.d.). Create.roblox.com. https://create.
roblox.com/docs/production/monetization.

MrNicNacWIKI, & Griffboy11. (2010, June 18). *Using an if statement.* Roblox Lua
Wiki. https://arebeexlua.fandom.com/wiki/Using_an_If_Statement.

Multiple conditions with else/if. (n.d.). Create.roblox.com. https://create.roblox.com/
docs/education/coding-3/multiple-conditions.

Nandanwar(Khadgi), J. (2022, September 30). *Roblox programming: A tool to learn
coding.* ELearning Industry. https://elearningindustry.com/roblox-program
ming-a-tool-to-learn-coding.

Nested loops. (n.d.). Create.roblox.com. https://create.roblox.com/docs/education/
coding-4/nested-loops.

Object properties. (n.d.). Create.roblox.com. https://create.roblox.com/docs/educa
tion/coding-1/object-properties.

Obstacle course. (2023, January 1). Roblox Wiki. https://roblox.fandom.com/
wiki/Obstacle_course.

Otaris, M. (2018, March 17). *Callback.* Roblox Wiki. https://roblox.fandom.com/wiki/Callback.

Parameters practice - buttons. (n.d.). Create.roblox.com. https://create.roblox.com/docs/education/coding-2/parameters-practice-buttons.

Parents and children. (n.d.). Create.roblox.com. https://create.roblox.com/docs/education/coding-1/parents-and-children.

Parts. (n.d.). Create.roblox.com. https://create.roblox.com/docs/building-and-visuals/studio-modeling/parts.

Paul. (2021, March 19). *Coding with kids. Coding with Kids.* https://www.codingwithkids.com/blog/2021/03/roblox-programming-parents-guide.html.

Repeating code with while loops. (n.d.). Create.roblox.com. https://create.roblox.com/docs/education/coding-4/repeating-code-with-while-loops.

Roblox_Educators. (2022). *Battle royale weapon.* https://create.roblox.com/marketplace/asset/10202913115/Battle-Royale-Weapon.

Roblox_Educators. (2022). *Graybox assets.* https://create.roblox.com/marketplace/asset/10202876758/Graybox-Assets.

Roblox Studio. (2023, February 17). *Roblox Support.* https://en.help.roblox.com/hc/en-us/articles/203313860-Roblox-Studio.

ropeccool. (2020). *Pink crystal.* https://create.roblox.com/marketplace/asset/5359904478/Pink-Crystal.

Rotate matrix elements. (2023, March 30). GeeksforGeeks. https://www.geeksforgeeks.org/rotate-matrix-elements/.

Selling items. (n.d.). Create.roblox.com. https://create.roblox.com/docs/education/adventure-game-series/selling-items.

ServerScriptService. (n.d.). Create.roblox.com. https://create.roblox.com/docs/reference/engine/classes/ServerScriptService.

Snap to grid. (n.d.). https://create.roblox.com/docs/education/build-it-play-it-create-and-destroy/snap-to-grid.

Sorting algorithms. (2023, March 21). GeeksforGeeks. https://www.geeksforgeeks.org/sorting-algorithms/?ref=lbp.

Starmaq. (2020a, March 16). *List of coding challenges.* DevForum. https://devforum.roblox.com/t/list-of-coding-challenges/485248.

Starmaq. (2020a, March 28). *Coding challenge #1: Numbers to French.* Devforum.roblox.com. https://devforum.roblox.com/t/coding-challenge-1-numbers-to-french/500012.

Starmaq. (2020b, April 20). *Coding challenge #2: It's sorting time!* DevForum. https://devforum.roblox.com/t/coding-challenge-2-its-sorting-time/533472.

Starmaq. (2020b, May 17). *Coding challenge #4: Non-repeating character.* Devforum.roblox.com. https://devforum.roblox.com/t/coding-challenge-4-non-repeating-character/580162/3.

Starmaq. (2020c, May 18). *Coding challenge #5: Rotating 90-degrees.* Devforum.roblox.com. https://devforum.roblox.com/t/coding-challenge-5-rotating-90-degrees/581975.

Starmaq. (2020d, May 25). *Coding challenge #6: First duplicate.* Devforum.roblox.com. https://devforum.roblox.com/t/coding-challenge-6-first-duplicate/593935.

Starmaq. (2020e, May 30). *Coding challenge #7: Pairs divisible by 5.* Devforum.roblox.com. https://devforum.roblox.com/t/coding-challenge-7-pairs-divisible-by-5/601127.

Starmaq. (2020f, July 12). *Coding challenge #8: snake_case to camelCase.* Devforum.roblox.com. https://devforum.roblox.com/t/coding-challenge-8-snakecase-to-camelcase/668949.

Starmaq. (2020g, July 13). *Coding challenge #9: Recamán's sequence.* Devforum.roblox.com. https://devforum.roblox.com/t/coding-challenge-9-recam%C3%A1ns-sequence/670384/3.

Starmaq. (2020h, July 20). *Coding challenge #11: Non-decreasing arrays.* Devforum.roblox.com. https://devforum.roblox.com/t/coding-challenge-11-non-decreasing-arrays/680261.

Starmaq. (2020i, July 28). *Coding challenge #12: Draw the multiplication.* Devforum.roblox.com. https://devforum.roblox.com/t/coding-challenge-12-draw-the-multiplication/694622.

Stieg, C. (2022, November 16). *Why Lua is so popular — & what you can make with it.* Codecademy News. https://www.codecademy.com/resources/blog/what-is-lua-programming-language-used-for/.

String. (n.d.). Create.roblox.com. https://create.roblox.com/docs/reference/engine/libraries/string#match.

Tables. (n.d.). Create.roblox.com. https://create.roblox.com/docs/scripting/luau/tables.

TechTarget Contributor. (2021, December 15). *What is loop?* WhatIs.com. https://www.techtarget.com/whatis/definition/loop.

Thundermaker300, & Otaris, M. (2021, July 18). *Dealing with debounce.* Roblox Wiki. https://roblox.fandom.com/wiki/Tutorial:Dealing_with_debounce.

Timers and events. (n.d.). Create.roblox.com. https://create.roblox.com/docs/education/battle-royale-series/timers-and-events.

Toolbox. (n.d.). Create.roblox.com. https://create.roblox.com/docs/studio/toolbox#asset-inspection.

Using events. (n.d.). Create.roblox.com. https://create.roblox.com/docs/scripting/events/using-events.

Variables. (n.d.). Create.roblox.com. https://create.roblox.com/docs/scripting/luau/variables.

Wickramasinghe, S. (2021, June 4). *The Lua programming language beginner's guide.* BMC Blogs. https://www.bmc.com/blogs/lua-programming-language/.

101 inspirational quotes about gaming & life. (2023, February 23). *Gracious Quotes.* https://graciousquotes.com/gaming/

Printed in Dunstable, United Kingdom

75092925R00251